AFRICAN-AMERICAN
REACTIONS
TO WAR IN ETHIOPIA
1936–1941

AFRICAN-AMERICAN REACTIONS TO WAR IN ETHIOPIA 1936–1941

JOSEPH E. HARRIS

LOUISIANA STATE UNIVERSITY PRESS *Baton Rouge and London*

Copyright © 1994 by Louisiana State University Press
All rights reserved
Manufactured in the United States of America
First printing
03 02 01 00 99 98 97 96 95 94   5 4 3 2 1

Designer: *Glynnis Phoebe*
Typeface: *Sabon*
Typesetter: *G & S Typesetters, Inc.*
Printer and binder: *Thomson-Shore, Inc.*

Library of Congress Cataloging-in-Publication Data

Harris, Joseph E., date.
   African-American reactions to war in Ethiopia, 1936–1941 /
Joseph E. Harris.
     p. cm.
   Includes bibliographical references and index.
   ISBN 0-8071-1832-X (alk. paper)
   1. Italo-Ethiopian War, 1935–1936—Afro-Americans. 2. United
States—Relations—Ethiopia. 3. Ethiopia—Relations—United States.
4. Afro-Americans—Politics and government. I. Title.
DT387.8.H36 1993
963'.056—dc20   93-10343
                                                                           CIP

The paper in this book meets the guidelines for permanence and durability of the Committee on Production Guidelines for Book Longevity of the Council on Library Resources.∞

To Rosemarie Pressley Harris

CONTENTS

PREFACE—xi

I   Early Encounters Between African Americans and Ethiopians—1

II   Ethiopia and the Pan-African Connection—19

III   Black Protests, Volunteers, and Recruitment—34

IV   Fund Raising—63

V   Italian-American Reactions—93

VI   African-American Envoys to England—104

VII The Emperor's Special Envoy for the Western Hemisphere—120

VIII African Americans in the Reconstruction of Ethiopia—142

CONCLUSION—153

APPENDIX A Ethiopian World Federation Locals: A Partial List—161

APPENDIX B Aviation Cadets Trained by John Robinson's Team—167

BIBLIOGRAPHICAL NOTE—169

INDEX—171

ILLUSTRATIONS

Following Page 84

Emperor Menelik II

Empress Zauditu Menelik

Emperor Haile Sellassie

Haile Sellassie and boys at court

Malaku Bayen

William M. Steen

Mignon Ford with sons and two of her adopted daughters

Hubert ("The Black Eagle") Julian

Ethiopian Research Council reception at Howard University, August 14, 1936

African Americans in Addis Ababa

African-American pilots in Addis Ababa

PREFACE

This study, which emerged out of years of research, owes much to a report I found in the William Leo Hansberry Papers that relates to the Ethiopian Research Council. The report led me to William M. Steen, secretary of the council, whose papers included copious and well-filed minutes for the organization, the principal link between Ethiopians and African Americans in the early years of the Italo-Ethiopian conflict. The Hansberry and Steen papers are housed with the respective families and in the Moorland-Spingarn Research Center, at Howard University.

As I explored those papers, I recognized how critical the Italo-Ethiopian War was in motivating the reaffirmation of a common historical identity for Africa and its diaspora. That perception led to a reexamination of the appeal of Ethiopia as a symbol of liberation for African peoples, an appeal that accelerated the mobilization of African peoples worldwide against the aggression of Italy. The mobilization of the 1930s became a reference point for the leaders of the freedom struggles in Africa and the Americas after World War II. The Italo-Ethiopian War thus represents a watershed in the history of African peoples.

Although this book examines primarily an aspect of the African diaspora, it also relates to the Italian diaspora in the United States. It is a study that demonstrates the significance of diasporas in both domestic and foreign affairs. Indeed, race, ethnicity, and class are all part of the phenomenon I investigate.

I am indebted to many people and organizations for their contributions to my project. I reaffirm my indebtedness to Hansberry and Steen. Mignon Ford has been a reservoir of inspiration and information, and so has David Talbot. Thurlow Tibbs, James William Cheeks, and Edgar D. Draper also provided helpful accounts of their experiences in Ethiopia. I am especially grateful to everyone who participated in personal interviews, most of whom are acknowledged in the text and footnotes. I offer special thanks to James Cheeks, Abiya Ford, and Malaku Bayen, Jr., for permitting me to include photographs from their collections.

Over the last several years, I have been awarded fellowships at the Woodrow Wilson International Center for Scholars, the National Humanities Center, and the Center for the Humanities and Social Sciences at Williams College, and I have benefited from a Reynolds Research Professorship in the African and Afro-American Studies Curriculum at the University of North Carolina, Chapel Hill. The support I received allowed me to conduct research into several matters, including that of this volume. I am deeply grateful to all the organizations and to their helpful and cordial staffs. I thank Howard University for granting the leave necessary for me to accept the awards.

As always, I received very congenial and useful assistance from the staffs of the Moorland-Spingarn Research Center and the Schomburg Center for Research in Black Culture.

AFRICAN-AMERICAN
REACTIONS
TO WAR IN ETHIOPIA
1936–1941

I
Early Encounters Between African Americans and Ethiopians

Historically, encounters between continental Africans and their descendants abroad have centered upon both a common origin and a shared social condition. The place of origin is Africa and the social condition includes slavery, colonialism, and denigratory discrimination. Europeans employed ancient myths, stereotypes, and the biblical account of the curse against Canaan's children to justify slavery and colonialism. Their position was that Africans had no meaningful history or culture and therefore needed to be Christianized and civilized. From the eighteenth century in particular, however, as more and more evidence surfaced about cultural achievements in Africa, white writers began to differentiate between Hamitic, northern Africans, including Ethiopians, and the "Negro" Africans to the south in order to explain civilized Africa without destroying the myths that undergirded European privilege.

Writers like Denis de Rivoire, Karl Dove, and Georg Schweinfurth observed in the nineteenth century that Ethiopians had "civilized customs" and must have descended from "Caucasians." One of the foremost among the many exponents of the division of Africa into Hamitic and non-Hamitic was C. G. Seligman, an English anthropologist and later a citizen of Germany. Seligman wrote that the Hamites "belong to the same great branch of mankind as the Whites." Such an idea allowed European scholars and writers to characterize Ethiopians as the cultural link between themselves and the non-Hamitic Africans who were regarded as the ancestors of African descendants in the diaspora.[1]

---

1. Edith Sanders, "The Hamitic Hypothesis: Its Origins and Functions in Time Perspective," *Journal of African History*, X, No. 4 (1969), 1–17; Harold Marcus, "The Black

The critical question for this study is the degree to which that conception was valid. How did Ethiopians perceive themselves, and how were they perceived by other Africans and their descendants?

The First African Americans in Ethiopia

Ethiopia's defeat of Italy in 1896 enhanced the fascination the African nation historically held for people of African descent. When Benito Sylvain, a Haitian poet, visited Ethiopia in 1897, he reportedly asked Emperor Menelik to agree to head an international organization of blacks working for the redemption of the race. Robert P. Skinner, a diplomat from the United States in Ethiopia at the time, recounted that the emperor's answer was to maintain that he was "not a negro. . . . I am a Caucasian," but other observers have questioned Skinner's account, in part because Menelik was "dark and Negroid" but also because, according to the black American bishop Alexander Walters, Sylvain registered at the Pan-African Congress in London in 1900 as a representative of the emperor. Menelik thus seems to have associated himself with black representatives at the congress.[2]

In any case, the emperor did support the idea of encouraging African Americans to visit Ethiopia and become involved in its affairs. Dr. Joseph Vitalien, an African American from Guadeloupe, for example, founded the first hospital in the country, served as Menelik's personal physician, and was invited by the emperor to become his minister of public health, though Vitalien declined the post.[3] Another African American, Daniel Robert Alexander, was the first permanent black settler from the United States on record there. Born in Missouri, Alexander lived in Chicago and settled in Ethiopia in April, 1909. William Henry Ellis, an African-American businessman who delivered the first treaty with the United States to Menelik

---

Men Who Turned White: European Attitudes Towards Ethiopians, 1850–1900," *Archiv Orientální*, XXXIX (1971).

2. Robert P. Skinner, *Abyssinia of To-day* (London, 1906), 130–32; Alexander Walters, *My Life and Work* (New York, 1917), 253; William Randolph Scott, "A Study of Afro-American and Ethiopian Relations, 1896–1914" (Ph.D. dissertation, Princeton University, 1971), 38–41.

3. Richard Pankhurst, "Menelik and the Utilisation of Foreign Skills in Ethiopia," *Journal of Ethiopian Studies*, V (1967), 65–67.

in 1905 and sought a land concession for black settlement and agricultural development, visited the country several times just after the turn of the century. When Menelik died in 1913, the New York *Times* reported that the funds he had in New York had been invested by Ellis.[4]

Still, that early interest could not easily be sustained, because there was no continuous diplomatic relationship between Ethiopia and the United States. Although an American consul general was appointed to Addis Ababa in 1906 and became a permanent resident in 1909, the consulate was closed from 1913 to 1927, owing to the limited commercial and diplomatic transactions it had to conduct. During the closure, the British legation handled American interests. Even when President Calvin Coolidge reestablished permanent American representation with the appointment of Addison E. Southard in 1927, relations between the two countries remained at a minimum.[5]

Ethiopian Missions to the United States

From about 1916, relations between the countries entered a new phase. Ras Tafari Makonnen, heir apparent to the Ethiopian throne, espoused an effort to get the United States to take a greater interest in his nation. That was in large measure a reaction to the Allied victory in World War I. The Ethiopian government decided in 1919 to send a goodwill mission to congratulate Belgium, England, France, and the United States on their success in the war. On each visit the mission sought ideas for reform in Ethiopia, and in the United States particularly the delegation expressed interest in obtaining assistance for developing national resources.[6]

The Dadjamatch Nadou, Empress Zauditu's nephew and the com-

---

4. *Voice of Ethiopia*, December 16, 1939; National Archives, RG 59, State Department Central File, Decimal File, 384.1115/16, Memorandum, August 13, 1935; Scott, "A Study of Afro-American and Ethiopian Relations," 45, 51–67; Pittsburgh *Courier*, February 8, 1936; National Archives, RG 59, State Department Central File, Decimal File, 884.602, Ellis to Knox, October 31, 1911; New York *Times*, December 17, 1913; *Amsterdam News*, February 8, 1936; "An American Promoter in Abyssinia," *Tuskegee Student*, March 12, 1904. Material in State Department files is hereafter cited with the decimal number, title, and date.

5. *Papers Relating to the Foreign Relations of the United States* (3 vols.; Washington, D.C., 1927), II, (5 vols.; Washington, D.C., 1933), II.

6. 033.8411, Visits of Abyssinian Officials to the U.S., 1910–1920.

mander of the Imperial Army, led the mission; others in the delegation were Ato Belanghetta Herouy Wolde Sellassie, mayor of Addis Ababa; Ato Kantiba Gabrou, mayor of Gondar; and Ato Sinkas, Nadou's secretary. This was the first official Ethiopian delegation to visit the United States.[7]

Prior to the visit, Southard, the American vice-consul in Aden, who had responsibility for the interests of the United States in Ethiopia, emphasized to Washington the importance of receiving the delegation hospitably. Recognizing that members could encounter racial discrimination in a land where race riots were then occurring, the vice-consul explained to the State Department that the delegates were "darkskinned men with the hair and some of the features of the negro, although the Abyssinian is not a negro." The intent was to distinguish the Ethiopians from American blacks in order to avoid any "offensive" encounter. Southard pointed out that the mission represented an independent and Christian country, and he voiced the hope that American businessmen would negotiate trade agreements with it. He mentioned his fear that racial incidents might adversely affect not only the mission but the developing relations between the countries.[8]

The same concern was broached in a report to the State Department from the American consul general in London, which the delegates visited prior to the United States. In describing the favorable reception accorded the delegation in London, the consul general wrote, "These distinguished Abyssinians wear their native costume and have refined faces and are easily distinguished from the ordinary Negroid type familiar in the United States."[9] He too urged the State Department to take precautions against difficulties arising from the American "color line."

In addition to trying to strengthen diplomatic and commercial relations, the mission served as the occasion for Ethiopians and African Americans to evaluate their relations. But since that was not part of the mission's official charge and was clearly not an aim of the State Department, the initiative in this regard rested with American blacks.

The African-American press gave good coverage to the delegation. It was of course a rare opportunity for African Americans to identify with official representatives of an independent African country and one that figured prominently in their heritage. Not surprisingly, the delegation was

---

7. Ibid.
8. 033.8411, Addison E. Southard to secretary of state, May 1, 1919.
9. 033.8411/18, Departure of Abyssinian Delegates to the U.S., June 27, 1919.

invited to speak publicly on its perception of blacks in the United States. Nadou affirmed that Ethiopians were of the "darker race . . . but not like American Black men. We are treated like white men."[10] His assertion does not seem to have been challenged, for although the delegates were of the "darker race," they were indeed treated by whites as whites, at least in certain circumstances and groups. But the Ethiopians' difference seems not to have impressed the National Democratic Club, in New York, which denied the delegation admittance to dine, because "they're black, we'll not have black men eating here."[11]

The African-American press was incensed. But the incident did eradicate the notion of a racial difference between African Americans and Ethiopians, at least in the United States. The New York *Times* carried the headline "Club Bars Heir to Abyssinian Throne" and described the club's cancellation of a dinner reservation "after learning the guests are Black." Although it was not the heir to the throne who was barred, the point was not lost on black Americans: "Because their skin was black, placing them in the same category as the American Race man" were words that removed any doubts about the racial commonality of the two groups.[12]

When the delegation visited the Metropolitan Baptist Church, in New York, it was well received by the African-American hosts. Herouy stated, "On the part of the Ethiopian Empire we desire to express the satisfaction we have felt on hearing of the wonderful progress the Africans have made in this country."[13] Although African Americans may have expected some reference to racial problems in the United States, especially given the race riots, Herouy behaved as a guest of the national government. It is noteworthy, though, that he referred to the blacks as Africans and not as Negroes. But when he credited the "independence" given blacks by the United States for their prosperity and educational achievements, he clearly misunderstood the history of the black American struggle.

Kantiba Gabrou made an appeal to blacks of the United States to emigrate to Ethiopia. Gabrou had been educated in Switzerland, where he acquired an international perspective, had met Sylvain in Ethiopia in 1897, and while attending the coronation of King Edward VII in London had

10. Chicago *Defender,* July 12, 1919.
11. *Ibid.,* August 9, 1919; New York *Times,* July 6, 1935, July 8, 1935, July 15, 1935.
12. Chicago *Defender,* August 9, 1919; New York *Times,* August 4, 1919.
13. Willis Huggins and John G. Jackson, *An Introduction to African Civilization* (New York, 1937), 87.

become acquainted with Ellis. His invitation was for black Americans to become involved in Ethiopia's development, and several blacks reported later that the Kantiba's appeal inspired their emigration to his homeland.[14] Some time later, the Persian consul general in New York, representing Ethiopia's interests in the United States, announced that Ras Tafari Makonnen, who was to become Emperor Haile Sellassie, had instructed him to inform black Americans that "we would welcome them back to Abyssinia, their fatherland. . . . There is plenty of room for them here and we are certain they would be of the greatest aid in restoring their ancient land to its pristine glory."[15] Another appeal from Ras Tafari was recorded at the convention of Marcus Garvey's Universal Negro Improvement Association in 1922: "I invite [African Americans] back to the homeland, particularly those qualified to help solve our big problems and to develop our vast resources. Teachers, artisans, mechanics, writers, musicians, professional men and women—all who are able to lend a hand in the constructive work which our country so deeply feels, and greatly needs."[16]

In 1927, another Ethiopian, Azaj Worknoh Martin, the ambassador to London, journeyed to the United States to pursue closer diplomatic ties and the construction of a dam on Lake Tsana. Martin had been educated in India, had received a medical degree at the University of Edinburgh, and had served as Emperor Menelik's physician. He had encountered racial insults that sensitized him to the problems of Africans and committed him to racial cooperation. He met with a delegation of African Americans in New York during his visit in 1927 and appealed to blacks to go to Ethiopia as farmers, engineers, mechanics, physicians, dentists, and the like. He assured them that as settlers they would receive free land and high wages. Nonetheless, his appeal met little visible response. Some observers have written that seventy or more blacks migrated in response to it, but Malaku Bayen remarked in his biography that Martin was "supposed to take back with him fifty-three Black men and women [but] did not succeed in getting even one person." That assertion is supported by Martin's daughter, Lia Workina Tedrous, who characterized her father as being very disappointed. She recounted that her father had told African Americans that

---

14. Scott, "A Study of Afro-American and Ethiopian Relations," 84; Dawit Gabrou (son of Kantiba Gabrou), interview with author, Washington, D.C., February, 1983.

15. *Home News*, June 7, 1922, in 815/436.

16. *Ibid.;* Amy Jacques Garvey, *Garvey and Garveyism* (New York, 1963), 105.

"we need you and you need us."[17] But if no African Americans migrated on that occasion, Martin's invitation and the response of the black press demonstrated an expanding consciousness of a shared interest and destiny between Ethiopians and African Americans.

African-American nationalists received a significant boost from the Ethiopian visits. The Star Order of Ethiopia and the Ethiopian Missionaries to Abyssinia, led by Cleveland Redding, seem to owe their origin at least in part to the contacts. There developed during this period, as well, a tendency to avoid the label Negro in favor of Ethiopian. One black American said, "I do not want to be called Negro, colored, or nigger. Either term is an insult to me or you. Our rightful name is Ethiopia[n]."[18] As the Nigerian political scientist Essien-Udom observed, for African Americans "to differentiate themselves from their 'Negro-ness' ha[d] become a means of escaping the abuses and insults of whites."[19] It was also a manifestation of identity and a way of solidifying support for political purposes. Although the Star Order of Ethiopia had the stated aim of migrating to Ethiopia, it does not seem to have achieved its goal. The group did, however, contribute to a higher level of black consciousness and interest in Ethiopia.

The early appeals and the tradition of African-American identification with Ethiopia prepared a base on which serious and more sustained efforts toward collaboration would be built in the 1930s. The coronation of the prince as emperor of Ethiopia in 1930 helped spark a renewal of activity. The prince had played a key role in organizing the missions of 1919 and 1927. In the 1930s, he encouraged the establishment of better commercial and diplomatic relations with the United States and in particular a stronger connection with African Americans.

Although Southard was skeptical about the meaning of Ethiopia's moves and uncertain about their substance, he, as the United States' new representative in Addis Ababa, prepared a lengthy assessment of the situa-

---

17. Jacques Garvey, *Garvey and Garveyism*, 273; 033.8411/3, 6, Special Missions, May, 1919; Scott, "A Study of Afro-American and Ethiopian Relations," 96–97; Huggins and Jackson, *An Introduction*, 88; Roi Ottley, *New World A-Coming* (New York, 1943), 107; *Pittsburgh Courier*, March 28, 1936; Malaku Bayen, *The March of Black Men* (New York, 1939), 5–6; Lia Workina Tedrous, interview with author, Washington, D.C., November 1, 1982.

18. Allan Spear, *Black Chicago* (New York, 1966), 193; Chicago Commission on Race Relations, *The Negro in Chicago* (1922), 480.

19. E. U. Essien-Udom, *Black Nationalism* (Chicago, 1962), 59.

tion for the State Department. According to him, there was a "new development in Ethiopian attitudes toward foreigners which appears to tend toward a distinct favoring of those with dark skins." He explained that previously the rulers had held dark skins in "contempt" and had been as disdainful of "foreign negroes as they were of their own negro subjects." The empress and others of the ruling class were, he said, and "still are, proud of their Semitic blood." He believed, however, that the prince was coming to the view "that the future of Ethiopia is bound up with domination by people with at least dark skins." Southard saw in this the government's recognition that modernization of the country required foreign technicians whose influence had to be contained. The prince had observed a "white arrogance" that, according to Southard, limited the usefulness of some foreigners. The solution seemed to be the involvement of blacks, who might "opt for Ethiopian nationality" and not display an arrogant superiority over the prince's compatriots.[20]

Southard believed that such thinking was influenced by Dr. Martin and by Ethiopians who in studying in the United States had seen racial problems firsthand and had met African Americans whose talents could help develop the country. The most influential United States–educated Ethiopian at the time was Bayen, who had studied at Muskingum College, in New Concord, Ohio, as well as at Ohio State University and Howard University's medical school. Bayen's influence increased significantly after the emperor's coronation, but even before it he had recruited two African-Americans teachers, Joseph Hall and William A. Jackson; a pilot, Hubert Julian; and a physician trained at Howard University, John West.[21] Bayen also recruited Dr. Reuben S. Young, an African-American physician who conducted a private practice in Addis Ababa for a few weeks before being appointed municipal health officer in Dire-Dawa. The mayor of that town, Bashawarad Hapte Wolde, had been Bayen's classmate at Muskingum College. Also in Dire-Dawa at the time was Cyril Price, a West Indian teacher who had spent twelve years in the United States.[22]

Southard believed that none of these blacks had been successful in Ethiopia and that each had become disillusioned after emigration. He also

20. 884.4016, Negroes/1, July 30, 1930.
21. *Ibid.*; 032, Joseph Hall/1, March 24, 1930; 484.11, Reuben S. Young/2, September 5, 1932; New York *Times*, July 1, 1930.
22. 484.11, Reuben S. Young/1, September 1, 1932, 2, September 5, 1932.

maintained that Bayen "greatly" exaggerated conditions and possibilities in Ethiopia, and he suggested that any offers to African Americans be investigated and confirmed by the American legation before individuals accepted them. He acknowledged, however, that qualified blacks could find employment if they were willing to accept a "certain humiliation" from Ethiopian officials and work for lower wages than they could earn in the United States.[23] Southard effectively confirmed a serious interest in the Ethiopian government in the recruitment of black technicians abroad, but he was skeptical about its plan and discouraged African Americans from accepting offers.

In 1930, the emperor sent a two-man delegation to the United States to negotiate for economic aid. The head of the delegation was Gabrou, who had been a member of the 1919 mission, and the other member was Bayen. Their specific objectives were to recruit a financial expert to administer the country's finances and to obtain a loan for the development of agriculture and the construction of roads. Because Bayen had knowledge of and experience in the United States, he was given the additional responsibility of presenting "to the American public the present-day problems of the Ethiopian Empire."[24]

Gabrou also wanted to pursue his earlier interest in African Americans by recruiting them as "colored assistants to white directors of finance, agriculture," and other areas, because "white Americans may in some cases prove to be too haughty and dictatorial." The Ethiopian government wanted white American resources without sacrificing dignity, and the hiring of African Americans looked like a means to that goal. The delegation held a number of meetings with officials at the State Department, the J. G. White Engineering Corporation, of New York, the Federal Reserve Bank, and other agencies. Everett A. Colson, a former financial adviser in Haiti, was engaged as the financial expert, but the delegation neither obtained a loan nor signed any African-American assistants. Gabrou's suggestion for "colored" recruits seems to have fallen on deaf ears at the State Department.[25]

But Ethiopia planned another mission, because the emperor wanted

23. 884.4016, Negroes/1, July 30, 1930.
24. 884.51-A/1, James L. Park to secretary of state, July 1, 1930, with Enclosure No. 3; 884.51-A/6, James L. Park to Wallace Murray, July 1, 1930.
25. 884.51-A/1, Park to secretary of state, July 1, 1930; 884.51-A/7, Paul Alling to James Clement Dunn, August 1, 1930; New York *Times,* September 28, 1930.

both to acknowledge gratefully the presence of an American ambassador, Colonel H. Murray Jacoby, at the imperial coronation in 1930 and to explore commercial ventures. It appeared at first that the minister for foreign affairs, Herouy Wolde Sellassie, would head the mission, and Southard, who had warned the State Department about possible racial incidents in connection with the mission in 1919, had to address the issue again. He wrote to the State Department "to mention my opinion that particular effort should be made—if [Herouy] actually ever arrives in the U.S.A.—to prevent any embarrassment on account of his color. He had some such experience in the United States when he was a member of the Mission which visited there just after the war."[26] The legation of the United States in Addis Ababa suggested that "the visitor's movements, entertainments, etc., be placed in [the] hands of a White American who will use tact to prevent any demonstration by Harlem or Howard University."[27] There was no explanation why Harlem and Howard University were singled out as risks, but both had a record of protest against racial discrimination and were regarded as well-informed, sensitive centers of African Americans. Southard offered his assistant, James L. Park, as chaperon for Herouy and mentioned the White Engineering Corporation as an understanding contact that might prove helpful. In addition, he suggested to Herouy and to the State Department that the visitor "don Ethiopian garb which would give him very much less of the appearance of an American darky."[28]

In the event, the emperor appointed his son-in-law, Ras Desta Demtu, and Ato Paulos Manamano, the consul general at Jerusalem, to the delegation. Because the State Department's racial concerns remained, it proposed that, in order to avoid problems like those "owing to the color of previous visitors from Ethiopia, [which] have marred their stay in this country, . . . a military aid be attached to Ras Desta Demtu." A State Department official was assigned to assist with "these protective duties," and the itinerary was well planned so that there was little free time. Demtu was carefully escorted, and the available record does not show any scheduled meetings with African Americans. Colonel and Mrs. Jacoby served as

26. 033.8411/80, Addison E. Southard to Wallace Murray, September 18, 1931.
27. 033.8411, List of Papers, Visits of Abyssinian Officials to U.S., 1930–1939.
28. 033.8411/80, Southard to Murray, September 18, 1931; New York *Times*, August 14, 1930, October 10, 1930, October 22, 1930, October 24, 1930, November 3, 1930, November 5, 1930, December 10, 1930.

his principal guides in New York; the State Department looked after him in Washington. Bayen provided most of the interpretation, and a military aide and police escort accompanied the delegation on official visits.[29]

In spite of the busy schedule of luncheons, receptions, tours, and meetings in Washington and New York, the delegation did meet a few blacks. In New York, a small group of African Americans led by Arthur P. Hayes and Willis Huggins visited Demtu at the Hotel Moritz on their own initiative. They related that the envoy was very much interested in African-American life, but they made no public remarks about any discussion of the possible emigration or recruitment of blacks.[30]

The Ethiopian missions established goodwill and raised the level of knowledge and awareness of their country in the United States. They attracted the interest of American businessmen and recruited a financial adviser. But whatever their diplomatic and commercial success, they also had the significant nonofficial effect of reinforcing African-American identification with Ethiopia and Africa, and they undermined the argument that Ethiopians resented being associated with American blacks. The missions contributed as well to the evolving international black network.

African Americans in Ethiopia: The Second Phase

The tempo of migration to Ethiopia had accelerated when Arnold Josiah Ford, an immigrant to the United States from Barbados, assumed the leadership of black Jews in New York City. Ford, a talented musician and composer, a writer and linguist, joined a small group of black Jews who believed that the Hebrews of the Old Testament were black and that African Americans descended either from them or from the Falashas, a group that practiced Judaism in Ethiopia. Ford's devotion to and knowledge of the faith, combined with his other talents and personal appeal, helped him organize some black Hebrews in Harlem into the congregation Beth B'nai Abraham. He also formed an adjunct, the Aurienoth Club (Angel of light club), which collected membership fees with a view to encouraging migra-

29. 033.8411, Special Mission/56, July 21, 1933, 84, July 26, 1933, 90, August 2, 1933.
30. Huggins and Jackson, *An Introduction*, 88, 89.

tion to the "promised land"—which turned out to be Ethiopia. Ford eventually organized some six hundred members.[31]

Ford's organizing efforts occurred during the 1920s, a time of nationwide racial tensions and conflicts, especially in the cities, where the competition for employment and social accommodations was intensified by postwar adjustments and communism. Ford and his colleagues, many of whom shared a Caribbean background, were attracted to the Universal Negro Improvement Association (UNIA), the nationalist movement of the Jamaican Marcus Garvey. The main attraction was the promise of black pride, African redemption, and self-help. Although Garvey and his followers focused primarily on West Africa, their thinking was influenced by Ethiopianism and pan-Africanism, and they were proud of Ethiopia as an independent African country. The anthem of UNIA was "Ode to Ethiopia," and one of its highest awards was the Distinguished Order of Ethiopia.

Pro-Ethiopian sentiment was heightened by the visits of the Ethiopian delegations to the United States. Ford himself is reputed to have met the delegation of 1919, but even if he did not, the delegation's impact on blacks in New York could not have excluded Ford and his followers. Dr. Martin's visit in 1927 further stimulated interest in emigration to Ethiopia, even if no one responded to his appeal.

Ford's chance meeting with Tamrat Emanuel, a Falasha scholar invited to New York by the American Jewish League, and a discussion with Gabrou, who led the Ethiopian mission to the United States in 1930, provided strong momentum for planning emigration. In spite of the opposition, skepticism, and apprehension of some European and American diplomats in Ethiopia, Ford pursued his goals. Through the collections his followers raised, he was able to attend the emperor's coronation in November, 1930, and he stayed to explore the possibility of African-American settlement. His principal contact in that regard was Gabrou.[32]

Among the members of Ford's congregation to accompany him were

---

31. FW 884.55/2, Special Agent Mullen to Special Agent in Charge A. R. Burr, February 19, 1932; William Randolph Scott, "Rabbi Arnold Ford's Back-to-Africa Movement: A Study of Black Emigration, 1930–1935" (Paper at annual meeting, Association for the Study of Afro-American Life and History, 1974).

32. FW 884.55/2, Mullen to Burr, February 19, 1932; 884.55/8, American Negroes in Ethiopia, May 7, 1932; 884.01A/8, Addison E. Southard to secretary of state, July 30, 1930; Scott, "Rabbi Arnold Ford's Back-to-Africa Movement."

Eudora Paris and Aron Jackson. In November 1931, Thomas Sandeford, Mignon Innis, and Mary Lynch followed, and soon thereafter Ford and Innis married. Two sons, Abiya (Abraham) and Yosef, were born in Ethiopia. But because Ford and his group had not made thorough arrangements before arrival, they were forced to rely on their own limited resources. While waiting for Gabrou to work out a grant of land for settlement, Ford, Paris, and Hattie Edwards Koffie, another immigrant from Harlem, gained a local renown as jazz musicians. Ford composed several pieces and played a number of instruments, displaying talents he had developed as music director at Garvey's Liberty Hall, in New York; Koffie played the piano, and Paris sang. The trio had the reputation of producing the "best dance music in Addis Ababa," and the emperor hired them for several soirees. In addition, Ford established himself as an expert piano tuner.[33]

In 1931, Gabrou could inform Ford that the emperor had approved a grant of eight hundred acres near Lake Tsana for settlement by African Americans. About then, Emmett Jones, president of the Rising Sun Club of Philadelphia, wrote to Gabrou for information about the prospects for black American settlement after hearing accounts from Dr. Charles I. West, the father of John West, who had served as a physician in the country. Gabrou explained that an area in the Lake Tsana region had been reserved for African Americans to develop an industrial and housing project and that the area was favorable for cattle and poultry raising as well as farming. Land grants were possible, Gabrou assured Jones, but land could not be purchased. He urged Jones to communicate with Ford, the "representative of the Ethiopian American Colony."[34]

It is not clear whether Ford himself made the arrangements for all the African-American emigrants, but some sixty-six of his followers came to settle the area. Most faced difficulties from the outset. So eager were many of them to emigrate and pioneer that they did not fully prepare for the cost of sea travel and stopovers along the way, of land transportation for household goods from Djibouti to Addis Ababa, and of the initial adjustments and the self-sustenance needed until employment became available. Even after the settlers had land, they had to clear it and build homes. Some of

33. FW 884.55/2, American Negroes, May 7, 1932.
34. FW 884.55/2, Mullen to Burr, February 19, 1932; FW 884.55/2, American Negroes, May 7, 1932; 884.55/15, 16, American Negroes in Ethiopia—Form of Land-Lease Offered Them by Kantiba Gabrou, June 15, 1933; *Voice of Ethiopia*, January 27, 1940.

them borrowed against their household goods and were swindled; others received credits they could not repay. By 1934, the economic situation had become so grave that Ford, ill for a number of months, and some of his followers faced legal action for failing to pay their rents.[35]

Ford explained in his petition to the court that the settlers had come to Ethiopia at the invitation of the state but that they had exhausted their funds. He had been supporting a number of others before his illness, but his funds were near depletion. Court testimony provided evidence against a number of Ethiopian cheats but also left no doubt about the naïveté of several settlers. Some of the pioneers returned in disillusionment to the United States, and the outbreak of war with Italy interrupted the court proceedings and encouraged others to leave. Two or three, however, remained through the war.[36]

Differences in language and culture had impeded the newcomers' adjustment. Since few of them had skills the Ethiopians would pay for, most had to settle for menial jobs and were unemployed for extended periods. In addition, the United States legation, partly because of its small staff and low diplomatic status but also as a result of the consul general's racist perceptions, failed to provide either sufficient information or the other assistance the American citizens deserved. In spite of everything, though, Mignon Ford and Joseph and Matilda Thomas asserted that they developed good relations with Ethiopians generally.[37]

The flow of African-American immigrants into the country and the problems their presence generated obviously caused the American consulate concern. During 1930 and 1931, the consul reported that about a hundred blacks from the United States and the West Indies had immigrated to Ethiopia. He found them "troublesome and often impecunious American negroes of whom the most objectionable appear to be British West Indian 'Garveyites' with American naturalization." He foresaw that the problem of blacks who had not found the promised land in Ethiopia was potentially

---

35. FO 915/436, VC/A/51647, Ford through H.B.M. Consul to the Honorable Tribunal Special, January 15, 1934.

36. *Ibid.*, with Appendixes A, B, C; FO 915/463, SC-4/34, 35, John Ricketts.

37. Some of the black repatriates referred not only to the derogatory labels the consul general applied to blacks but to his "coolness" and "inconsiderate attitude toward blacks": Thurlow Tibbs, interview with author, Washington, D.C., November, 1982; David Talbot, Mignon Ford, interviews with author, Addis Ababa, March, 1983; Joseph Thomas, Matilda Thomas, interview with author, New York, July 29, 1983.

damaging to the prestige of the United States and would continue a drain on the limited funds of the legation.[38]

The consul's reports led the State Department to explore the possibility of having the passport division "restrict or refuse" passports to blacks planning to travel to Ethiopia. The consulate calculated that among recent immigrants, at least eight were from New York and five from Cleveland: a number of others had not registered at the consulate. The State Department was aware that emigration to Ethiopia received special encouragement from organizations and persons in New York. It was particularly concerned about the number of West Indians involved, possibly 50 percent, and about the way many of them had been naturalized in the United States only shortly before obtaining passports. One inference the Department of State thought possible was that the West Indians were acquiring American citizenship for protection in Ethiopia. Another possibility was that the British were refusing or delaying the issuance of passports to British West Indians until they had proof that the applicant could pay for passage and would not become a public charge.[39]

Wilbur J. Carr, of the passport division, informed Southard, the consul, that the only step his office could take was to circulate to the press the consul's concern about the unfavorable conditions in Ethiopia and the information that many of the émigrés had become indigent. Carr also mentioned that it was possible to seek the cancellation of a passport if the holder, after five years of naturalization, returned to the country of birth or went to another foreign country to establish residence.[40]

The State Department followed up by publicizing the facts that might discourage blacks from leaving for Ethiopia. In addition, clerks in the passport agency were under instruction to examine closely all "colored applicants," questioning their intent, explaining conditions in the country, and inquiring where the applicant received information about employment opportunities. New York was the target of extraordinary vigilance by the agency.[41]

38. 884.55/7, Addison E. Southard to secretary of state, November 2, 1931; 884.55/20, Report of Migratory Movement in Ethiopia; FW 884.55/3, Addison E. Southard to secretary of state, October 7, 1931; Scott, "Rabbi Arnold Ford's Back-to-Africa Movement."

39. FW 884.55/3, Southard to secretary of state, October 7, 1931.

40. FW 884.55/3, Wilbur J. Carr to Addison E. Southard, January 21, 1932; 884.55/4, Wallace Murray to Castle, January 18, 1932.

41. FW 884.55/4, Murray to Castle, January 18, 1932, with Press Release, September

The State Department also had special agents investigate the situation, especially the "inspiration" behind the black migration to Ethiopia. One special agent reported that newspapers and magazines were sparking the interest of prospective emigrants, the *National Geographic* magazine in particular, in which a general article by Southard had attracted attention. In addition, the agent recorded that Ford had organized groups to make migration and settlement in Ethiopia easier. He identified Gabrou as behind that project.[42]

Southard pointed out another source of inspiration, the longtime Ethiopian resident Daniel Alexander. An Ethiopian had found and brought to Southard two letters addressed to Alexander, to whom Southard had returned them, but only after he had read them. One letter had asserted that "quite a few" African Americans wanted to migrate to Ethiopia because of depressed economic conditions in the United States. The writer asked Alexander to explain the procedures and the resources available to immigrants. In the second letter, Lewis Livingstone, of Chicago, wrote, "We have here just what is needed for Africa," namely, skills. Livingstone clearly had communicated with Alexander previously, for he referred to earlier letters Alexander had not answered. He also mentioned mutual acquaintances and included some newspaper clippings concerning which he requested "your answer," and assured Alexander, "Our Ethiopian club is giving an exhibition [in Chicago] in October." A number of African Americans already in Ethiopia used Alexander's address for correspondence, and two settlers confirmed that Alexander was a persuasive force behind African-American settlement in the country.[43]

Another promoter of black emigration to Ethiopia was the Pioneers of Aethiopia, in New York City. Although the origin and place of that organization's founding are unclear, the founder and president was F. A. Cowan. What little documentation is available suggests that the Pioneers had grandiose plans and an international appeal. In September, 1931, Cowan wrote

---

21, 1932; 884.55/2, R. B. Shipley to Newsome, passport agent, January 20, 1932, R. B. Shipley to Hoyt, February 13, 1932; 884.55/6, Hoyt to R. B. Shipley, February 15, 1932.

42. FW 884.55/2, Mullen to Burr, February 19, 1932; 884.55/8, Hodgdon to R. C. Bannerman, June 23, 1932; Addison E. Southard, "Modern Ethiopia," *National Geographic*, June, 1931, pp. 679–738.

43. 884.55/12, Copies of Letters Written by American Negroes, October 8, 1932 (Full text of the two letters in *Voice of Ethiopia*, January 20, 1940); Ford, interview with author, March, 1983; Joseph Thomas and Matilda Thomas, interview with author, June, 1983.

to Lawrence Beckford, a Jamaican tailor in Puerto Cabeza, Nicaragua, explaining the purpose of the group and spelling out how to arrange passage to Ethiopia. He named Dr. N. P. Willis as a local source of additional information. Cowan rhapsodized, "Aethiopia stretches out her hand for you, calling you to come. The possibilities are very unlimited. Tradesmen and businessmen are greatly in demand. The Pioneers offer you all the land that you can intelligently handle, free, and tax free for seven years."[44] He gave the cost of passage as $215 and explained that the customary conveniences were not available but that the opportunity to build was. "We are pioneers. We are builders," he stressed. He added that the Pioneer Lumber Company and the Pioneer Shoemaking Company had already been formed and that nearly a hundred men and women had settled in. The hundred settlers may have been an exaggeration, but a German firm in Ethiopia had received an inquiry from the Pioneers about the price of machinery for sawmills, brickyards, tanneries, and so on.[45] There is no doubt that extensive plans were afoot.

In 1932, the American consul in Djibouti apprised Southard that Beckford, the Jamaican tailor in Nicaragua, had sought advice about traveling to Liberia. He and his wife had accepted Cowan's invitation to settle in Ethiopia but had become disillusioned.[46] Further research may uncover the Beckfords' aspirations and fate, but they were plainly committed to black reunion in Africa.

David D. Erwin, the national president of the Pacific Movement of the Eastern World, in St. Louis, also put out feelers about migration to Ethiopia. The exact profile of Erwin's organization is unclear, but he wrote to the secretary of state, Cordell Hull, explaining that, because of the lack of economic opportunity in the United States, thousands of blacks were ready to colonize lands in Ethiopia. Mrs. M. L. Gordon estimated to President Roosevelt that the United States could be relieved of 400,000 blacks if it granted permission for them to emigrate.[47]

Hattie Koffie, repatriated from Ethiopia in September, 1934, when Italy's invasion of Ethiopia appeared imminent, settled for a time in Columbus, Ohio, but continued to envision a flourishing community of African

44. 884.55/2, Pioneers of Aethiopia, December 5, 1931.
45. *Ibid.;* 884.55/9, Pioneers of Aethiopia—Inspiration, June 7, 1932.
46. 884.55/9, Pioneers of Aethiopia—Inspiration, June 7, 1932.
47. 884.52/9, David D. Erwin to Cordell Hull, September 3, 1935; 884.51/10, M. L. Gordon to the White House, December 23, 1935.

Americans in Ethiopia. She sought support from both Roosevelt and Hull for her proposal to have the American government purchase the homes of African Americans at the market prices of the United States so that the sellers could buy property in Ethiopia, where the exchange rate favored the dollar. She also asked the American government to try to influence the emperor to provide passage for the settlers. With incentives like those, Koffie believed that black Americans would migrate and would be able to develop schools, community centers, and such to stimulate development in the country.[48]

What settlers arrived in Ethiopia during this period hardly had time to accommodate to the social, economic, and political problems in the country before suffering the repercussions of the military skirmish with Italy at Walwal in December, 1934. Full-scale war broke out in October, 1935. From late 1934, the legation of the United States in Addis Ababa had become increasingly apprehensive about American citizens in Ethiopia. Because of the likelihood of war with Italy, the State Department undertook to assist its nationals to migrate. Most of the African Americans had already returned, however, and those still in the country were listed as indigent and in need of funds for travel. The State Department, through several inquiries and appeals, persuaded the American Red Cross to provide $2,500 to cover the transportation costs for the fifteen or so African Americans left there. The Federal Emergency Relief Administration and Travelers Aid cooperated by providing lodging for the group. After about six months, the State Department notified the Red Cross that ten American blacks had returned to the United States at a cost of $2,302.90; it returned the unspent $197.10 with thanks.[49]

What had been an ambitious emerging community of African Americans in Ethiopia in the early 1930s had by late 1934 become a small, largely destitute, and demoralized group uneasy about their status and about conditions in a poor country threatened by war. By 1935, only two or three of the expatriates remained in Ethiopia.

    48. FW 765.84/552, Hattie Edwards Koffie to President Roosevelt, January 22, 1936; Hattie Edwards Koffie to minister of foreign affairs, Washington, D.C., July 15, 1935.
    49. 384.115/1, Telegram, June 6, 1935, 2, Memorandum for Wallace Murray, May 20, 1935, 4, 5, 6, 16-1/2, 33A, William Phillips to Cary T. Grayson, June 11, 1935.

11

Ethiopia and the Pan-African Connection

Pan-Africanism acquired an international structure in 1900 when Henry Sylvester Williams, of Trinidad, and W. E. B. Du Bois, of the United States, convened in London a group of African people from the continent and the diaspora to discuss various issues of common concern, including the social and political rights of Africans in the colonized world. The Pan-African Congress of 1919 and several congresses in the 1920s expanded African political consciousness and increased the ranks of adherents both in Africa and outside. Because the Ethiopians, however, were already independent, they did not figure strongly among the participants in the movement. Yet Africans and African Americans had for centuries regarded Ethiopia as a symbol of black liberation. Many Africans and African Americans had been inspired by a part of Ps. 68:31, "Ethiopia shall soon stretch out her hands unto God," which was interpreted as a prophecy of success in the struggle against slavery and colonial oppression. The Ethiopian churches, which had proliferated through much of central and southern Africa during the nineteenth century, were breakaway Christian churches that were infused with a sense of African issues and traditions and that operated under African leaders. Europeans regarded these churches and their leaders as antichristian rebels against the colonial system.

In the Americas, Ethiopianism had a similar impact. African Americans too saw Ps. 68:31 as prophesying the redemption of African people on the continent and in the diaspora. Ethiopia's defeat of the invading Italians in 1896 and its continued independence when the rest of Africa fell to colonial rule gave credence to the role of Ethiopia as liberator. From colonial days, some African Americans had styled themselves and their organizations Ethiopian and had made reference to Ethiopia in literature and song. That Ethiopia was a Christian state reinforced its appeal. Many African-American churches raised money for Ethiopia—which sometimes meant Africa as a whole. The noted scholar St. Clair Drake has labeled this pan-Africanism with a small *p*. It was not structured as an international organization but was strong and influential anyway. By the 1930s, however, that brand of pan-Africanism had converged with the larger, more politically oriented Pan-Africanism.

The Ethiopian Research Council

In 1934, a group of Africans and African Americans organized the Ethiopian Research Council in Washington, D.C., to disseminate "information on the history, civilization, and diplomatic relations of Ethiopia in Ancient and Modern Times." The founders' statement declared that Ethiopia was "one of the oldest living civilizations in the world . . . and in the Classical Age it was universally regarded as one of the greatest and most powerful nations of the earth," and the statement continued that "Ethiopians of subsequent centuries succeeded in preserving their culture and their liberties, in the face of numerous attempted invasions." Because Ethiopia was "playing a prominent part" in "certain recent international developments," the council would, the statement said, "for the moment, concern itself primarily with the task of assembling and disseminating" information about contemporary Ethiopian affairs.[1]

The council's formation was on the eve of Italy's aggression against Ethiopia. A unit of an estimated six hundred men from Italy's neighboring colony of Somaliland clashed with the Ethiopian contingent for control of the wells at Walwal.[2] Although the frontier was undemarcated, maps of the time showed the well area to be about a hundred kilometers inside

---

1. Ethiopian Research Council, Memorandum, Washington, n.d. The Ethiopian Research Council files are hereafter cited as ERC. Most of the sources in those files are in the William Leo Hansberry Collection, which is in the possession of Hansberry's family in Washington, D.C. Other ERC materials are in the Moorland-Spingarn Research Center, at Howard University.

2. Angelo del Boca, *The Ethiopian War, 1935–1941*, trans. P. D. Cummins (Chicago, 1969); Brice Harris, *The United States and the Italo-Ethiopian Crisis* (Stanford, Calif., 1964), 1–9.

Ethiopia's boundaries. The timing suited Italy's African policy, since a disarray among the European powers let Mussolini act without fear of reprisal. Mussolini had an "Adowa complex," a compulsive urge to avenge Italy's humiliating defeat by Ethiopia in 1896, but he and his supporters were also under the sway of a "nostalgia for ancient Rome" and a desire for greatness. Furthermore, he argued that Italy was overpopulated and needed overseas territories for expansion. With the fascists established in Italy, Hitler ascendant in Germany, and the Geneva Disarmament Conference a failure in October, 1933, Ethiopia was a low policy priority for all the European powers except Italy, which as early as 1925 had had a plan to establish a protectorate there.[3]

For the United States, Ethiopia was of even less concern. Since there were no American colonies on the continent, the skirmish did not cause any territorial anxiety; American trade and investments in Ethiopia were inconsequential; very few American citizens visited the country, and fewer still resided there; knowledge about the country was limited and distorted; the United States was in a period of isolation and was pursuing a policy of noninvolvement. Besides, 1936 was an election year, and neither of the major political parties was prepared to risk alienating voters over Ethiopia. The Democrats, having regained control of the government after over a decade, sought votes from both African Americans and Italian Americans, two groups that were especially sensitive to the situation but that also offered very different proposals for its resolution. The political reality counseled discretion, especially since President Roosevelt placed a higher priority on his domestic policies.

When Mussolini decided that the time was ripe for aggression against Ethiopia, he sent General Emilio de Bono to Eritrea, an Italian colony on Ethiopia's northern border. Arriving as high commissioner, Bono was within three months appointed commander in chief of the Italian armed forces in Africa. Then came the Walwal incident, at odds with the ostensible pursuit of peace by Italy that had resulted in the Italo-Ethiopian Treaty of Friendship, Conciliation, and Arbitration of 1928. On August 29, 1934, the American military attaché's office in Italy warned the State Department that "the Italian Army have drawn up plans for the military conquest and occupation of Abyssinia [and] the contemplated operation will

3. Denis Mack Smith, *Mussolini: A Biography* (New York, 1983), 98.

be undertaken whenever Abyssinia commits an 'overt act.'"[4] Walwal provided the pretext Italy had been waiting for.

In what followed, the Ethiopian Research Council was fortunate in the quality of its leadership. Its president was William Leo Hansberry, a pioneer historian of Africa who had joined the Department of History at Howard University in 1922. He had inaugurated the African-civilization section. For the next forty years he pioneered in research about Africa, and he introduced a host of African, mainly Ethiopian, courses into the curriculum. His classes drew large numbers of students, including Africans.[5]

Hansberry took a special interest in his foreign students, because he hoped they would return to their homelands to apply the perspectives and skills they acquired at Howard. He served as counselor to many African students and helped raise money for their education. He wrote letters directly to the heads of government in Ethiopia and Liberia, the only African nations that had gained independence prior to World War II, in which he successfully appealed for financial support for the two countries' students.[6]

One student who was influenced by Hansberry was Malaku Bayen, possibly the first Ethiopian student to matriculate in the United States, and the first at Howard University. He was a cousin, page, and attendant to the crown prince and regent of Ethiopia, shortly to become Emperor Haile Sellassie. Bayen's pan-African perspective was implanted before he arrived in the United States and he owed it in part to Ambassador Workneh Martin, who in 1927 had told Bayen that "the greatest service you could render your country would be to influence thousands of Black people in the U.S.A. and the West Indies and let them come and help us develop Ethiopia."[7] Bayen has written, "My belief in Race Solidarity caused me to select Howard University for my studies, in order that I might have a closer contact with my people."[8] In 1935, he wrote to the African-American jour-

---

4. Harris, *The United States and the Italo-Ethiopian Crisis*, 1–9. See also George Padmore's several articles in *Crisis*, XLIV (1937), and Nathaniel Peffer, "R.I.P. Ethiopia," *Opportunity*, XIV (1936).

5. Joseph E. Harris, *Pillars in Ethiopian History: The William Leo Hansberry African History Notebook* (Washington, D.C., 1974), Chapter 1.

6. Ibid., 3, 19–20.

7. Malaku Bayen, *The March of Black Men* (New York, 1939), 3–8; William M. Steen, "Howard Men and Ethiopia," *Howard University Alumni Journal*, Winter, 1935–36, p. 4.

8. Ibid.

nalist Claude Barnett, "I hope to make it one of my points to have our government convinced that their cooperation with western Negroes would be a quick solution to our need."[9]

Bayen entered Howard University's medical school in 1929, after his studies at Muskingum College and Ohio State University. He returned to Ethiopia, however, in 1930 and was appointed to the two-man mission that the Kantiba Gabrou led. When he returned to Howard's medical school, he was assigned the additional responsibility of presenting Ethiopia to the American people, and he carried out his commission until he graduated in 1935.

While Bayen was at the medical school, he met Hansberry. The two men obviously had much in common—pan-African perspectives and a commitment to Ethiopia in particular. Their views were shared by Ralph Bunche, a political scientist and Africanist at Howard; Gilbert Balfour Bovell, a classmate of Bayen's in Howard's medical school; William M. Steen, one of Hansberry's history students, with a concentration in Africa; Makonnen Haile, an Ethiopian studying commerce at New York University; and Engueda Johannes, an Ethiopian student in veterinary science at Cornell University. These were the men who joined Bayen and Hansberry in organizing the Ethiopian Research Council.[10]

Bayen was listed as founder of the group, but because he returned to Ethiopia just a few months later, he did not continue to play a major role in its activities in the United States. But he did represent the organization in Ethiopia and followed up its requests there. It was because of him that the emperor and his government responded as willingly to the council's activities as they did. In the United States, general responsibility rested with Hansberry, the president. Steen, as secretary, oversaw the day-to-day activities of the organization.

An examination of the council's available correspondence reveals that Hansberry and Steen most often determined policy, which Steen implemented. As assistant secretary, Howard Moore, a State Department employee, prepared a number of requests and commentaries on matters pertaining to foreign affairs. Associate members in Ethiopia, Uganda, Nigeria, and several cities in the United States joined the cause. Bunche was the

---

9. Malaku Bayen to Claude Barnett, March 3, 1935, in Barnett Papers, Chicago Historical Society (Microfilm at Moorland-Spingarn Research Center, Howard University).
10. Howard Moore to Azaj Workneh Martin, September 30, 1935, in ERC.

adviser on international affairs; Dr. George M. Jones was the technical adviser for health affairs.

Claude A. De. M. Lewis, a technical adviser and cartographer, was probably the most loyal and consistent representative outside Washington, D.C.[11] He and his partner, Alvin C. Gary, operated an export business in New York City, the Haitian-American Appliance Company, which sought to increase business with Haitians and Ethiopians. Lewis was employed as well in the engineering division of the Department of Sanitation of New York City. Both positions brought him into direct contact with a number of engineers and other professionals, both black and white, on whom he could draw.

An avid reader of newspapers, Lewis frequently reported to Steen on, and sent clippings from, the black and white press. He especially watched the newspaper coverage of Ethiopian issues and collected flyers and posters on Ethiopian events. Periodically he visited Steen and Hansberry to discuss the activities of pro-Ethiopian organizations and to help settle questions about fund raising.

Lewis was responsible for printing the council's materials. He also advised the council on engineering matters, including airplanes, communications, and nonaviational transportation, providing technical knowledge of the sort that became critical when the council assisted Ethiopia's war effort. Lewis later subjected to critical examination a road-building plan some Swiss engineers were proposing to the Ethiopian government, and he went on to devise his own scheme for railroad and highway construction for submission to the emperor.

Robert F. S. Harris, earlier a journalist with the New York *Herald*, had experience and contacts that gave him access to news and to prominent people. He served as the council's principal adviser on publicity, identifying pro- and anti-Ethiopian groups and visiting with Steen and reporting to him about their activities. He was also secretary of the Committee for Ethiopia, probably the first organization established specifically to collect funds for Ethiopia's defense against Italy. In addition, he proposed a number of fund-raising ideas to the council, recruited physicians as potential volunteers in Ethiopia, and initiated negotiations for medical supplies the council wished to send.

---

11. This and the following biographical data are, unless otherwise stated, derived from extensive correspondence in the ERC files, supplemented by oral and written testimonies and newspaper accounts.

Willis Huggins' name appears in several letters, reports, and other documents. The council's correspondence referred to him as one of its New York representatives, and he submitted reports on a trip he took to England and France, and to Geneva, where he presented the League of Nations with an appeal in behalf of Ethiopia. Huggins was a history teacher at Bushwick High School, in New York City, and he was one of the best-informed Americans of the time on Africa. With Henry Jackson, he was the author of *Introduction to African Civilizations,* in which he described some of his pro-Ethiopian activities. He was active in a number of other organizations, including the Friends of Ethiopia.

Bayen, Hansberry, Steen, Lewis, Harris, and Huggins were the core around which other African Americans and Ethiopians, as well as some non-Ethiopian Africans, rallied to help the council achieve its objectives of promoting the study and dissemination of information about Ethiopia and cultivating a friendly constituency for that country in the United States and abroad.[12]

From the beginning, the council was a nonprofit organization of volunteers. Meetings at first took place in private homes, in Hansberry's office at Howard University, and in similar small forums. Within a year, however, the council had expanded its network to several cities in the United States and abroad. Affiliates included the Rising Sun Clubs, of Boston and Philadelphia; the Peace Movement, of Chicago; the Medical Committee for the Defense of Ethiopia, in New York; L'Amour pour la Patrie, in Addis Ababa; the Conseil de Recherche d'Ethiopie, in Addis Ababa; the Comité d'Action Ethiopienne, in Paris; and the Istmo-African Bureau and Pioneering Club, in Ancon, a town in the Panama Canal Zone.[13]

The council established relations with several foreign correspondents, mostly Africans in European countries and Ethiopia, who sent reports for evaluation and distribution by the information bureau and historical service. The council's main publication was the *Digest,* which ran analytic summaries of stories on Ethiopia that had appeared in newspapers and magazines. The council printed maps of Ethiopian boundaries, railroad and highway networks, and ports and cities; it also published the constitution and fact sheets on Ethiopian history and the war with Italy.[14] As an

---

12. Ethiopian Research Council Mimeograph, April 27, 1935, p. 1, in ERC; Moore to Martin, September 30, 1935, in ERC.
13. Listed on the Ethiopian Research Council's letterhead, June 1, 1936.
14. Ethiopian Research Council Mimeograph, April 27, 1935, p. 1, in ERC.

information resource, it had a far greater impact than surviving documentation can confirm. Inquiries by telephone and mail kept the limited staff busy, but there is no record of the telephone calls. The correspondence that remains includes a wide range of queries about history, geography, social and political developments, population, education, and military statistics. There were also innumerable requests for Ethiopian flags and photographs of the emperor.

In responding to general inquiries, the council frequently recommended Ernest Work's *Ethiopia: A Pawn in European Diplomacy*. But the most popular of its own publications was Steen's *Cartographic Summary Map*, regarding the Italo-Ethiopian War. It sold for fifteen cents, and the proceeds from its sale went to support the Ethiopian cause. The council's publications were peddled at churches and lodges and at the meetings and rallies of the NAACP and social and study groups, as well as door to door and on the streets. The incentive of one-third of the sales as commission no doubt boosted circulation in the depression years of the 1930s. Hundreds of maps were ordered by NAACP chapters, the UNIA, and other groups, and by teachers and researchers.

The council received letters from persons who could hardly afford the cost of a stamp but who wanted to declare their solidarity. "We are Ethiopians," they frequently said. "Our brothers in Ethiopia" was a phrase that recurred in the letters. Even before the war there were requests about travel to and services in Ethiopia. The council helped to entrench and expand African and Ethiopian consciousness and identification among rank-and-file African Americans.[15]

Although letters from various parts of the United States affirmed support for the organization and occasionally included money to assist it, there seems to have been extended correspondence with only three of the affiliates: the Rising Sun Clubs, in Philadelphia and Boston, and the Istmo-African Bureau and Pioneering Club, in the Canal Zone.

The Philadelphia club was organized in 1936 by Andrew Cook, a dealer in resalable goods. The earliest correspondence, dated March 5, 1936, describes the planning for a large meeting to coordinate fund raising

---

15. J. W. Edwards, Hollandale, Miss., to Ethiopian Research Council, August 30, 1935, J. H. Welch, Wilmington, Del., to Howard Moore, August 6, 1935, Causey to Ethiopian Research Council, Detroit, n.d., Howard Moore to Smith, Forsyth, Ga., November 18, 1935, Howard Moore to Sufi Abdul Hamid, New York, June 20, 1935, all in ERC.

for the Ethiopian resistance. Hansberry, an invited speaker, served as assistant chairman of the meeting, which convened at Child's Memorial Baptist Church. Lij Tasfaye Zaphiro, an attaché of the Ethiopian embassy in London, was the main speaker.[16] Joint sponsors of the meeting with the Rising Sun Club were the International Council of Women of Darker Races, the Philadelphia Committee for the Defense of Ethiopia, the National Negro Congress, and the Booker T. Washington Memorial Association. These organizations were Philadelphia branches of national groups. The Rising Sun Club frequently coordinated combined gatherings.[17]

As early as May, 1936, Fannie Harris, the president of the Rising Sun Club in Boston, submitted a report to the Ethiopian Research Council on new members and donations. The club's members came from the greater Boston area, including Cambridge and Brookline. Steen thanked Harris and tendered congratulations on the club's progress, but he also made it his business to ask how many copies of the Ethiopian constitution the members wanted.[18]

In 1931, C. C. Moulton, the president of the chapter of Garvey's UNIA in Ancon, had formed the Istmo-African Bureau and Pioneering Club to "organize African groups for the good and welfare of Africans at home and abroad, especially in connection with Ethiopia." Later the same year, Moulton had approached Arnold Josiah Ford to inquire about the availability of land for settlement in Ethiopia, and about the possibility of finding work at a dam construction project on Lake Tsana. His overtures came to nothing, however, because of the skirmish at Walwal in 1934.[19] In May, 1935, Moulton wrote to Hansberry that the Istmo-African Bureau had learned about the council from reading the Pittsburgh *Courier* and wanted to have an association "with our Brethren in the United States" so as to keep abreast of developments in Ethiopia and contribute where possible. The size of Moulton's following is uncertain, but it seems to have been large enough to draw notice in the Canal Zone: "We are up in arms against the Fascist bellicose designs in Ethiopia, and recently one of our affiliated clubs created a stir here that brought about diplomatic investigations as it

16. Emmett Jones to William Leo Hansberry, March 5, 1936, in ERC.
17. *Ibid.*; Charles Mackey to Ethiopian Research Council, March 12, 1936, Emmett Jones to Ethiopian Research Council, March 31, 1936, both in ERC.
18. Robert F. S. Harris to Howard Moore, October 30, 1935, Howard Moore to Robert F. S. Harris, November 2, 1935, both in ERC.
19. C. C. Moulton to John Shaw, November 26, 1935, in ERC.

was feared that the whole Negro populace was out to create revolutionary conditions on account of Mussolini's aggression. . . . We are waiting for anything to start, at which time we are determined at least to create a boycott against all Italian goods in Panama, so far as our people is concerned, since we are the largest group of buyers in this country."[20] Steen sent his customary reply on the history, leadership, and general activities of the council, and he informed Moulton that affiliation had been established. He suggested maintaining a connection by mail and cable.[21]

There remains much to learn about Moulton and the rallies he reported and about whether or not Panamanian groups sent contributions to Ethiopia. He seems to have been committed but frustrated by his unsuccessful tries at uniting the factions in the area for the Ethiopian cause. He wrote criticizing Huggins' attempts to bring a branch of the Friends of Ethiopia to Panama. Moulton also seems to have felt that two other local groups, the Ethiopian Pioneering Club and the Ethiopian Defense Committee, had put a strain upon his position. He developed his case in the *Panama American* and the *Panama Star and Herald*.[22]

The strategic role of the Ethiopian Research Council was as a clearinghouse for information and a facilitator and coordinator of activities for the benefit of Ethiopia. But it also deepened the consciousness of African Americans as blacks and Africans.

The Young Ethiopian Movement

Prior to World War I, only a few Ethiopians had established contacts with the western world and even fewer had cultivated relations with blacks in the diaspora. Western influences had begun to penetrate the country during the nineteenth century in the form of missionaries, soldiers, skilled workers, advisers, and a few immigrant settlers and adventurers. Ethiopians increasingly attended mission schools, and some pursued higher education abroad with the assistance of missionaries, foreign governments, and the emperor. The informal and formal education of Ethiopians was

---

20. C. C. Moulton to William Leo Hansberry, May 29, 1935, Moulton to Shaw, November 26, 1935, both in ERC.

21. William Steen to C. C. Moulton, April 1, 1936, Moulton to Shaw, November 26, 1935, both in ERC.

22. Moulton to Shaw, November 26, 1935, in ERC.

enriched by their acquaintance with modern developments and their engagement with the ideas of social, economic, and political change. On returning to Ethiopia, the students compared conditions abroad with those in their country and became more critical of their leaders. They became the seed for an influential western-oriented elite and, later in the twentieth century, a small but consequential intelligentsia.

One member of the early western-educated elite was Afework Gebre Eyessus, who had been sent to Europe with two other students in 1894. A specialist in literature and art, he wrote at least five books, one of them *A Guide for Travellers Visiting Ethiopia* (in both Amharic and French) in 1908, in which he deplored the lagging development of Ethiopia and criticized the authorities for conservatism and "selfishness." At about the same time, European observers were beginning to notice that other western-educated Ethiopians had a similar desire for more rapid change in their country.[23] And in the same year that *A Guide for Travellers* was published, Emperor Menelik introduced a modern educational system, opening the way to an expanded pool of educated elite, who would agitate for even more rapid change.

In a report to the American secretary of state in 1929, Southard called attention to the growing numbers of young Ethiopians who had been educated in the French Roman Catholic mission schools in Dire Dawa and Harrar. They were filling the increasing roster of clerical and other governmental posts for which a modern education was indispensable. The ability to speak French, which the emperor spoke and admired, and to a lesser extent Italian and English, was esteemed to have considerable value.[24] That gave the French particular influence in the government and country. The French had investments everywhere and had constructed the first railroad link to the Red Sea coast. The American consul regarded the French inroads a cause for concern.

But one of the great limitations of the United States in combating this situation, according to Southard, was the "unpleasantness of our alleged color prejudices should [Ethiopians] elect to go to the United States for an education." He explained that "our alleged prejudices . . .

---

23. Girma Amare, "The Modern Ethiopian Intelligentsia and Its Evolution" (Paper prepared for the Interdisciplinary Seminar of the Faculties of Arts and Education, Haile Selassie I University [now University of Addis Ababa], 1966–67).

24. 884.404/26, Addison E. Southard to secretary of state, December 5, 1929.

have become fairly well disseminated during recent years in Ethiopia and have retarded . . . our potential influence here," and he mentioned his conviction that other foreign nationals were "inclined to encourage" a racist image of the United States. Southard acknowledged that the "discouraging of such influence is, accordingly, one of this Legation's more delicate duties."[25]

A small but significant group of Ethiopian intellectuals known as the Young Ethiopian Movement was judged xenophobic by Southard in 1930. The consul identified the movement, which had one of its springs in resentment over the emperor's lavish coronation, as a group educated abroad or in the foreign Christian missions who held subordinate but influential executive positions in the government and bridled at the arrival of foreign advisers commanding "extravagant salaries."[26] He believed that a feeling of racial inferiority in reaction to white behavior abroad and in Ethiopia lay behind the movement. The consul named a number of foreign-educated Ethiopians, including Bayen, who had taken offense at the racial discrimination they faced in Europe and the United States and wanted greater opportunities to apply their knowledge and skills in their own country. They were aware of their limited numbers and the restricted resources in their country and were indignant over the large salaries accorded foreign advisers and the lavish style in which the emperor entertained. What particularly worried Southard was that the movement seemed to be gaining a sway over the emperor, leading him to restrict the use of foreign advisers in favor of black experts. Bayen had succeeded in having African-American technicians appointed by the government.[27]

One member of the Young Ethiopian Movement had written, "We see the foreigners who have come to our country influence our people. They spread their influence over the inhabitants of the city and the provinces. By this fact the latter are chastised and reproached, without their having any domination or power over the foreigners. By such methods they lead the people just like a shepherd leads his flock. Now a study of the different governments and methods of colonization will show us that the people

25. Ibid.
26. 884.4016/2, Addison E. Southard to secretary of state, November 24, 1930; 884.01A/14, Addison E. Southard to secretary of state, November 24, 1930.
27. 884.01A/14, Southard to secretary of state, November 24, 1930; 884.01A/8, Addison E. Southard to secretary of state, July 30, 1930.

were first counselled by this influence. . . . Let us destroy foreign influence by our lives and deaths."[28]

In 1932, the Ethiopian government had over a hundred foreign employees, but only a few were given the prestigious title of adviser. Dr. Johannes Kolmodin, a Swede, was a political adviser in the Ministry of Foreign Affairs. Frank de Halpert, who was British, was an adviser in the Ministry of the Interior. Jacques Auberson, from Switzerland, was an adviser in the Ministry of Justice. Everett A. Colson, of the United States, was an adviser in the Ministry of Finance. Professor Ernest Work was an adviser on education. In addition, several foreign engineers and draftsmen (mostly Russian), aviators (mostly French), teachers (mostly Egyptian), public-works technicians (most Italian, Russian, and German), and military aides (mostly Belgian) were among the employees of the municipal government of Addis Ababa.[29]

As a result of pressure from the Young Ethiopian Movement, the emperor had by 1932 encouraged the recruitment of more African-American technicians, limited the number of foreign advisers, and dismissed some; in one case negotiations for a Belgian mining adviser reportedly failed as a result of the influence of the movement. Southard regarded the trend as "regrettable," because it was "based on the false premise that the 'Young Ethiopians' themselves are educationally qualified to guide the development of the government."[30] What the movement wanted was a strong central government with a constitutional foundation, and a civil service drawn from western-educated Ethiopians.

By 1934, Southard had concluded that the movement "definitely promises to engender a national resistance to foreign influence here." It had a "loosely formed organization" that attracted the participation of some prominent Ethiopian officials. Influential government positions usually went to persons of high family rank, whereas the early student leaders were mostly from families of lower, even peasant, status. The student leaders had acquired their education from missionaries, unlike most of the elite Ethiopians at the time. But the movement had the potential of bridging the

28. 884.01A/14, Southard to secretary of state, November 24, 1930, with enclosure.
29. 884.01A/22, Addison E. Southard to secretary of state, January 23, 1932. See also Harold Marcus, *Haile Sellassie I: The Formative Years, 1892–1936* (Berkeley and Los Angeles, 1987), 138.
30. Marcus, *Haile Sellassie*, 138.

gulf between the classes, especially since the holders of the most powerful positions increasingly needed the linguistic and other skills of the western-educated students. There was therefore a diminishing disdain for mission and western education and a gradual acceptance of the social mobility the less privileged but educated classes were achieving.

At the same time, high-level officials remained suspicious of foreign-educated subordinates with strong ties to the foreign community in Addis Ababa. Ethiopians educated abroad were sometimes accused of divided loyalties, with the result that they occasionally became vocal against intrusion from outside, as a proof of their patriotism.[31] At work were a deep sense of Ethiopian national pride and consciousness, sensitivity to the increasing foreign influence in the country, and a realization of the country's vulnerability in international affairs.

As Ethiopia became a more active party in the international sphere, the leadership faced the challenge of keeping national identity, development, and independence in balance. The foreign-educated students added to the complexity of the task, because they had not only experienced racial discrimination firsthand but had also observed that Europeans were not the superior beings that many Ethiopians had imagined. The students had seen European and American poverty, crime, and illiteracy. They had witnessed social ills unapparent in their interaction with foreign missionaries and diplomats in Ethiopia. As one Ethiopian remarked to Southard, "You foreigners have your peasants and your ignorant classes just as we have. . . . We do not recognize merely a white skin as carrying with it any kind of superiority."[32] In the 1930s, the spreading presence in Addis Ababa of western newspapers, magazines, and foreign visitors, including black Americans, sharpened the awareness of both the positive and the negative that white foreigners brought, and underlined the need to assert national perspectives and to reckon the potential of a pan-African connection.

Within a short time, Southard produced the name of the leader of the movement and the names of other important members. Kidane Mariam Aberra, a Tigrean from the Italian colony of Eritrea, was the leader. He had arrived in Addis Ababa in 1925 and had become director general of the Ministry of Education. His most prominent confederates included

---

31. 884.4016/6, Addison E. Southard to secretary of state, February 12, 1934.
32. *Ibid.*

Wolde Giorgis, secretary-general of the Foreign Office; Makonnen Hapte Wolde, director general of the Ministry of Commerce; Ayela Gabre, Chief judge of the Mixed Court; and Bashawarad Hapte Wolde, the American-educated former-mayor of Dire Dawa.[33] How effective this group might have become is debatable, for the war limited their prospects before they had a chance. In 1937, General Rodolfo Graziani ordered the massacre of many Ethiopians, including many of the educated. What is clear, however, is that western intellectual currents and influence had gained a foothold in Ethiopia in the early 1930s.

By the time of Italy's invasion in 1935, the forces of modernization had taken root. The emperor, himself inclined toward reform, increasingly sent students abroad for an education and accommodated much of their insistence about drawing upon the expertise of Ethiopian nationals. Those who studied abroad also persuaded the emperor to recruit African-American technicians, in spite of their denigration by officials of the State Department of the United States. Although the war stalled the trends of the early 1930s, Ethiopians were being pulled into the pan-African orbit.

33. *Ibid.*

III

Black Protests, Volunteers, and Recruitment

The invasion of Ethiopia ignited an emotional reaction among Africans and among descendants of Africans around the world, strengthening the bonds of pan-Africanism.[1] Africans who were themselves under colonial rule expressed indignation. Ethiopia held a historical appeal for them, and they were especially proud that the country had been a member of the League of Nations from 1923 and had signed a treaty of friendship and arbitration with Italy in 1928. When Italy ignored that treaty, however, and Britain and France urged Ethiopia to recognize Italy's claim over Walwal, pay an indemnity, and apologize for the incident, African teachers, doctors, lawyers, journalists, civil servants, and other intellectuals were outraged. They quickly identified with the Ethiopians.

Their outrage intensified when, after the war began, Britain and France refused to supply the country with arms even though it had become clear that Ethiopia's armaments could not match Italy's. Then came the failure of the limited sanctions imposed by the League (which did not include oil, the one commodity through which there could have been leverage over Italy), the Hoare-Laval compromise (which would have made Ethiopia a colony), and Britain's recognition of the conquest, in May,

---

1. Among the many valuable books on the Italo-Ethiopian War are Angelo del Boca's *The Ethiopian War, 1935–1941*, trans. P. D. Cummins (Chicago, 1969), Brice Harris' *The United States and the Italo-Ethiopian Crisis* (Stanford, Calif., 1964), F. Hardie's *The Abyssinian Crisis* (London, 1974), Alberto Sbacchi's *Ethiopia Under Mussolini: Fascism and the Colonial Experience* (London, 1985), and S. K. B. Asante's *The Pan African Protest: West Africa and the Italo-Ethiopian Crisis, 1934–1941* (London, 1977). See also Harold Marcus, *Haile Sellassie I: The Formative Years, 1892–1936* (Berkeley and Los Angeles, 1987), Chapter 8.

1936. All that not only ensured the conquest by Italy but also severely shook the confidence of African intellectuals in the leadership of the imperial powers.[2]

Mrs. G. S. Wynter Shackleford, on behalf of the Prominent Lagos Women's Society, sent a protest to the League of Nations, and the Ethiopia Relief Fund Committee of Enugu, Nigeria, passed a protest resolution. At a meeting in Accra, African politicians and veterans threatened not to "take up arms to defend European nations" if Britain recognized the conquest. And the dean of African journalism, Nnamdi Azikiwe, mobilized his newspapers in the Gold Coast and Nigeria to denounce the powers and to inform the African public of the injustice they had perpetrated. As one scholar has written, "It was the Italo-Ethiopian controversy which provided a testing-time for the articulate nationalist groups, broadened their horizon, and intensified their nationalism, which took on a more pan-African perspective."[3]

Italy's aggression against Ethiopia also sparked a number of protests, demonstrations, physical clashes, boycotts, fund-raising activities, and recruitment and volunteer efforts in the African diaspora. Barbados' *Advocate* reported that on August 1, 1935, a mass meeting in Saint Lucia passed a resolution expressing grave concern over the crisis and deep sentiment for Ethiopia. A similar report came from Trinidad, where resolutions condemned Mussolini's actions and called on Britain to intercede. On August 17, the *Advocate* carried an extended account of resolutions passed at Aggrey House, in London, by "students and others of African descent." The resolutions condemned Italy, pledged support to Ethiopia, and called for the establishment of an Abyssinian relief fund. "Coloured people in England, in America, in Africa, and in the West Indies" were called on for support.[4]

One article in the *Advocate* judged that sentiment in favor of Ethiopia could bulk large in the West Indies because the communities were over-

---

2. S. K. B. Asante, "The Italo-Ethiopian Conflict: A Case Study in British West African Response to Crisis Diplomacy in the 1930s," *Journal of African History*, XV (1974); M. B. Akpan, "Ethiopia and Liberia, 1914–1935: Two Independent African States in the Colonial Era," in *General History of Africa*, ed. A. Adu Boahen (8 vols.; Paris and Berkeley, 1985), VII.

3. Asante, "The Italo-Ethiopian Conflict," 301.

4. *Barbados Advocate*, August 2, 1935, August 17, 1935. For reactions in Africa, see Asante, *The Pan African Protest*.

whelmingly of African descent. Attention was called to an article in London's *Sunday Times* that had said, "As the European power ruling the greatest number of African subjects, we have quite a special interest in the matter. An Italo-Abyssinian war would be a war between black and white. . . . Reverses to the Italians—if such occurred—would excite the most dangerous feelings. Speedy victory for them won by mass bloodshed would be very unsettling, too; and equally so would the prolonged guerrilla warfare."[5]

The *New Statesman and Nation* voiced the opinion that "to coloured people everywhere, the war would seem a concerted attack of white against black." The *Advocate* observed that such a war would stir up "national and racial animosities throughout the world. It threatens a clash of colour, judging from the resentment which Negroes throughout the West Indies, in England and America are registering."[6]

On September 12, 1935, the American consul in Jamaica sent the secretary of state the report "Public Reactions in West Indies to the Italo-Ethiopian Question," with newspaper clippings about mass meetings that had adopted a number of resolutions sympathetic to Ethiopia. Among Jamaica's predominantly black population the feeling ran strong against Italy and assumed sharp racial overtones. According to one report, the rumor was that "the white man and the black man are going to have a war."[7] Just over a month later, after the war had begun, the consul sent another report to the State Department, "Reactions in Jamaica to Italian Ethiopian War." It remarked, "Jamaica's sympathies go out spontaneously to her stricken Abyssinian brother." It related that the local paper, the *Daily Gleaner*, had been filled with war news "for several weeks and supported sanctions. Blacks were observed reading the news on bulletin boards."[8]

The press, especially *Plain Talk* and *The People*, stimulated popular interest in the war among middle-class as well as rank-and-file Trinidadians. *Plain Talk*, edited by Alfred Mends, a Garveyite, carried a series of articles under the title "In Defense of Abyssinia and Its History." *The People* was edited by the former New York Garveyite Leonard F. Walcott,

5. London *Sunday Times,* July 21, 1935.
6. *New Statesman and Nation,* July 20, 1935; *Barbados Advocate,* August 24, 1935.
7. 765.84/1481 1/2, Public Reactions in West Indies to the Italo-Ethiopian Question, September 12, 1935.
8. 765.84/2037, Reaction in Jamaica to Italian-Ethiopian War, October 15, 1935.

who had returned to Trinidad in 1933. Walcott patterned his paper after Garvey's *Negro World* and published reprints from the *Blackman*. Also active in the campaign was Amy Jacques Garvey, who led a number of initiatives in Jamaica, including some with recruitment as their aim.[9]

Several protest organizations in Trinidad made the Ethiopian cause popular, among them the Trinidad Citizens Committee, the Afro–West Indian League, the Friends of Ethiopia, the West Indian Youth Welfare League, and the Negro Welfare Social and Cultural Association. Typical of the materials the Negro Welfare Social and Cultural Association distributed was a handbill appealing to Trinidadians to "join a protest meeting. . . . Thousands of Abyssinian peasants . . . are being slaughtered by the bombing of the Fascist butcher Mussolini. . . . Only the united action of all Negroes and oppressed people can stop this horrible mass murder."[10]

Trinidadians boycotted Italian businesses, refused to service Italian ships, organized fund-raising campaigns, and sent funds to the Ethiopian ambassador in England; former servicemen offered to join Ethiopia's military. In general, Trinidadians expressed an identity with Africa, with Ethiopians in particular. Anti-Italian protests and demonstrations also occurred in British Guiana (Guyana), Grenada, and Saint Vincent, and among Trinidadians in Venezuela.[11]

Such reactions were multiplied many times over in the United States. Militants voiced their support for Ethiopia directly, vociferously, and sometimes violently, and the established civil-rights organizations, like the National Association for the Advancement of Colored People, supported the cause as well. The NAACP's official publication, *Crisis,* informed the public about events in Ethiopia through articles, reviews, commentaries, and the like. In addition, the organization's board petitioned the League of Nations to safeguard Ethiopia's rights as a member of that body, it criticized the Soviet Union for supporting the Italians, and it lodged protests with Congress and urged its own membership to write to their congressional representatives in opposition to neutrality legislation that it held would benefit Italy. These were heady days for the NAACP as it shouldered

---

9. Brian L. Friday, "The Impact of the Italo-Ethiopian Crisis on Trinidad, 1934–1937" (Ph.D. dissertation, Dalhousie University, 1986), 9.
10. *Ibid.,* 11, 56, 98.
11. *Ibid.,* 74, 101, 110.

the principal responsibility for promoting civil rights. Concerns like unemployment, voting rights, and antilynching legislation occupied most of its attention.¹²

Several months before Italy invaded Ethiopia, African Americans through much of the country began writing to the Ethiopian Research Council about the possibility of enlisting in the emperor's armed forces. They wanted to know whether Ethiopia was "willing to use us [African Americans] in defense against Italy." And they raised questions premised on the assumption that it was: "Why is it that some preparation is not made in order to prepare us?" "Why is no transportation provided?" "Will I violate United States laws by enlisting?" "What must I do to enlist?" One simply stated, "I am a descendant of Africa and interested in our country." Another requested "information regarding going to Abyssinia, passport and the best route." Still another wrote, "Anything in defense of the African Race I am willing to support and you may call on me anytime to do so." There was the declaration "I want to go to the land that my your [sic] father came from." The Pacific Movement of Philadelphia sent a flyer to the emperor and a copy to the council: "We earnestly pledge to you our support and assistance in every way possible for the cause of Ethiopia, our mother land, that we will dye if necessary for her protection to which we are interested."¹³

Sufi Abdul Hamid, a particularly visible black activist in New York City, wrote to Bayen urging Haile Sellassie to serve as the worldwide leader of blacks, who would "die for him and his cause." Hamid asked whether he should communicate directly with the emperor.¹⁴ British subjects "of the African race" in the United States also expressed a "desire to defend the King and Ethiopia and fellow countrymen in Africa."¹⁵

12. James W. Ivy, "Traditional NAACP Interest in Africa as Reflected in the Pages of the *Crisis*," in *Africa As Seen by American Negroes,* ed. American Society of African Culture (Paris, 1958); Rodney A. Ross, "Black Americans and Haiti, Liberia, the Virgin Islands, and Ethiopia, 1929–1936" (Ph.D. dissertation, University of Chicago, 1975); "Neutrality Bill Amendment Would Aid Italy in War" (NAACP Press Release, n.d., in Files for 1935, ERC). For a general discussion of the NAACP, see Warren D. St. James, *The National Association for the Advancement of Colored People: A Case Study in Pressure Groups* (New York, 1958).

13. Pacific Movement, Philadelphia, "To the King of Ethiopia," September 9, 1935, in ERC.

14. Sufi Abdul Hamid, International Black League, to Malaku Bayen, February 26, 1935, in ERC.

15. Selwyn W. Lucas to Malaku Bayen, March 25, 1935, in ERC.

Not all communications concerned military enlistment. Samuel Albert, of New York City, wanted to open a factory in Ethiopia to produce ammunition and chemical products. He asked about the procedures he would have to follow and the arrangements that would be necessary, and he wanted to know what the country was like and what kind of reception he would be apt to find there.[16] Arthur Smith, of Bakersville, California, wrote that a group of "tradesmen" were interested in serving Ethiopia in the event of war.[17] After Harry and Pearle Broome, of Hattiesburg, Mississippi, wrote to the Ethiopian government and received no reply, they let the council know that they desired to go to Africa. Harry was a carpenter and cabinetmaker, and Pearle was a "feltmaker and designer." Not only were they prepared to serve the emperor, they said, but there were "thousands of others waiting to do likewise."[18]

The Broomes traveled about, exhorting African Americans to consider service to the emperor. Lige Green, also of Hattiesburg, heard the Broomes speak and wrote that he was "doing all I can to get all the names I can to enlist them for the Ethiopian war."[19] Another Hattiesburg resident, Mae Hicks, wrote on behalf of a "large group of young girls and boys" who constituted a club that had the education of its members as its purpose. They had heard a speech by the Broomes and wanted help so that they could "come home." They longed to live "among our own color and nation of peoples over there."[20]

Some African Americans acquainted the council with their opinions about the war and about the position the United States was taking. Joseph Green Johnson, of Baltimore, arrived at the conclusion that the United States "will not help Ethiopia because she is black. She won't do no more for Ethiopia than she will do to stop mob rule in the south." He decided that blacks should unite in the way Marcus Garvey had advocated. Johnson recalled how he had wanted to go to Africa from when he was a small boy; he saw the war as an opportunity to fulfill a dream and to help at the same time. He showed a familiarity with Ethiopian history that was uncommon among Americans. Recalling Ethiopian's defeat of Italy in 1896,

16. Albert Samuel to Ethiopian Research Council, July 5, 1935, in ERC.
17. Arthur Smith to Ethiopian Research Council, July 16, 1935, in ERC.
18. Harry L. Broome and Pearl F. Broome to Ethiopian Research Council, August 24, 1935, in ERC.
19. Lige Green to Ethiopian Research Council, August 26, 1935, in ERC.
20. R. Mae Hicks to Ethiopian Research Council, September 19, 1935, in ERC.

he was troubled that Ethiopia had not realized that Italy would seek revenge.[21]

As secretary of the council, William M. Steen tried to respond adequately to the flood of inquiries. He sent out maps and fact sheets with his correspondence. He sometimes enclosed pictures of the emperor and an Ethiopian flag. But the distance from Ethiopia, a woeful lack of funds, an inadequate mode of communication, the thin network of dedicated members, and the shielding of policy makers and even their assistants from them were all obstacles to obtaining and disseminating the information people sought. Still, the organization provided prudent, helpful, and consistent answers.

When war was near but the details of Ethiopian policy were still unclear, the council could tell aspiring soldiers only that the "Imperial Government has not yet worked out a policy governing foreign enlistments in the Imperial Army." It could express thanks "on behalf of the Imperial Government for the interest Negroes throughout the world" had shown, but it always had to deliver the disappointing news that "no recruiting is underway." Later, it had to cite the neutrality laws of the United States as a deterrent to enlistment. The council did not equivocate about its attitude toward the neutrality laws: it made it altogether plain that it did not encourage a violation of them.[22]

On the commercial opportunities of Ethiopia, the council explained that it was possible to obtain a permit to operate there provided that the license did not conflict with rights the imperial government had already granted. It referred several persons to the Société Nationale d'Ethiopie, in Addis Ababa, which financed—and purchased interests in—business projects. The council itself furnished information on labor, the standard of living, and legalities affecting the purchase and rental of property.[23]

The council almost invariably encouraged its correspondents to look to the future with optimism: "Ethiopia will accept with open arms her black brothers from America, after the war, for she will need the help of all in rebuilding herself." The council explained that the "situation prevents the acceptance by the Imperial Government of immigrants. How-

21. Joseph Green Johnson to Ethiopian Research Council, July 8, 1935, in ERC.
22. Howard Moore, acting secretary, Ethiopian Research Council, to Selwyn W. Lucas, June 17, 1935, Howard Moore to R. Mae Hicks, October 10, 1935, Howard Moore to Arthur Smith, July 20, 1935, Howard Moore to Jim Bradley, September 16, 1935, all in ERC.
23. Howard Moore to Albert Smith, July 8, 1935, in ERC.

ever, after the war subsides, it is expected that American Negroes will be given a chance to take up residence in Ethiopia and participate in her rebuilding."[24]

Some African Americans addressed inquiries and opinions to the White House. As early as July, 1934, Dan Homes wrote to President Roosevelt asking, "Why can't the black people fight against Italy? . . . We have fought out for the white peoples, why can't you help the black people out?"[25] Since this letter was written prior to the Walwal incident, it is not evident what prompted the writer, unless he had heard that in the event of war, government regulations would prevent blacks from enlisting. Reacting a year later to the neutrality legislation and in particular to an earlier statement that an "American citizen shall be deemed to have expatriated himself when he had been naturalized in any foreign state in conformity with its laws, or when he had taken an oath of allegiance to any foreign state," Orhardo Andrews, of New York City, wrote to put the viewpoint of the "majority of the Ethiopians or Africans who are residing in this country" on record: "First the Africans who are residing [here] and all over the West did not come here voluntarily, but by an act of kidnapping which today is punishable in the United States by death. . . . As for loosing our citizenship of this country, we don't give a nick about that. This citizenship is of no value to us. . . . If your country can not protect us when we are citizens and living here, why should we worry about it[?]" Showing a keen knowledge of history and contemporary affairs, Andrews continued, "The Ethiopians who lives in the United States fought for this country in the Civil War, the Revolutionary [War], the War of 1812, the Mexican, the Spanish American and the World War and yet they are treated the [same] way after every war[;] . . . you were the head into drawing of the Kellogg Peace Pact Treaty and now have deferred from your treaty. What must the world think of you?" He informed the president that "we the Ethiopians are going to continue recruiting regardless of consequences, and what [is] more some of us will go even if we have to pay our fare from our labor and savings of years."[26]

Writing from Madison, Illinois, Sam Buck reminded President Roose-

---

24. Howard Moore to Will W. Trimble, October 19, 1935, Howard Moore to H. B. Williams, October 10, 1935, both in ERC.
25. 884.2221/13, Dan Homes to Roosevelt government, July 18, 1935.
26. 884.2221/12, Orlando Andrews to President Roosevelt, n.d.

velt that blacks fought in the Spanish-American War, in Haiti, and in World War I, and he asked, "Why cannot American Ethiopians help their Black Race?" He appealed to the president and Congress "to make it possible that we as Negroes of the United [States] may have the privilege to enlist."[27]

Dr. H. Randall, of Kansas City, Kansas, writing as an "American Colored man," felt that his "duty" had been set before him, and he announced that he was "ready to go at the sound of the bell." Randall appealed for a proclamation to be issued for all "colored Americans at once."[28]

Letters like these to the president were referred to the Department of State, which sent standard acknowledgments calling attention to the legislation forbidding enlistment in foreign armies. The State Department also received a number of inquiries directly from African Americans. Some of them offered nonmilitary service, like W. P. Perkins, of Macon, Georgia, who wrote, "I am a carpenter. . . . I am a colored person. Please send me over to Ethiopia to help in construction." Walter Johnson, of Plainfield, New Jersey, asserted, "My brother and myself, of the colored race, are planning to go to Ethiopia, if transport can be arranged, in the hope that we might in some way be of use to our colored brethren, there as nurses or otherwise. We do not plan to enter the army, as we believe that is forbidden to American citizens." Johnson inquired if "the people of Ethiopia resent the sympathies of the colored people of the United States," as they were alleged to "in a book recently written by a Dr. [Carleton] Coon."[29]

A letter to the State Department from R. R. Walker, of Kansas City, Missouri, asked if there would "be any objection in this country should any African-American volunteer for military service in aid of his ancestral home." Henry Kimble, of Cincinnati, raised the question "Can I get permission . . . to open a recruiting office of enlisting men for service in Africa. I have made a survey of the city, and I find there is a great number of men . . . and they ambition is to join the Ethiopian army. . . . The ways [and] means of transportation has been figure[d] out. I want to have efficient."[30]

27. 884.2221/12, Sam Buck to President Roosevelt, July 20, 1935.
28. 884.2221/33, A. H. Randall to President Roosevelt, October 7, 1935.
29. 884.208/8, W. P. Perkins, Macon, Georgia, to State Department, October 6, 1935; 884.208/9, Walter Johnson, Plainfield, N.J., to State Department, October 7, 1935.
30. 884.2221/7; Memorandum by Wallace Murray, July 16, 1935; 884.2221/14, R. R. Walker to secretary of state, July 20, 1935; 884.2221/10, Henry Kimble to secretary of state, July 19, 1935.

Arthur P. Hayes, who graduated with cadet training at the Dunbar High School in the District of Columbia and received B.S. and M.A. degrees at Columbia University, had served in the United States Army and was honorably discharged. He became a captain in the reserves and requested the State Department's assistance in support of his attempt to win consideration for a military post with the Ethiopian government. Hayes's record was impressive. He had studied in the Ph.D. program at Columbia, served as professor of military science and tactics at Lincoln University, in Missouri, at Tuskegee Institute, in Alabama, and at Prairie View State College, in Texas; he had also been an instructor for the Army Extension School for black reserve officers in 1932. His overseas experience included service in the Philippines, and at one time he worked under Colonel (later General) Benjamin O. Davis. But he became frustrated over his assignments and concluded that he could contribute more and receive better recognition in Ethiopia.[31] There is no sign that the State Department gave him any support. Anyway, he never served in Ethiopia.

From Bartlesville, Oklahoma, Shellie Nelson, a high-school teacher, wrote, "I am the representative of an organization of Bartlesville Negroes who are desirous of entering the conflict." An inquiry came from John A. Diaz, of Tucson, Arizona, affirming that "50,000 Americans of African descent [are] ready to leave for Ethiopia for the expressed purpose of defending that country's independence. . . . In my lectures I come in contact with numerous African-Americans, ex-soldiers, mechanics, and professionals, who are eager to go to the aid of Ethiopia in her hour of suffering."[32] Diaz signed his letter as organizer of the Association for Ethiopia's Independence.

Joseph C. Coles, of the Detroit Committee for Aid to Ethiopia, wrote to Secretary of State Cordell Hull that "there are a number of sympathizers here of Ethiopian people . . . and [they] are desirous of doing something tangible in expressing this sympathy." Coles wanted to know if his committee would be transgressing "the laws by raising funds, recruiting volunteers, and [doing] other things" that his group deemed necessary.[33]

An exceptionally militant piece of correspondence came from the In-

---

31. 884.20/20, Arthur P. Hayes, New York, to secretary of state, July 19, 1935.

32. 884.2221/16, Shellie Nelson to Department of State, July 25, 1935; 884.2221/46, John A. Diaz to Cordell Hull, December 30, 1935.

33. 884.2221/23, Joseph C. Coles to secretary of state, August 24, 1935.

ternational African Progressive Association, of Beckley, West Virginia. That organization wrote to Secretary Hull that

> the Black Man in America is not an alien in any State or District anywhere in Africa, he was simply taken away against his will . . . the black man in America is an aborigine, indigenous to Africa, torn from home[;] . . . he has never sworn allegiance to the New World. . . . The black race is a much despised race by the white races[.] . . . What is the big reason that the U.S. objects to the Ethiopians in America going to the aid of his brothers in defending their ancient kingdom, against their enemies?
>
> Our emperor Haile Selassie is calling upon the descendants of the very Africans who were seized and brought to this country by violence[;] . . . the insistent call of the Africans at home must be answered by the Africans abroad. . . . It is all black folks['] duty to defend Africa, whether at home or abroad[;] Africa is the home of the black folks.[31]

This unsigned message came from an organization in a small town of a small, conservative, poor state. The International African Progressive Association manifestly had an articulate leadership that was aware of the relationship between Africa and its diaspora. Africa for Africans, the idea of Africa as home for African Americans, had emerged as a concept in this country around the 1850s. And *black* as the label for African Americans was an idea in the black legacy that would gain momentum in the 1960s and 1970s. But the State Department seemed to attach little importance to this correspondence, for there is no record of a response to it.

In Fort Worth, "Negroes met to consider going to Ethiopia . . . to spill their blood in behalf of our native land." Walter J. Davis, a World War I veteran and the apparent leader of the meeting, said that the gathering was called to "protest against the threatened war." He drafted an open letter, which was distributed:

> My dear Emperor:
> I herewith ask your permission to organize a company of men, by voluntary enlistment, for military duty in behalf of your

34. 884.2221/12, president general, I.A.P.A., to Cordell Hull, July 24, 1935.

country. There are a large number of local colored men who are ready to spill their blood.... We are ready at your command, and will request only that your government pay the transportation expense to Ethiopia."[35]

From neighboring Okmulgee, Randolph Mitchell, an African American, reported that "100 Negroes of that city had signed to fight for Ethiopia in event of war and that a state-wide recruiting movement was under way."[36]

Observing that many African Americans were interested in enlistment, Robert Lee Vann, the publisher of the Pittsburgh *Courier,* requested information from the State Department on regulations governing the enlistment of citizens of the United States in foreign armies. The department did not deviate from the position it had adhered to throughout. It cited the relevant statutes of the United States, stated the purpose of the neutrality legislation, and stressed the security risks in Ethiopia. The usual reply was simply to present the relevant section of Title 18 of the United States Code: Section 21 (Criminal Code, Section 9), which provided that any citizen accepting a commission to serve against a country or territory at peace with the United States could be fined up to two thousand dollars and imprisoned up to three years. It also regularly cited Section 2 of the Act of March 2, 1907, regarding the loss of American citizenship by an oath of allegiance to a foreign country.

The State Department sought to discourage travel to Ethiopia even for nonmilitary purposes and when there was no intention of taking an oath of allegiance. A typical statement during the period was that "the Department has considered it necessary to advise American citizens to leave Ethiopia, and since it cannot therefore encourage the entrance of additional American citizens into that country at the present time it has been deemed advisable not to issue passports in general to persons who decide to proceed to Ethiopia."[37] No official position seems to have been in force for citizens already holding passports. The strategy, however, was to discourage recruitment and travel without exacerbating a highly sensitive and difficult matter—especially during the election year of 1936.

35. New York *Times,* July 14, 1935.
36. *Ibid.*
37. 884.2221/31, Wallace Murray to Norman Yoder, October 16, 1935; Philadelphia *Tribune,* June 13, 1935, p. 1.

A few cases of recruitment, however, did cause deep concern on the part of the Department of State and the Department of Justice. Evidence of cooperation between Ethiopian students in the United States and African Americans came to light early in 1935. Malaku Bayen, while a medical student at Howard University, was turning out to be an important liaison with African Americans and with the State Department. He sought to ensure that the department received information reflective of the Ethiopian perspective. In December, 1934, he confided to the Division of Near Eastern Affairs of the State Department that he had a telegram from the Ethiopian government explaining how the Walwal incident occurred. He stressed that he thought the matter "extremely grave," for Italy had been "planning the attack for a long time." He also offered his judgment that neither the British nor the French would oppose the Italian aggression.[38] Bayen's entrée to the State Department aimed not only at promoting the Ethiopian perspective but at winning American support despite his country's lack of official representation.

At the same time, Bayen was establishing an African-American connection. He was especially popular as a spokesman for Ethiopia at African-American gatherings. His commitment to black solidarity led him to welcome black expressions of support, which sometimes included a desire to enlist in the emperor's forces. To one group he said, "The American Negro, through racial kinship, is duty-bound to support Abyssinia." That kind of statement caused some journalists to portray him as the emperor's representative enrolling volunteers. On one occasion he felt compelled to respond to the editor of the *Afro-American,* "I think it is a fine spirit for the American to be showing, inasmuch as Ethiopia is contending for a principle. I am sure that my country would be pleased to know of such willingness. I do not see why the Ethiopian Government would refuse such help provided such volunteers can find a way to keep within American neutrality laws."[39] But Bayen was quick to explain to the State Department that he did not intend his statements to be interpreted as recruiting volunteers. He was eager, though, that African-American sympathies not be dampened. Whatever signal he wanted to give, several African Americans claimed to have been recruited because of him and his speeches.

One case that caused the United States government concern involved

38. 765.84/100, December 17, 1934.
39. 765.84/178, February 23, 1935; *Afro-American,* February 23, 1935.

C. Malcolm Ashe and Dutton Ferguson, both African Americans. Not much is known about Ashe except that he had a student pilot's license. Dutton Ferguson, who graduated from Howard University in 1929, was acquainted with Bayen and by 1936 had become editor for the Washington *Tribune,* a black American newspaper in the District of Columbia. He and Ashe acted on what they took to be a suggestion by Bayen that African Americans might be used by Ethiopia against Italy. They wrote to the Department of Commerce for a list of black pilots. They then sent some thirty letters to pilots on that list, inquiring about their availability and interest in serving in Ethiopia.[40] The FBI launched an investigation and discovered that several letters had gone to students enrolled in commercial aviation at Roosevelt Field, on Long Island. According to the instructor, Ernest Nathan, a transport pilot who also operated an auto parts business, he had drafted a model negative reply.[41] Nathan also explained that although Lola Jackson had told a journalist "she planned to go" to Ethiopia if she could be helpful there, she had no such plans. Cy Caldwell, an associate editor for *Aero-Digest,* also assured the FBI that Nathan's students were not considering service in Ethiopia. Nathan's and Caldwell's assessments were reinforced by interviews the FBI conducted with some of the students. Leonard L. Yates, of the Bronx, had responded to Ashe but received no further correspondence. Thomas Mills had not responded. It is not clear whether Archie Smith, Harry Ross, Herbert Osborn, or Robert Thomas had. All the students denied any interest in enlisting for service in Ethiopia, however.[42] Ashe and Dutton told the FBI that they simply wanted to identify pilots and determine their availability for Ethiopia in the event of war. Both men said that the Department of Commerce and the Department of War had held that their efforts were not illegal. Apparently the FBI was satisfied, for it declared the matter closed.[43]

What caused the FBI greater concern was a group of organizations and street speakers in New York City. One bureau report by T. H. Tracy mentioned that "street speakers were a common feature of Harlem, except in cold or inclement weather." The 32nd precinct, on West 135th Street, had an officer who maintained close contact with the street speakers, whom he

40. 884.2221/52, March 30, 1936.
41. 884.2221/50, February 17, 1936.
42. 884.2221/51, April 10, 1936; New York *Times,* July 25, 1935.
43. 884.2221/52, March 30, 1936.

regarded as "petty racketeers." The report explained that black officers could not gather much information and that white officers had even less success. Most of the street speakers, according to Tracy, were blacks from the Caribbean affiliated with the Garvey movement. The principal speakers were James Thornhill, of the Universal Negro Improvement Association; William Jordan, of the Ethiopian Pacifist Movement; Ira Kemp, of the African Patriotic League; Reggie Thomas, of a local branch of the International Labor Defense; and Charles T. Romney, of the American Civil Rights Association. The report called Sufi Abdul Hamid, of the International Black League, a "decidedly interesting" speaker who dressed like an Arab and was a "linguist" commanding "about six languages." Samuel Daniels was described as founder and spokesman of the Pan-African Reconstruction Association (PARA), the "largest and most active of the new organizations." Other active groups included the Afro-American Producers' and Consumers' League and the Ethiopian Guild of the Latter-Day Garveyites.[44]

Tracy reported that officers listened to all the speeches, in order to gauge activity in Harlem. His allegation was that the Italo-Ethiopian War served to attract crowds who contributed money that resulted in little more than the personal gain of some individuals. What most of the speakers called for was the boycotting of white businesses, especially those operated by Italians. Evidently the recommended tactic bore results, because some Italians were forced to move their businesses from Harlem and some of the larger stores were forced to employ blacks for the first time. But according to the report, "very little recruitment" was conducted, because the police kept the speakers "informed of the law."[45]

The most popular venues for street speakers in New York were at 130th Street and Seventh Avenue, where as many as five hundred listeners and spectators sometimes congregated, and at 132nd Street and Lenox Avenue, 133rd Street and Lenox Avenue, 138th Street and Lenox Avenue, 143rd Street and Seventh Avenue, 138th Street and Seventh Avenue, and 135th Street and Seventh Avenue. Pictures of Haile Sellassie and books on black history were for sale at the meetings. The normal pattern was for the speakers to perform nightly until about eleven and then to adjourn to a more secluded place with the "more faithful." In refuges like the long, dark sidewalk next to a school on Lenox Avenue between 134th Street and

44. 884.2221/51, April 10, 1936.
45. Ibid.

135th Street, groups of between five and twenty-five persons could discuss matters more privately. Whites were not welcome then.[46]

Hamid and Daniels became preoccupations of the FBI. Hamid, who was born in Pennsylvania, appears to have been self-trained, especially in languages, and he was a charismatic speaker capable of attracting large audiences. Although the bureau listed him as being involved in several organizations, he seems to have played a key role mainly in the African Legion and the International Black League. Investigators gave his headquarters as Dunbar Hall, on Seventh Avenue.[47]

Hamid also extended his efforts to the South. The New York *Herald Tribune* carried a story about his launching a campaign in Goldsboro, North Carolina, to raise funds for a plane for T. H. Hawkins, a flier in Harlem who had been born in Wilmington, North Carolina. The Goldsboro *News-Argus* referred to Hamid as the "Black Hitler of Harlem" because of his "radical" and "fiery" racial comments and his passionate recounting of the causes of the Italo-Ethiopian War. Later interviews by FBI agents showed that Hamid's audiences in North Carolina did not regard his remarks as either radical or fiery. Whether he adjusted his speeches to the fervor of his audience or whether what was radical and fiery depended on the listener, he was well received by several African-American groups, including the African Methodist Episcopal church in Goldsboro, Dillard High School, and the "colored Baptist Church in Mt. Olive."[48] He made a number of unconfirmable claims, however. He spoke of having a summer camp in upstate New York for training recruits, and in Goldsboro he gave assurances that he had a food production plant in Harlem and that he had "sent [Hubert Julian] to Ethiopia" to train pilots. The last of these assertions was pure fabrication, casting doubt on the others, since there is no evidence substantiating them. Hamid also had a prison record for petty offenses, including "preaching Atheism without a license." But he was popular to street audiences in Harlem particularly. It is possible that the police or the FBI harassed Hamid to contain him, for there were stretches of time when the police did not report seeing him on the streets.[49]

Daniels attracted the attention of the FBI when the United States at-

46. 884.2221/50, February 17, 1936.
47. Ibid.
48. Ibid.; New York *Herald Tribune*, August 31, 1935; Goldsboro (N.C.) *News-Argus*, August 30, 1935; J. Edgar Hoover to Hon. Stephen T. Early, secretary to the president, Memorandum on Colonel Hubert Fauntleroy Julian, November 13, 1940.
49. 884.2221/50, February 17, 1936.

torney's office in New York sent to the attorney general's office, in Washington, some information, including a newspaper clipping, about Daniels' involvement in recruitment activities. The attorney's office in New York "deemed it advisable to submit the matter for consideration before taking any steps." The clipping showed a group of blacks looking at a sign labeled, Ethiopian Volunteers Register Here! Daniels and PARA were apparently enlisting volunteers, who paid twenty-five cents "for office overhead."[50]

Daniels said he was born in Tanganyika and became an American citizen in 1924. He seems to have traveled in Europe and possibly the Caribbean. The New York *Evening Journal* mentioned his "clipped English accent which he picked up in London after he fled his tribal home in Africa."[51] Daniels hoped PARA would help "bind Liberia and Abyssinia together industrially." What he meant by that and how he planned to achieve it remain unclear. Police officers and businessmen interviewed by the FBI related that in the beginning the organization was "very active with large crowds of people around, blacks and whites," and that there was considerable talk about military enlistments for Ethiopia. At that early period there were nightly meetings in the street and at Daniels' headquarters, on West 135th Street. A PARA truck passing up and down the streets of Harlem advertised the organization and its activities. According to Daniels, there were fifty thousand military volunteers in Detroit and seventy-five hundred in Chicago. He spoke of his plans to obtain a ship to transport the volunteers to Ethiopia.[52]

On July 11, 1935, the New York *Evening Journal* bore the headline "Harlem Calls for Men to Fight Duce," under which it was observed that "porters, mechanics, bottlewashers, and cooks 'paid' twenty-five cents to register." Four days later, on July 15, the New York *Times* carried a story on a rally that PARA had organized in Harlem at the Trade and Commerce Building, on Seventh Avenue, to elicit support for Ethiopia. Among the speakers was the Reverend Harold H. Williamson, an organizer for PARA, who exhorted, "Let's get right up and tell why we want to knock out Mussolini like Joe Louis did Carnera." Daniels urged African-American "technicians and industrialists to apply their skill in a Negro land—Libe-

50. 884.2221/8, July 19, 1935.
51. 884.2221/50, February 17, 1936; New York *Evening Journal*, July 11, 1935.
52. 884.2221/50, February 17, 1936.

ria or Abyssinia, preferably, Abyssinia." He conceded that it was illegal for Ethiopia to recruit in the United States, but he maintained that volunteers would be "welcome and accepted." Transportation was to be "guaranteed." He also appealed for shoes for the Ethiopians. Some of the speakers extolled Marcus Garvey; a frequent assertion was that "Africa is for Africans." Several participants said they would fight for Ethiopia. One speaker allowed that he liked "the word African. No more Negroes or shines 'an coons.' African!"[53]

During the summer of 1935, not only PARA but other groups were aggressively asserting themselves. In New Haven, newspapers reported planning for a rally by PARA. Accounts multiplied about the recruitment of volunteers and the raising of funds for airplanes. But by the time the war officially began, on October 3, the United States had left no doubt about its determination not to be drawn into the hostilities and had communicated to Americans, directly through legislation, public announcements, and investigations, that the government would not countenance involvement and was unable to guarantee personal security in Ethiopia. The press and police officials, especially the latter, made sure that the American policy on recruitment and service in foreign armed forces was known by those likely to enlist.[54]

Although the attorney general's office concluded that Daniels was "engaged in a petty racket" and made no serious effort to recruit, it felt that the "violent nature of the social propaganda" rife at the meetings would become more virulent if it interviewed Daniels. It also feared that Daniels would depict an interview as proving his "victimization," to rally others around him.[55] In the end, the FBI did not take additional action against him, because it saw no serious danger in the enlistment he was conducting and did not regard his "racket" as inflicting enough pain to compel facing the indignation and controversy that would have attended its suppression.

What seems to have been another potential national recruitment movement was led by the Universal Multitechnic Association (UMA), a religiously based organization whose objective was "to study and discover means of bettering humanity and to apply these findings to the uplift of all people." The UMA called on all major social institutions—churches,

53. Ibid.
54. Ibid.; 884.2221/51, April 10, 1936.
55. 884.2221/22, September 13, 1935.

states, schools, businesses, and homes—to reexamine themselves and adjust to the "human society" of the day. Although its aims were lofty and vague, and the means of achieving them were murky, the organization succeeded in attracting a following, largely because of its emphasis on self-help and social programs in poor communities.[56]

The origins of the UMA are obscure, but it was in existence in Washington, D.C., by July, 1935, with an office on Eleventh Street in the northwest sector of the city. The organization seems to have had a relationship with the Good Samaritans, which produced a pamphlet, *The Good Samaritan,* that the UMA distributed. The Good Samaritans were located on D Street in the northwest quadrant, and it appealed for clothes and furniture for the needy, and toys for children, and arranged for the delivery of the donations. It also sought funds for establishing a camp for young boys and girls. Both the UMA and the Good Samaritans were influenced by Jane Addams and the work at Hull House.[57]

The FBI turned its attention to the UMA's alleged recruitment activities. The Washington *Times* carried an article on July 13, 1935, with the caption "Colored Group Recruits Here for Ethiopia." According to the story, a group of over two hundred, headed by former Howard University students, was mounting a "boycott and war move against Italy." The newspaper identified the group as the UMA, which it said had opened a recruitment office in the 1300 block of U Street, N.W.[58] It listed J. Van Bruner as president, James Y. Eaton as vice-president, Bernard Hampton as secretary, and the Reverend Ulyses S. Edwards as treasurer. The specific aim, it reported, was "to recruit several thousand volunteers and sympathizers." As the "first colored group to give its active support to the Ethiopian cause," the organization had passed at an earlier meeting a "resolution urging a boycott of all Italian merchants in Washington and vicinity who refuse to protest in writing to [the] Italian government officials against the invasion of Abyssinia." The *Times* also mentioned that the association had decided to establish branches in Maryland and Virginia.[59]

On July 14, the Washington *Herald* informed its readers that "white recruits [were] ready to fight for Abyssinia." Walter Isham, a former truck

---

56. 884.2221/6, Memorandum with Attachments, July 17, 1935.
57. Ibid.; *Good Samaritan,* July 13, 1935.
58. Washington *Times,* July 13, 1935.
59. Ibid.

driver, explained that he liked "to be where there's trouble." He remembered "hearing his father . . . talk of his own youth in Abyssinia . . . and now a second-hand nostalgia has seized him." The *Herald* wondered if the UMA would "receive white recruits" as well.[60]

When the Department of State began receiving reports about the U Street recruitment operation, it initiated an investigation. Charles H. Simmons, a white man, told it that he had enlisted and that his transportation to Ethiopia would be paid. He added that he would receive no salary but would be covered by a thousand-dollar life insurance policy. The Justice Department began an immediate investigation.[61] Its inquiry confirmed that Edwards, Eaton, and Bruner were leaders of the UMA, but they all denied inducing anyone to enlist for service in the Ethiopian army. They maintained that they had only collected names of sympathizers with the Ethiopian cause. It was not their intention to violate American statutes, they assured the Justice Department.[62]

But according to the Washington *Times* the enlistment had been going on for several weeks and the department was unsure whether to proceed against it. One official, Frank Parrish, had been informed that recruitment was occurring in New York and other cities, but his position was that "we probably will take no action unless the State Department requests that we do."[63] Parrish also observed that the "recruiting in Harlem, New York, according to reports I have received, has all the earmarks of a racket. . . . What puzzles me is the interest of the colored people in the Italo-Ethiopian developments. The reigning House of Ethiopia, unless I'm mistaken, does not belong to the colored race, but rather is Semitic. This appeal to the colored people along race lines seems to me to be all poppycock."[64]

On July 30, the FBI submitted a copy of its report on the UMA to the State Department. Edwards and his associates seem to have convinced the bureau that their activities were not ill intentioned and did not violate the law. Edwards insisted that the names and addresses of sympathizers were collected for possible future reference and that there was no obligation on anyone's part. There was no commitment to issue insurance poli-

60. Washington *Herald*, July 14, 1935.
61. 884.2221/3, Memorandum, July 16, 1935; 884.2221/4, Wallace Murray to William Phillips, July 16, 1935.
62. 884.2221/6, Memorandum, July 17, 1935.
63. *Ibid.*; 884.2221/5, Memorandum, July 18, 1935.
64. Washington *Times*, July 17, 1935.

cies, and such funds "could not possibly be raised by the association." Edwards stressed that there were no plans to hold mass meetings or to collect funds, munitions, or supplies in behalf of the Ethiopian cause. The FBI ruled, "This case is closed subject to being reopened if the Bureau or Department desires further investigation."[65] There appears to have been no desire to continue the investigation.

Obviously, considerable exploration of ways to join Ethiopia's armed forces took place among black Americans. In the final analysis, though, economic depression and increasingly persistent government restraints and harassment prevented all but two African Americans from participating in the war. The two who went to fight were pilots, Hubert Julian and John Robinson. Julian, who was born in Trinidad, migrated to the United States in 1921; Robinson, who was born in Florida and educated at Tuskegee Institute, resided for many years in Chicago.

Julian, an early supporter of Garveyism in New York and a largely self-trained pilot and parachute jumper, organized a number of flying and jumping exhibitions that earned him the title of Black Eagle. Bayen heard about Julian's exhibitions and recruited him as a pilot for the emperor in 1930. Hiring was part of the general campaign to employ African Americans in Ethiopia. When Julian arrived in Addis Ababa, he attested to the United States legation that he had several years' experience as a flyer and trainer and that he was the only black with a flying license in the United States. Neither of his statements was correct, however. His flying experience was very limited and not consistently successful, and at the time he had received only a student pilot's permit such as others too had obtained for ten dollars. The permit merely indicated interest in seeking a regular license later. Julian acquired his license in 1935.[66]

Within two weeks, Julian succeeded in having the emperor arrange and witness his successful parachute jump. That won him a medal, the Order of Menelik. Ethiopian officials, the local media, and the diplomatic community were highly impressed by Julian's performance. The French diplomats and aviation advisers, however, were conspicuously cool to the demonstration of prowess, and no doubt for good reason. Not only had

---

65. 884.2221/5, Phillips to attorney general, August 2, 1935; 884.2221/22, legal adviser, State Department, September 13, 1935; 166.121/54A, Paul Alling to Addison E. Southard, July 29, 1930; 166.121/47, Park to secretary of state, May 26, 1930.
66. 166.121/49, James L. Park to secretary of state, June 4, 1930.

Julian expressed disdain for the French advisers, the French were anxious about their future in Ethiopia. The American chargé d'affaires had informed the State Department that the emperor wanted to break the French monopoly in the country's aviation program.[67]

After the successful jump, Bayen received a sizable allocation of funds for the introduction of an aviation training program under Julian, who later maintained that the emperor had awarded him the title of colonel. Julian hoped to use his prestige to help him sell aircraft to the emperor. On leaving Ethiopia a few weeks later for a short visit to the United States, he portrayed himself as chief of the Ethiopian air service, with authorization to purchase planes for the government.[68] His statements caused the American consul to inquire into their authenticity. The Ethiopian minister of the foreign office answered, "I have the honor to inform you that on his departure Mr. Julian received from the Emperor *only* a promise for an ordinary job, for which he might have qualifications, in a Department of the Government, and that he has not been given any other orders."[69]

The American legation had been pleased with the positive image of the United States that Julian's early impact fostered, though he was really a British subject from Trinidad and only identified locally as an American. Concern began to grow, however, about his "boastfulness." The foreign minister's statement made the legation even more suspicious and more attentive to the aviator's activities and claims.

When Julian returned, the Ethiopian government put him to work installing electric-light poles for the coronation. In spite of his self-advertisement, he did not have a high-level position and was probably not close to the emperor. It is a telling detail that he had no role in arranging the flying program for the Ethiopian student pilots at the emperor's coronation. If he had been chief of the air service, he would have been involved. He would not have been reduced to making an unauthorized flight in the emperor's favorite aircraft, which, to the embarrassment of the emperor, he crashed at the ceremony. According to the Ministry of Foreign Affairs, the government at first considered disciplining Julian and fining him for the cost of the plane. The eventual decision was to "expel him from the

67. *Ibid.;* 166.121/50, James L. Park to secretary of state, July 12, 1930; 166.121/57, James L. Park to secretary of state, July 7, 1930.
68. 166.121/62, Addison E. Southard to secretary of state, September 15, 1930.
69. 166.121/64, Addison E. Southard to secretary of state, October 14, 1930; 166.121/65, Addison E. Southard to secretary of state, October 20, 1930.

country," however, and "to have nothing to do with Mr. Julian." The Black Eagle later denied that he had been forced to leave.[70]

Although Julian was embittered and critical of the Ethiopian government, he returned to the country when the war began in 1935, planning to join the emperor's armed forces. In spite of his and others' statements, there seems no evidence that he became supervisor of the Ethiopian air force, nor does it appear that he had any combat duty. He may have helped train ground troops, but the idea that he assumed an important position and fought for Ethiopia very likely goes back to gullible journalists eager to accept flamboyant rumors about the Black Eagle's exploits.[71]

John Robinson was a man of a different cast. Although he had been denied entrance to several pilot classes in the United States because he was black, he persisted, eventually becoming the first black graduate of the Curtiss-Wright Aeronautical School, in Chicago. Later he was one of the school's instructors.[72] Robinson was not a headliner. He did not perform in exhibitions but taught others and flew private planes. He was much less widely known than Julian, but he gained considerably more experience as a pilot.

When Bayen was in medical school, he wrote to Claude Barnett, the publisher and director of the Associated Negro Publishers (ANP), an African-American news agency, expressing interest in black technicians: "As I see it now, my country will not get very far with the help that is rendered by the white man for the development of the country." Bayen elaborated on his country's need for chemists, mechanics, engineers, and other such specialists, and he requested Barnett's assistance in identifying and selecting black candidates: "I hope to make one of my points to have our Government convinced that their cooperation with western Negroes would be

70. 166.121/65, Southard to secretary of state, October 20, 1930. For Julian's account, see *The Black Eagle: Colonel Hubert Julian, as Told to John Bulloch* (London, 1964), 90–91.

71. John Peer Nugent has explained in *The Black Eagle* (New York, 1971) that Julian trained ground troops, was appointed military governor of Ambo, and participated in combat. Nugent, however, presented no documentation for the assertions in the book, many of them at variance with available evidence. He did not explain his methodology, although it seems that the book resulted from interviews with Julian, who must be regarded as a highly questionable, if not unreliable, source. See *The Black Eagle*, 95–100.

72. James William Cheeks, unpublished manuscript; John Robinson, "Wings Over Ethiopia," *New Masses*, July 7, 1936; James William Cheeks', Thurlow Evans Tibbs', and William Steen's interviews with author, 1981–85.

a quick solution to our need." Barnett recommended Robinson, whom Bayen interviewed and selected as a pilot. The two men sailed together for Ethiopia on May 2, 1935.[73]

Bayen and Barnett had discussed the utility of informing African Americans about developments in Ethiopia. Bayen had agreed to translate Ethiopian news items for Barnett, and the publisher had arranged for Robinson to serve as a reporter for the ANP in Ethiopia. Robinson went to Ethiopia with more than one mission.[74]

Notwithstanding the experience the Ethiopian government had had with Julian, it received Robinson well, appointing him a pilot in the Ethiopian air force, which at the time may have included only nineteen vintage planes. Robinson flew several missions for the emperor, and some say that during the war he was the principal means of communication between the government and the front lines of battle. Reportedly, he also flew the emperor on several reconnaissance inspections over the battle zones. On two occasions, his plane may have taken hits, but he sustained no serious injuries. Because of his aeronautical virtuosity, he became known as the Brown Condor.[75]

Unlike the Black Eagle, whose departure brought relief to the Ethiopians and whose return to the United States elicited denunciations of him as a coward and a traitor, Robinson was popular among both Ethiopians and Americans. The Brown Condor received a hero's welcome in the United States, and he was determined to support the cause to the end. Over the following years, he toured the nation as a lecturer and fund raiser for Ethiopian defense and played a large role in the organization and development of the Ethiopian World Federation. He returned to Ethiopia to participate in its postwar reconstruction and died there in 1954.

There is a final, somewhat tragic note on Julian. In November, 1935, a rumor circulated in Addis Ababa that a high-ranking American was in league with Italians to assassinate the emperor. Although Julian was not a high-ranking official, suspicion came to rest on him, especially after a

---

73. Claude Barnett to Malaku Bayen, January 8, 1935, Malaku Bayen to Claude Barnett, May 6, 1935, both in Barnett Papers, Chicago Historical Society (Microfilm at Moorland-Spingarn Research Center, Howard University).

74. Claude Barnett to Malaku Bayen, February 5, 1935, Malaku Bayen to Claude Barnett, January 21, 1935, January 30, 1935, William Robinson to Claude Barnett, November 21, 1935, all in Barnett Papers.

75. Robinson to Barnett, November 21, 1935, in Barnett Papers; Robinson, "Wings."

newspaper reported that the suspect was a "colored American." Although Julian was among those the government interrogated in its investigation, it filed no charges against him. Still, it had become clear that his presence in the country was a burden on him and on his hosts. In November, 1935, he left on short notice, after a stay of only four months.[76]

In view of Julian's unremitting efforts to obtain a ranking position in the armed forces and his posturing about his influence in the country, his frustration over the the way he had been treated is understandable. He felt that his "service and knowledge were not appreciated," and he became openly critical of the Ethiopians. Calling the country backward, he predicted an Italian victory. He was careful, though, not to attack the emperor, whom he admired but thought poorly advised. It was because of his public attacks on the country and the war effort, and his "threatened 'exposure' of conditions in Ethiopia," that a number of African Americans denounced him as a "traitor" and "Judas."[77]

In the United States, Julian announced a national tour to lecture on Ethiopia and his experiences there, at a fee of a thousand dollars an appearance. As flamboyant as ever, dressing and traveling in style, he struck pro-Ethiopian leaders and their groups as a threat to the fund-raising efforts being launched. Some African Americans talked of blocking the tour and appealed to the State Department to deport Julian. Willis Huggins announced that mass meetings were being planned to discredit him.[78] None of this, however, silenced the Black Eagle. If anything, he was emboldened. One newspaper account quoted him as saying, "It would certainly be an act of God if some well-meaning civilized nation would go to Ethiopia and try to lift that country out of the rut of backwardness. . . . That mission of mercy could certainly be performed without the aid of guns and the ruthless destruction of life, limb and property." He argued, "His majesty, Haile Selassie, is all that an honorable, sincere, courageous human being could be, but he is being weighted down with tremendous handicaps of internal strife, brought on by the lack of discipline, class hatred, and many other outmoded evils which go to make a backward and non-progressive country." Julian hurled his strongest criticisms against the

76. Nugent, *The Black Eagle*, 101–103.
77. Philadelphia *Tribune*, November 14, 1935, December 19, 1935, February 6, 1936. For Julian's explanations, see *The Black Eagle: Colonel Hubert Julian as Told to John Bulloch*, 113–16.
78. *The Black Eagle: Colonel Hubert Julian as Told to John Bulloch*, 113–16.

award of key government positions to whites: "There surely must be something radically wrong when a human being volunteers to die, if need be, for a country that is populated by black people from the ruler down to the most humble peasant, and that human being finds . . . that all government jobs and positions of responsibility are being held by white men."[79]

The class conflict and internal strife that Julian perceived did hobble Ethiopia, as they did many other countries. But Julian worsened the problems by his ineptitude, his gross exaggerations of his skills and contacts, his intrigues, and his distortions of the facts. Several whites occupied crucial advisory positions in the government, but Ethiopians also held responsible posts. The truth was that Ethiopians—Bayen and others—recognized that not enough of their countrymen possessed the skills the nation required.

Many African Americans no doubt shared some of Julian's dissatisfactions with the Ethiopian regime, including those about the autocratic and feudal manner in which it proceeded. But Paul Robeson probably expressed the sentiments of most: "There may be serious problems—slavery, for example—but Ethiopia could work out her own problems in time. There is no reason to believe that Italy can work them out for her."[80]

Rebuffed by the greater number of African Americans, Julian sailed for France in January, 1936, and in June he announced in Naples that he had become an Italian citizen with the name Huberto Fauntleroyana Juliano. That was the last piece of evidence many people, especially among African Americans, needed for believing that the Black Eagle was an agent of the Italians. They thought they at last understood why he had been able to travel in luxury, dazzle with his wardrobe, and flaunt a fat wallet.[81]

The Federal Bureau of Investigation had decided that Julian was a personality to be watched: "Subject who fought in the Ethiopian Air Force for Haile Sellassie during the war with Italy is reported to have visited the N.Y.C. Italian Consul General after his return to the U.S. in [19]36 and to have been given three free trips to Italy thereafter on Italian Line Ships.

79. News clipping in Hubert Julian File, Moorland-Spingarn Research Center, Howard University.
80. New York *Herald Tribune*, January 12, 1936.
81. *Ibid.*, January 13, 1936, January 18, 1936; Pittsburgh *Courier*, January 1, 1936, January 11, 1936; New York *Times*, June 19, 1936; William Randolph Scott, "Hubert F. Julian and the Italo-Ethiopian War: A Dark Episode in Pan-African Relations," *UMOJA*, n.s., XI (Summer, 1978), 89.

The Consul General is reported to have financed him to the extent of $1500 for propaganda work among the Negroes in Harlem, N.Y.C. where he is said now to be continuing pro Axis speeches and attempting to cause Negro dissatisfaction."[82]

Julian later tried to pass off his involvement with the Italians as a stratagem he had devised with Bayen to win an audience with Mussolini so he could assassinate him. But nothing corroborates that story. Bayen, who appears to have severed relations with Julian after the plane crash in 1930, had repudiated him in public speeches and was to denounce him as a fraud in his book. Julian's attempt at vindicating himself appears in his autobiography, published nearly thirty years after the events. The book is poorly documented and is very sketchy and inaccurate on many matters.[83] Without independent confirmation, that source remains unreliable, especially in view of Julian's well-documented distortions earlier in his life.

The Black Eagle probably had the best of intentions at the outset, but his misunderstanding of the Ethiopian milieu, his several disheartening encounters in the country, and his diminished prestige in the United States and Ethiopia after he had greatly exaggerated his status all contributed toward making him an easy prey for the Italians. His penchant for grandiose schemes renders it at least conceivable that he thought he could carry out the assassination of Mussolini, however preposterous that seems in light of his many other failed ventures. Julian was naïve and confused by the momentous events into which he had been thrust. He seems to have had virtually no pro-Italian effect on African Americans and may have fortified black resolve regarding the Ethiopian cause.

Ironically, though, a greater number of African Americans fought in an approximately concurrent non-African war than participated in Ethiopia's resistance. Just over two months after Sellassie's self-imposed exile and nine months after Italy's full-scale invasion, the Spanish civil war erupted. About a hundred African Americans volunteered for combat in what was essentially an internal conflict in Spain. How is it possible to account for the heavier involvement of black Americans there than in Africa? In the first place, the Spanish recruitment was much better organized

---

82. Department of the Army, Intelligence, and Security Command, Dossier No. X8438938, pp. 104, 105.

83. Malaku Bayen, *The March of Black Men* (New York, 1939), 6; *The Black Eagle: Colonel Hubert Julian as Told to John Bulloch*, 113–16.

and financed and centered on a transnational objective. It was a worldwide effort promoted in large measure by the Comintern, which instructed Communist parties everywhere to recruit volunteers to fight fascism in Spain. Conscious of the menace of European fascism and nazism and alarmed by Italy's victory over Ethiopia, an estimated thirty to forty thousand came from England, continental Europe, Canada, Latin America, and the United States. The Socialist party in the United States, under Eugene Debs, solicited funds and sought volunteers. The labor unions were a wellspring of contenders against fascism, as were the college and university campuses, where the fight for democracy became, for some, a moral crusade.[84] Some of the participants were Communists, some were not. But the appeal was strong for all, and it had a powerful resonance with the concerns of black Americans. Leonard L. Yates, who had been approached earlier about serving in Ethiopia and who joined the contest in Spain, wrote afterward, "It is a sad indictment of American politics that the only political platform that seemed to recognize the reality of my life belonged to the Communist Party." Its call for equal rights, the vote, and an end to segregation, discrimination, and lynchings was attuned to the experiences of black Americans.[85] Some black volunteers also recalled that enlisting in the Spanish civil war compensated for their debarment from the Ethiopian conflict by American law.

Between January, 1937, and October, 1938, something in the neighborhood of a hundred African Americans fought in Spain with other Americans in the Abraham Lincoln and George Washington battalions—later merged as the Lincoln-Washington Battalion—and in other units of the International Brigades. Along with the moral appeal, the promised compensation drew some during the depression years. But the desire to combat fascism and racism seemed the major motivation for risking the loss of life. One who fell was Oliver Law, a black American commander of the Lincoln-Washington Battalion.[86]

The United States had no compelling financial interest in Ethiopia, but

---

84. F. Jay Taylor, *The United States and the Spanish Civil War* (New York, 1956), 104, 106; Hugh Thomas, *The Spanish Civil War* (New York, 1961), 298; Gabriel Jackson, *The Spanish Republic and the Civil War* (Princeton, 1965), 336–38; Richard Traina, *American Diplomacy and the Spanish Civil War* (Bloomington, Ind., 1968), 88.

85. James Yates, *Mississippi to Madrid* (Seattle, 1989), 98–99.

86. Taylor, *The United States*, 102–103, 109; Thomas, *The Spanish Civil War*, 461, 464–65; Yates, *Mississippi to Madrid*, 137, 138.

there were an estimated seventy million dollars of American investments in Spain. American citizens remained in Spain throughout the civil war. The government of the United States attempted to follow a policy of neutrality and nonintervention, but the Roosevelt administration is thought to have been sympathetic to the Spanish Republicans and to have known that supplies and volunteers were arriving to assist them.[87] In the Ethiopian conflict the American government was more vigilant, enforcing special restrictions against travel.

But the lasting importance of the black activism in behalf of Ethiopia arises less out of the numbers enlisted than out of the demonstration it afforded of a pan-African commitment on the part of African Americans, the diaspora, and the residents of the African colonies, and across class lines. That commitment extended beyond the emotional response to unite in battle and persisted in fund raising, in diplomatic activities, and in postwar reconstruction.

Writing in *Foreign Affairs,* W. E. B. Du Bois captured both the historical significance of the war and the reality of the black condition: "Italy has forced the world into a position where, whether or not she wins, race hate will increase. . . . Black men and brown men have indeed been aroused as seldom before. . . . If there were any chance effectively to recruit men, money and machines of war among the one hundred millions of Africans out side of Ethiopia, the result would be enormous."[88]

87. Taylor, *The United States,* 54, 108.
88. W. E. B. Du Bois, "Inter-Racial Implications of the Ethiopian Crisis: A Negro View," *Foreign Affairs,* XIV (1936), 88.

IV

Fund Raising

Months before October 3, 1935, and the outbreak of the war, a small number of African-American groups had organized to address what they foresaw would be Ethiopia's need for assistance. Some African Americans had even explored the possibility of floating loans in behalf of the African nation. In May, 1935, the chief of the commercial division of the State Department reported on a telephone call from the Commercial Trading Company, of New York City, a firm that was engaged in the export business in the West Indies and wanted information about fund raising for Ethiopia. Anthony Crawford, an African American and one of the company's owners, had become interested in raising a subscription to make a gift of commercial aircraft to the emperor.[1] A few months later, Thomas H. Wyatt, president of the Helping Hand Finance Corporation, in Philadelphia, inquired if the State Department had objections to the floating of a ten-million-dollar loan for Ethiopia. The State Department told both Wyatt and Crawford that the requirements and procedures had to conform with the regulations of the Securities and Exchange Commission. There is nothing to show that either initiative went beyond that point.[2]

Collaborative activity, however, yielded more. In New York City as early as December, 1934, several Harlem groups, including UNIA, the YMCA, the Elks, and the League of Struggle for Negro Rights, organized the Provisional Committee for the Defense of Ethiopia. The cooperating

---

1. 884.113/80, Telegram, May 16, 1935; 884.113/81, Memorandum and Telegram, May 24, 1935; 884.113/82, Anthony Crawford to secretary of state, May 28, 1935.
2. 884.51/37, 38, 42, 43, 46 1/2, Letters and Memoranda, August 8–29, 1935.

groups sponsored a rally that attracted thousands of Harlemites who wished to protest Italy's mobilization for war against Ethiopia. The speakers were Adam Clayton Powell, the minister of the Abyssinian Baptist Church; Joel A. Rogers, a journalist; Willis Huggins, a historian; A. L. King, of UNIA; and James W. Ford, of the Communist party.[3] The rally adopted resolutions to supply Ethiopia with money, arms, and ammunition rather than manpower; to send protests to Mussolini, the League of Nations, Secretary of State Cordell Hull, and the mayor of New York City; to organize a fifty-thousand-person parade in Harlem; and to urge Harlemites to spend no money that might fall into the hands of Italian fascists ready to use it "to stab our brothers in the back." Similar rallies occurred in Harlem again during the spring and summer of 1935.[4]

In July, 1935, the Provisional Committee for the Defense of Ethiopia, the Committee for Ethiopia, and the American League Against War and Fascism sent Huggins to Geneva to present a petition to the League of Nations seeking restraints on Italy and support for Ethiopia, the dispatch of a commission to report on the boundary dispute between the two countries, and the body's resolve to conform to its covenant. While in Europe, Huggins established contact with two high Ethiopian officials—Azaj Workneh Martin, minister to the Court of Saint James's, and Tecle-Hawariate, minister to France and delegate to the League of Nations. Both ministers voiced support for Huggins' mission and encouraged him to proceed with fund raising in the United States. Martin called on "colored people" to help the Ethiopian cause and Tecle-Hawariate "unofficially" affirmed that the emperor regarded himself as the "Guardian of the interests of black men everywhere." In London, Huggins consulted as well with Amy Jacques Garvey, the widow of Marcus Garvey, and with Lapido Solanke, leader of the West African Students Union.[5]

The Huggins mission represented a significant extension of African-American involvement in international affairs. Never before had such an

---

3. *Amsterdam News,* March 2, 1935, p. 1, March 9, 1935, p. 1. For a good general and concise survey of fund raising, see Rodney A. Ross, "Black American Relief, 1935–1936," *Ethiopia Observer,* XV (1972), 122–31. See also New York *Times,* July 14, 1935, July 22, 1935.

4. New York *Times,* January 25, 1935, July 14, 1935, July 22, 1935.

5. 765.84/965; 884.51/40; *Afro-American,* July 27, 1935; Willis Huggins and John G. Jackson, *An Introduction to African Civilization* (New York, 1937), 90, 91; *The Friends of Ethiopia in America* (New York, n.d.), 5.

unequivocal statement on the relationship between Africans and their descendants in the diaspora made its way to the highest level of international deliberation with the support of organizations of mass constituency. The introduction of the appeal that Huggins bore read, "Africans and persons of African descent throughout the world, have always looked with pride at the Empire of Ethiopia, which alone of all the ancient empires of black men in Africa, still maintains its independence."[6] Huggins' presentation was judicious, clearly drawing the relationship between the fate of Ethiopia and the position of the black world at the same time that it focused on the Italian menace and the imperative that the League act in the name of peace and justice.

In addition to projecting an international black presence, the Huggins mission, by winning endorsement from the Ethiopian ministers in London and Paris, reinforced the evolving connection between Ethiopians and African Americans, thereby providing an added incentive for fund raising. From Geneva, Huggins wrote to William M. Steen, secretary of the Ethiopian Research Council, that consultations with Martin and Tecle-Hawariate were fruitful, and on October 5, 1935, after his return to the United States, he organized the Friends of Ethiopia in America (FEA), with headquarters on Seventh Avenue in New York City. The purpose of the FEA was to mobilize pro-Ethiopian sentiment and raise money for supplies for the Ethiopian cause. By the end of November, the organization boasted of having founded locals in 106 cities in nineteen states.[7] George Schuyler, publisher of the Pittsburgh *Courier,* lent his support. He pointed out that "what Ethiopia needs is money. She has man-power, grit, determination and intelligence." His conclusion was that there was "no excuse this time that any Negro community can give for not having a branch of the Friends of Ethiopia."[8]

Huggins hoped to develop connections he had made, during his European visits, with two deputies in the French Assembly, Galandou Diouf, from Senegal, and Candace Gratien, from Guadeloupe, with the Haitian delegate to the League of Nations, General de Nemours, with the minister from Haiti to France, Constantin Mayard, and with members of the International African Friends of Abyssinia, in London. Huggins

---

6. Huggins and Jackson, *An Introduction,* 91.
7. *The Friends of Ethiopia,* 2, 11.
8. Pittsburgh *Courier,* November 23, 1935.

and the International African Friends of Abyssinia seem to have planned joint fund raising, for Amy Garvey, George Padmore, a writer and pan-Africanist from Trinidad, and Ismael Mohammad Said, a pan-Africanist from Somalia— all of them in the London group—scheduled a visit to New York to meet with Huggins and John Payne, an African-American singer and activist. The meeting does not seem to have occurred, however.[9]

The extent of fund raising by the FEA is undocumented. Minutes and reports for the organization are unavailable, and public reports on money collected or supplies sent to Ethiopia are few. In one of the FEA's official publications, however, there is a reference to a contribution to American Aid to Ethiopia for the purchase and shipment of a hospital truck. The FEA also had affiliations with the International Friends of Abyssinia, the Save the Children Fund, the American Pro-Falasha Committee, the Ethiopian Research Council, and other groups, to any of which Huggins may have contributed funds. He at one time envisioned cooperating with the Universal Ethiopian Students Association to conduct a National Ethiopian Week to raise money.[10] But in the context of the publicity Huggins cultivated, his good terms with the Pittsburgh *Courier,* his wide lecture circuit, and the attention the public paid to his activities, the dearth of information about funds raised suggests that he had limited success in that area.

Robert F. S. Harris, of New York, led a more successful fund-raising effort. Harris, an African American who had served as an assistant editor of the New York *Herald,* was secretary of the biracial Committee for Ethiopia. Although the membership roster listed the Reverend G. Ashton Oldham, of Albany, as chairman, and the Reverend Adam Clayton Powell as vice-chairman, most of the group's publicity centered upon Harris, who by 1935 was a free-lance journalist in the city. He spoke of having visited Ethiopia, and he had established channels of communication with Martin.[11]

The stated objectives of the Committee for Ethiopia were to mobilize public opinion against Italy's aggressive acts, to urge the League of Nations to support Ethiopia, to set aside a nationwide day of prayer for the coun-

---

9. Willis Huggins to William Steen, August 4, 1935, August 16, 1935, in ERC; 884.142/58 1/2, 108; 765.84/853, Prentiss B. Gilbert to Gray, August 15, 1935; *The Friends of Ethiopia,* 11.

10. *New York Age,* November 23, 1935; *The Friends of Ethiopia,* 11.

11. 884.142/18, A. R. Burr to R. C. Bannerman, September 3, 1935 (Special agent report to the State Department).

try, to prevent communists from using the crisis to expand their influence among African Americans, to disseminate information about the nation, and to purchase and ship medical supplies in the case of war. The achievement of those objectives would require fund raising, which Harris said was to begin if war occurred, "then and only then."[12]

Harris opened an office on East 45th Street in New York City, with the Manhattan Art Press. He announced that branches were operational in a number of states, relying considerably on Red Cross members. Unsolicited funds came in, and Harris solicited contributions as well. He sent over 5,000 circulars to church ministers and distributed some 250,000 copies of a public appeal to President Roosevelt.[13] The organization called on the United States to invoke the Kellogg-Briand Pact against war, and it coordinated a day of prayer in the United States and the West Indies, which was held on August 18, 1935. The date chosen was the Sunday preceding the release of the League of Nations' conciliation report on the war. Haile Sellassie cooperated by calling for prayers of peace and national independence, and he attended a parallel service in Addis Ababa. Harris was instrumental in synchronizing the events.[14]

The organization had received enough funds by August to arrange the purchase and shipment to Ethiopia of antiseptic articles. The Squibb Company furnished the supplies, which were sent aboard the Franco-Iberian Line's *Ingria*. A picture in the New York *Times* showed Harris and a colleague, Dr. Lewis L. Shapiro, the medical director for the group, checking the consignment, over which a Red Cross flag was draped. The goods seem to be the first confirmed shipment of supplies from the United States to Ethiopia during the crisis.[15]

The Red Cross flag, however, aroused considerable controversy. Officials of the American Red Cross cautioned Harris that only their organization had the right to use the Red Cross flag and emblem. They admonished him for misrepresenting his organization and misleading the public into thinking it had a Red Cross affiliation that it did not. Harris' defense was that the flag belonged to Dr. Shapiro, who had served with the Red

12. *Ibid.*; 765.84/456, Robert F. S. Harris to Henry A. Lardner, July 1, 1935.

13. 884.142/18, Burr to Bannerman, September 3, 1935.

14. 765.84/1220, C. Van H. Engert to Cordell Hull, August 20, 1935; 884.142/18-A, "Exhibit A," Burr to Bannerman, September 3, 1935; *Afro-American*, August 24, 1935.

15. 884.142/19, Photo—Article Enclosure, 1935; 884.142/18, Burr to Bannerman, September 3, 1935.

Cross during World War I, but he consented to desist from tenuous uses of it and of the Red Cross emblem.

Intent to deceive would be hard to prove, especially since the supplies went to the Ethiopian Red Cross. But Harris faced an investigation, during which he acknowledged that he expected personal gain from his campaign. He explained to the investigator, though, that he did not skim a profit from the funds collected but instead hoped the emperor would reward him with a coffee concession and a radio franchise.[16] The controversy seems to have subsided without substantial adverse effects.

During the early stage of Harris' efforts, the Ethiopian Research Council became aware of the Committee for Ethiopia. Howard Moore wrote Harris that the council had followed the committee's work from early July and knew about the shipment of medical supplies. He revealed that the council had provided information to Ethiopia about that, and he assured Harris that although the council had only modest resources, it had important contacts. He offered Harris the privacy of a secret code for communicating with Addis Ababa. Not even the Ethiopian consul general had that code, he confided. It had come from Bayen. Moore offered to encipher Harris' messages and return them for dispatch, and to unscramble messages from Addis Ababa. He stressed that he was proposing a service in the interest of Ethiopia and that no publicity should attend to it. He labeled his letter, Strictly Confidential.[17]

Harris' reply was that he regretted he had not received Moore's letter before sending a cable to the Ethiopian government: FOUR MILLION PEOPLE COMMITTEE FOR ETHIOPIA SUPPORT ETHIOPIAN OPPOSITION TO ITALY STOP STARTING DRIVE FOR MEDICAL SUPPORT STOP CABLE COMMISSION COMMITTEE ACT FOR ETHIOPIAN RED CROSS IN AMERICA. The manifest purpose of the cable was to obtain official Ethiopian endorsement for the committee, and Harris appealed for Moore's help in the matter. He enlarged on how he planned to raise a million dollars to purchase medicines, surgical supplies, concentrated foods, hospital equipment, mule litters, and other materials, and he enumerated supplies that would be sent later and requested a list of urgent needs from Ethiopia. He accepted with alacrity Moore's offer to put his correspondence in cipher.[18]

16. 884.142/18, 19, Memorandum with Attachment, August 29, 1935.
17. Howard Moore to Robert F. S. Harris, August 16, 1935, in ERC.
18. Robert F. S. Harris to Howard Moore, August 17, 1935, in ERC.

Harris had been collecting the names of physicians and nurses who might become volunteers. He had the idea of establishing a branch of the Ethiopian Red Cross in the United States, but he wanted the emperor to request that, or at least endorse it, so as to ensure more effective publicity and support among Americans.[19]

Moore desired to assist Harris, but he made clear that the Ethiopian government wished only arrangements that the Italian government could not use as a pretext for aggression or as a wedge for cracking the sympathy Ethiopia enjoyed in the United States and elsewhere. Ethiopia wanted "to play it safe," in the hope that world opinion would support its cause. Moore promised to cable Addis Ababa for a list of its greatest needs, and he commented on the climatic conditions that required special kinds of supplies to be effective.[20]

Moore sent a cable to Ethiopia for Harris: PLEDGE ONE MILLION DOLLAR MEDICAL SUPPLY TEN HOSPITAL FIELD UNITS OR AWAIT INSTRUCTIONS VIA MARTIN WILL SHIP CARE OF ETHIOPIAN RED CROSS ADVISE. A cable arrived from Ethiopia: SHIP SUPPLIES TO MARTIN FOR RESHIPMENT ON BRITISH VESSELS THEREBY AVOIDING ITALIAN CONFISCATION IMPERIAL GOVERNMENT GRATEFUL TO HARRIS COMMITTEE.[21] Harris also designed and sent to Moore, and to Martin, in London, plans for a project to raise money by issuing Ethiopian stamps for collectors in sets of five each. Harris had discussed the plan with a stamp dealer and had received estimates for the cost of engraving and printing, but the government apparently decided against launching the scheme.[22]

Harris, who became a member of the Ethiopian Research Council, involved himself in what appears to have been the only concrete initiative by a council member for the acquisition of arms for Ethiopia. In a letter to Moore in 1935, he observed that he could obtain hand grenades, gas masks, rifle ammunition, Lee Enfield rifles with bayonets, MC-28 Colts, infantry guns mounted on wheels and adaptable as antiaircraft weapons, and shells. He suggested that William Leo Hansberry, the group's president, and Martin compare his figures "with quotations forwarded from New York by other people." The only response in the council's files is to the

---

19. Robert F. S. Harris to Howard Moore, August 19, 1935, in ERC.
20. Howard Moore to Robert F. S. Harris, August, 19, 1935, in ERC.
21. Howard Moore to Robert F. S. Harris, October 5, 1935, in ERC.
22. Robert F. S. Harris to Howard Moore, October 28, 1935, in ERC.

effect that Moore received the letter and would keep it "confidential."[23]

That the idea of acquiring weaponry occurred to council officers is unsurprising, what with the grim prospects of Ethiopia's war efforts. The nature and tone of Harris' letter lend themselves to the supposition that there had been prior discussion of the matter, but Moore was especially sensitive to the government's opposition, especially after its declaration of neutrality. All parties knew of the risk involved in approaching arms dealers who might have links to the State Department. A fair assumption is that the council explored the avenues of support open to it and reserved its options.

The Committee on the Ethiopian Crisis comprised representatives of the Federal Council of Churches of Christ in America, several Jewish groups, the League of Nations Society, and a number of peace organizations. In close relationship with John Shaw, a white naturalized American with commercial connections in Ethiopia, it adopted objectives its chairman, Emory Ross, distinguished as support for the secretary of state in his efforts to maintain peace, and preparation of an apparatus that, in the event of war between Ethiopia and Italy, would collect funds for medical and other nonmilitary aid to the African nation. The Committee on the Ethiopian Crisis opposed Harris' actions and sought to prevent "irresponsible groups and individuals" from "soliciting funds for the Ethiopian cause without any authorization."[24]

Ross, who had experience in Africa and served as secretary of the welfare committee of the Federal Council of Churches of Christ, had access to many people in and out of government circles. The other members of the Committee on the Ethiopian Crisis were Thomas Jesse Jones, of the Phelps-Stokes Fund; Sidney E. Goldstein, of the American Conference of Rabbis; George E. Haynes, of the Federal Council of Churches; and Thomas A. Lambie, of the United Presbyterian Mission and the Sudan Interior Mission, both in Ethiopia. Haynes was the only African American in the body, and Lambie was field director of the mission in the Sudan. Ross presented the plans of the committee to officials of the Red Cross, which supported them. He could also announce that the Near Eastern Foundation and other groups had assured him of their backing. When he inquired of the State Department whether the contemplated fund-raising operation

---

23. Robert F. S. Harris to Howard Moore, October 30, 1935, in ERC.

24. 884.142/25, Memorandum, September 5, 1935; 884.142/26, Memorandum, September 16, 1935.

would violate American neutrality laws, the department answered that so long as it collected funds for nonmilitary purposes, it seemed to be in conformity with regulations. But the State Department emphasized that it did not want to imply its approval of or acquiescence in the plan.[25]

The way at least provisionally cleared, the group organized American Aid for Ethiopia (AAE) in 1935, with Dr. William J. Schieffelin, a wealthy New York philanthropist, as chairman. Again Haynes was the only African American, this time on the board of directors. AAE arranged affiliation with the Friends of Ethiopia in America, which was awarded recognition by Shaw. The FEA sent medical supplies and a Ford ambulance to Ethiopia in November, 1935.[26]

In 1935, Colonel H. Murray Jacoby, who five years earlier had been the United States' special ambassador to the coronation of Haile Sellassie, accepted an invitation from the Ethiopian minister of foreign affairs to become the American representative of the Ethiopian Red Cross. Jacoby conferred with officials of the American Red Cross, which approved his plan to organize a committee to collect funds for personnel and medical supplies. He also decided to affiliate with AAE.[27]

After the outbreak of hostilities on October 3, the International Committee of the Red Cross, in accordance with the Treaty of Geneva, asked both Italy and Ethiopia if they wanted Red Cross assistance. Italy replied that its own resources were sufficient, but Ethiopia, whose doctors were mostly foreigners based in missionary hospitals and whose pool of motorized ambulances was insufficient, accepted help. The emperor in addition transmitted a request to Harris for help in securing American medical supplies and volunteers.[28] On October 10, Cary T. Grayson, chairman of the American Red Cross, opened his organization to contributions designated for the Ethiopian Red Cross's relief efforts. The American Red Cross had no plans to send personnel and was doubtful that the level of the American public's interest would sustain fund raising on a large scale.[29]

25. 884.142/26; 884.142/28, legal adviser to Wallace Murray, September 18, 1935; 765.84/929, Memorandum, August 17, 1935.

26. 884.142/48 1/2, James McClintock, American Red Cross, to William Phillips, State Department, December 3, 1935; 884.142/26; New York Times, October 13, 1935, November 27, 1935.

27. 884.142/30, Memorandum, October 2, 1935.

28. 884.142/33 1/2, American Red Cross News Release, October 10, 1935; New York Times, October 7, 1935, p. 7.

29. 884.142/33 1/2, American Red Cross News Release, October 10, 1935.

Interest among African Americans, however, was strong, and one of their most successful fund-raising organizations was the Medical Committee for the Defense of Ethiopia (Medcom), to whose president, Dr. J. J. Jones, a dentist, Moore wrote on August 16, 1935. Moore underlined the Ethiopian Research Council's interest in Medcom's plans for getting medical assistance to Ethiopia, and he offered use of his privacy code to the organization. Moore stressed the council's interest in trained technicians, doctors, and nurses, and its opposition to recruitment that violated the law. He emphasized that what he had said "should not be publicized, so we shall trust you and your associates to keep this information 'STRICTLY CONFIDENTIAL.'"[30]

Dr. Arnold Donawa, secretary of Medcom, replied for Jones that the organization was assembling volunteers for Ethiopia and wanted to communicate with the authorities there concerning logistics. At Donawa's request, the council transcribed and sent a wire in cipher: "Group of medical men ready to go to Ethiopia. Desire information concerning provisions of your government for transportation and maintenance."[31] Steen and Hansberry were pleased to be working with Donawa, whom they knew as a former dean at Howard University's school of dentistry.

Moore repeatedly stressed the importance of secrecy, because he had qualms that the Department of State might withhold visas. He inquired of Donawa how many doctors were slated to go, who they were, how long they would stay, and what pay they would accept. In response to his anxieties, Donawa reassured him of Medcom's intent to carry the matter through. Moore advised against informing Shaw.[32]

Moore and Donawa met and agreed to coordinate efforts. Medcom was to raise the money, recruit and screen volunteers, and provide information to the council, which would coordinate other groups and give general support as needed. Donawa was able to tell Moore that on October 22, Medcom and the Provisional Committee for the Defense of Ethiopia had shipped 1,450 pounds of medical supplies to Ethiopia, including bandages prepared by "our nurses" and properly sterilized before shipment, tetanus antitoxins, sutures, live extract, germicidal soaps, castile and other soaps, biochloride tablets, potassium permanganate tablets, Mercurochrome, and

---

30. Howard Moore to Dr. J. J. Jones, August 16, 1935, in ERC.
31. Dr. Arnold Donawa to Howard Moore, August 24, 1935, in ERC.
32. Howard Moore to Dr. Arnold Donawa, September 13, 1935, in ERC.

Fund Raising

other antiseptics and germicides. They had followed the council's advice and consigned the supplies to Lambie, the American missionary who had become secretary-general of the Ethiopian Red Cross. Their shipment arrived in November, and another shipment was planned within a month.[33]

Medcom became increasingly active in cultivating "sentiment in favor of Ethiopia." There was palpable concern about the negative image Ethiopia was receiving in the press, especially in the Hearst newspapers. Medcom was among the groups fearing that the bad publicity would be turned into a justification for Italy's aggression. To forestall that, it sponsored a dance at the Savoy Ballroom, in New York, which about two thousand persons attended, adopting two resolutions. One protested to President Roosevelt against a reported refusal by the State Department to allow the shipment of two air ambulances to Ethiopia and called for the lifting of the embargo on arms to the country, and the second summoned "all fair-minded, peace-loving people to boycott the Hearst press."[34]

Steen did not hide the council's desire to have "Negroes get some recognition for what they do in this crisis. That is why we have steered away from such mixed groups as the American Aid for Ethiopia."[35] Donawa believed that "Negroes in America should take the lead in coming to the defense of their Negro brothers in Ethiopia, and we have that constantly in mind in our activities. We recognize also the necessity for cultivating the assistance of all those sincerely interested in aiding Ethiopia, and are out to win this support of our efforts."[36]

Within a month, the Pittsburgh *Courier* carried the news that another African-American group, the Chicago Society for the Aid of Ethiopia, under the chairmanship of Dr. Julian Lewis, had shipped medical supplies.[37] The proliferation of fund-raising activities inevitably led to intense competition and conflict. Shaw in particular became frustrated and angry. At his first conference with State Department officials in connection with his commission to serve as Ethiopia's consul general, he expressed concern over the number of persons and organizations raising funds for Ethiopia and over their tactics. He professed to have investigated them all, and "ex-

33. Pittsburgh *Courier*, December 14, 1935.
34. Dr. Arnold Donawa to Howard Moore, November 6, 1935, Dr. Arnold Donawa to William Steen, November 29, 1935, both in ERC; *New York Age*, November 30, 1935, p. 1.
35. Dr. Arnold Donawa to Howard Moore, November 6, 1935, in ERC.
36. William Steen to Dr. Arnold Donawa, November 25, 1935, in ERC.
37. Dr. Arnold Donawa to William Steen, November 29, 1935, in ERC.

cept in one case" he found "none of them was responsible or reliable." Only the Committee on the Ethiopian Crisis won his approbation. Shaw singled out Harris for particular censure. He thought that Harris had newspaper support beyond his merits because of his journalistic background. He also regarded Harris as a schemer who counted on using the Ethiopian crisis for personal profit.[38]

Harris took an equally dim view of Shaw, whom he regarded as an opportunist collecting his cut on the purchases he made for Ethiopia. Shaw accused Harris of circulating stories to that effect, and Harris later maintained that a vendor had accused Shaw of demanding a commission. But Harris did not produce any proof, and Shaw denied wrongdoing. Shaw also criticized Jacoby "for assisting in slamming him." In fact, Wallace Murray, of the Division of Near Eastern Affairs in the State Department, had received information from Henry A. Lardner, vice-president of the J. G. White Engineering Corporation, which had a concession in Ethiopia, that Jacoby's interest in fund raising arose from his desire to smooth the way toward construction of a dam on Lake Tsana. Lardner, who acted periodically as an informant for Murray, was on good terms with Shaw, Ross, and others in and out of the government.[39]

The Department of State worried about reconciling all that was going on with the country's officially neutral stance. The State Department believed that the emperor had given Harris written authorization to collect funds, that the Ethiopian minister in London had encouraged others to seek funds, that Jacoby was interested in behalf of the Ethiopian Red Cross and because he wanted the concession for a dam at Lake Tsana, and that the American Red Cross and several small groups were about to collect funds. The role of Shaw, the consul general, was not clear, though.

What Shaw visualized was a central organization to collect funds, and he hoped that the nascent American Aid to Ethiopia would become that organization. When he presented his views to Murray, the State Department, eager to have the situation clarified, cabled the legation in Addis Ababa for a statement of the Ethiopian government's position. The department's suggestion that the consul general assume greater control re-

---

38. 884.142/25, Memorandum, September 5, 1935; 884.142/39, Henry A. Lardner to Wallace Murray, October 11, 1935.

39. 884.142/33, 34, 39, Memoranda, October 10–11, 1935.

ceived the endorsement of Ethiopia's foreign minister, who conveyed instructions to Shaw.[40]

The problem abated with the formation of American Aid to Ethiopia and the consent by the American Red Cross to receive contributions. Harris announced that the Committee for Ethiopia would cease its own collections, to reduce confusion, and he urged his sympathizers to contribute to the Red Cross. Harris confided to Moore that he had representatives in nine states but that, because they were also Red Cross representatives, it would have been costly and probably unproductive to continue a separate effort. The implicit admission was that the Red Cross was better organized and better funded to perform the task.[41]

But Harris was unwilling to retire altogether from fund raising. He pledged to Moore that he would continue his propaganda campaign in behalf of Ethiopia, and he pointed out that a "100%" African-American organization, the National Committee for Ethiopia, was raising funds in a way that left no doubt that American blacks were behind Ethiopia.[42] The wish to ensure that African-American support for African causes was visible lay at the base of much of what Harris and others were doing.

Still, because the quantity and quality of African American support remained problematic, Harris continued to give pro-Ethiopian speeches and to seek the mobilization of black and other groups. He sent the Ethiopian Research Council copies of pro-Ethiopian flyers by Yugoslavs in the United States and urged black journalists to spread the word regarding Ethiopia's plight.[43] About then, the American legation in Ethiopia fielded an inquiry by the emperor's office to whether the council was "favorably known" by the American Red Cross. The council was proposing to contribute a hospital unit with doctors, and it may be that the council had sent the cable with its offer directly to the government, either in care of the foreign minister, Belaten Gheta Herouy, or in care of the emperor's private secretary, Lorenzo Taezoz. Those were the usual addresses of the council's cables, but the communication had in the main been through

40. 884.142/35A, Telegram, October 11, 1935; 884.142/41, Telegram, October 18, 1935.
41. Robert F. S. Harris to Howard Moore, October 23, 1935, in ERC; New York *Times*, October 14, 1935.
42. New York *Times*, October 14, 1935.
43. Harris to Moore, October 23, 1935, in ERC.

Bayen, who at the time was on the battlefront and unavailable to vouch for the council.[44]

The State Department went to the American Red Cross for enlightenment about the organization that Addis Ababa was trying to vet. The Red Cross's vice-president, James McClintock, learned a little from Shaw, but Shaw's knowledge was limited. He had literature referring to an "address in the colored residential section of Washington." The conclusion was that the council "was a negro organization and one of numerous small, inactive and probably more inadequately financed groups which proposed to engage in relief work on behalf of Ethiopia." The cable to Addis Ababa added the confidential note "It has been suggested that Ethiopian Research Council may be seeking letter of endorsement from Emperor for use in obtaining contributions."[45]

Shaw's input could not have helped the council, especially at a time when Shaw and others had an eye on a monopoly in fund raising. The council was indeed "inadequately financed," but it was by no means "inactive." Moore was serious in asking Harris for the whereabouts of a company that could handle the purchase of a hospital field unit, and he wanted Harris' opinion whether Shaw would issue visas to a "Negro unit." Harris saw no impediments, and he estimated the cost of the hospital unit at three thousand dollars. He also gave prices on supplies.[46]

Harris and Moore wished to organize a group of physicians and nurses to accompany the hospital unit to Ethiopia. The idea was to seek volunteers, in large measure from Howard University's alumni. Ralph Bunche and Hansberry were to take the lead and secure the approval of Mordecai Johnson, Howard's president. The hope was that Johnson's reputation and Bayen's ties to the school as an alumnus would make a forcible enough impression on a sufficient number of physicians and nurses to staff the field hospital. Both Harris and Moore cabled names and received estimates on costs for both travel and salaries. The purchase of hospital planes also came under consideration. But the United States had declared its neutrality, and Canada, which seems to have held promise as a supplier earlier, was by then supporting the sanctions of the League of Nations. During

44. 884.142/57, C. Van H. Engert to secretary of state, November 14, 1935, with telegram; Howard Moore to Robert F. S. Harris, October 24, 1935, in ERC.

45. 884.142/57, Telegrams, November 14, 1935, November 19, 1935.

46. Robert F. S. Harris to Howard Moore, August 8, 1935, Howard Moore to Robert F. S. Harris, October 24, 1935, both in ERC.

this planning, Harris accepted Moore's invitation to become an adviser to the council and to list the Committee for Ethiopia as an affiliate.[47]

The interests of Harris and Shaw remained a source of friction and made the consul increasingly unacceptable to African Americans, who had been disappointed when he was appointed. They had difficulty understanding why Shaw, a naturalized English-born American citizen, was representing Ethiopia. What they did not realize was that he had connections with Ethiopia stemming from his skin-and-fur import business. He also had good relationships with bankers in the United States. His advantages must have seemed, to some minds, to exceed those of prospective African-American candidates, and even of Ethiopians. It is somewhat surprising, though, that no Ethiopian won the nod of Addis Ababa, especially since several Ethiopian nationals had visited the United States on official missions. The African-American community had tried, however, to make the best of the appointment. Shortly after its disclosure, Moore had written a letter to Shaw expressing pleasure and the hope for "your cooperation."[48] At the same time, the council had sent Shaw a brief history of itself, highlighting Bayen's role in its founding, mentioning the membership of other Ethiopian members, and spelling out its objectives. Moore told Shaw of the coded cable service and indicated Huggins as the New York representative.[49] He declared that the council had neither "profit-making nor money-raising" purposes and that no one drew a salary, and he continued, "In addition, we do not approve of the so-called recruiting schemes because (1) they are in violation of American neutrality laws; (2) they are not in the best interests of the Imperial Government; and (3) . . . such activities are ironic . . . in view of the fact that the Imperial Government has not the equipment for the millions of splendid warriors which it has available."[50]

When Shaw requested further information, Moore revealed that the council had offered three groups use of the secret code: the Committee for Ethiopia, the American Committee on the Ethiopian Crisis, and the Medical Committee for the Defense of Ethiopia. Moore told Shaw about the cables Medcom had sent, and added that Bayen had consulted with the

---

47. Howard Moore to Robert F. S. Harris, November 2, 1935, in ERC.

48. 884.142/51, A. R. Burr to R. C. Bannerman, July 23, 1935; Howard Moore to John Shaw, September 15, 1935, in ERC.

49. Moore to Shaw, September 15, 1935, in ERC; Steen Memorandum, July 15, 1935, in ERC.

50. Moore to Shaw, September 15, 1935, in ERC.

emperor about employing American doctors, nurses, aviators, and other technicians. Inviting the consul's suggestions, he concluded, "We hope that a method of cooperation may be arranged between your office and the Council."[51]

Moore later acquainted Shaw with the organization's idea of sponsoring a hospital unit for the war zone. He observed that the council had collected the names of doctors and nurses who might accompany the unit. A new group, Ethiopian Emergency Medical Aid, was to formulate plans. Hansberry was its chairman, George M. Jones, an architect and engineer at Howard University, was executive secretary, and Mordecai Johnson was treasurer. The intention was that the planning body would also take responsibility for raising funds for the council, but in the end it seems not to have become operational.[52]

Moore and others on the council had been chary of relations with the consul general, and he no doubt had felt reciprocal apprehensions. As early as September, some on the council had complained of Shaw that, "being a naturalized American, he has no conception of the feeling of kinship which the millions of American Negroes feel that they have with Ethiopia." Shaw on several occasions voiced his frustration over the number of organizations formed to help Ethiopia. His misgivings became more acute when he learned about the council's plan for a hospital unit. He pronounced his pleasure that the council was addressing the need, but he explained that in order to prevent "unauthorized persons from soliciting funds in the name of Ethiopia," a new centralized body was receiving all donations. Although Shaw did not direct the council to affiliate with American Aid for Ethiopia, the body to which he referred, his hopes were clear when he requested that Moore "confer with me before making any commitments" so as not to duplicate aid.[53]

The role assigned American Aid for Ethiopia required the leaders of the Ethiopian Research Council to clarify the council's raison d'être. In a letter to Shaw, Hansberry commended efforts to suppress the activities of "questionable organizations"; he also acknowledged that Aid for Ethiopia deserved to have the council wish it success. He argued, however, that the

51. John Shaw to Howard Moore, September 16, 1935, Howard Moore to John Shaw, September 17, 1935, both in ERC.
52. William Leo Hansberry to John Shaw, November 22, 1935, in ERC.
53. William Steen to Azaj Workneh Martin, September 30, 1935, John Shaw to Ethiopian Research Council, November 25, 1935, both in ERC.

council's ventures did not duplicate but supplemented the efforts of others. It was necessary, Hansberry submitted, that "American citizens of African and Ethiopian descent" mount campaigns aimed at the "colored" people, many of whom had expressed their desire for that kind of approach. Other groups, Hansberry noted, lacked a comparable rapport with African Americans and would probably not be able to mobilize those who needed a "more direct and distinctive part" in the cause. Shaw did not give explicit approval when Hansberry requested his assent, but he kept channels open with the council and its officers. He alerted James McClintock, vice-chairman of the American Red Cross, that Hansberry and his colleagues "seem to attach some importance to forming an organization of their own people."[54]

The failure of Shaw and others to understand why African Americans attached the importance they did to organizing and directing their own programs engendered suspicions, diverted energies into defending the different groups' prerogatives, exacerbated race relations, and complicated the fund-raising efforts by blacks and whites in the United States. The visit of Lij Tasfaye Zaphiro underscored the problems that were impeding action. Zaphiro, first secretary of the Ethiopian legation in London and private secretary to Martin, the Ethiopian minister in London, arrived in the United States in December, 1935. His visit seems to have been part of Martin's response to appeals in the United States for some official direction of the fund raising. Huggins had briefed Martin, who had written to the Associated Negro Publishers, of which Claude Barnett was president, "I desire to inform the Colored people of America that Dr. Huggins has been introduced to me . . . and I would like to thank the colored people [for their support]."[55] Although Zaphiro's trip to the United States had the objective of appealing to all Americans, it sought to pay special attention to African Americans. Zaphiro himself wanted to "convince Americans of the racial link between Ethiopians and negroes."[56]

Shaw, as consul general, was responsible for receiving the envoy and helping to arrange his program. Unmindful of or insensitive to what African Americans would think, he placed Zaphiro in the Waldorf-Astoria,

54. William Leo Hansberry to John Shaw, November 29, 1935, in ERC; 884.142/67, James McClintock to Wallace Murray, November 23, 1935.
55. Azaj Workneh Martin to Associated Negro Publishers, August 19, 1935, in Barnett Papers.
56. *New York Age,* December 21, 1935.

where he was inaccessible to most blacks, since even those who could afford the hotel were not sure they would escape racial insult there. From Shaw's point of view however, the Waldorf accorded the envoy status and was well located to attract influential and wealthy whites. But white contributors did not respond as Shaw had hoped. Still, because the consul had already had an unpleasant encounter with Robert Harris and had been criticized by African Americans who opposed his appointment as consul general, he very likely looked at the choice of hotel as ensuring his control and influence over Zaphiro and thus enhancing his position as the highest Ethiopian official in the country.

Shaw introduced Zaphiro to prominent white Americans and aligned him with American Aid for Ethiopia. The envoy at first followed Shaw's itinerary but found he was raising the most money from speeches and appeals to black groups in New York, Boston, Philadelphia, Chicago, St. Louis, and other cities. Contributions also arrived at the consulate by mail. Zaphiro told Hansberry and Steen that by March, three months after his arrival, he had turned in over five thousand dollars to Shaw for American Aid for Ethiopia.[57] In order to be in closer contact with African Americans, the group on whose generosity he most depended, he moved to Harlem within a couple of weeks. That seems to be when his relations with Shaw began to deteriorate perceptibly. Addressing some three thousand persons at the Abyssinian Baptist Church, in Harlem, Zaphiro said, "We were happy when your Dr. Huggins came to see us in London last August and hoped that you would heed the message given him by our Legation. We have found much obstruction and many jealousies from which we wish you to abstain."[58]

What prompted Zaphiro to lament obstruction and jealousies were his experiences with Shaw's group. Zaphiro had become convinced that blacks would not support any white-led group from which they received "no credit for their work." To help pay for a shipment by American Aid for Ethiopia of a tent hospital unit, with X-ray and other equipment, a Ford ambulance truck, and bandages and dressings prepared by Harlem volunteers, blacks had conducted dances and solicited funds, but they had

---

57. Hansberry Report, March 7, 1936, in ERC; Memorandum for Dr. Malaku Bayen on the Activities of John H. Shaw, Ethiopian Consul General in New York City, prepared by the Ethiopian Research Council, n.d., in ERC, hereafter cited as Memorandum for Bayen.
58. *New York Age,* January 4, 1936.

received no publicity for their efforts. Only Shaw and Major General John O'Ryan, the former police commissioner of New York City, had been featured in the papers.[59] Zaphiro's move to Harlem thus coincided with a frustration and resentment that African Americans felt not only about Shaw but about American Aid for Ethiopia as well. Zaphiro, Jones, Phillip Savory, and others organized United Aid for Ethiopia, to bring the several black-led groups into coordination. Zaphiro was chairman and Savory treasurer. The new group's immediate goal was to raise five thousand dollars for medical supplies.[60]

Differences between Shaw and Zaphiro continued to grow. The State Department had demonstrated some concern about the envoy's status in December when it cabled the legation in Addis Ababa for comments relevant to his proposed trip. The American representative, C. Van H. Engert, consulted with the Ethiopian foreign minister, who had not been informed about the trip but concluded that it was on behalf of Martin. In early March, Secretary of State Hull cabled Addis Ababa that the envoy was lecturing and collecting funds and that Shaw was unable to determine his status. Shaw had also apprised the State Department that Zaphiro was meeting living expenses by deducting what he needed from the revenue his lectures brought in and only then passing the collections along. This was a sensitive point for Shaw, who complained that the Ethiopian government had not provided money to operate the consulate and that he had used over seven thousand dollars of his own that he wanted reimbursed.[61]

In between a number of fund-raising appearances in Philadelphia in March, Zaphiro confided to Hansberry that his relationship with Shaw had deteriorated drastically. He felt that the consul was attempting to stop his lectures and indeed was working to have him deported. He admitted that he considered Shaw a "hinderance [sic] to the Ethiopian movement in America" and implied that the consul manipulated price quotations for munitions in the interest of his own profits.[62]

Hansberry sympathized entirely with Zaphiro and explained that he thought the problem lay in Shaw's not being paid a salary but receiving a percentage of the charges for visas and ship papers. Because few people

59. Hansberry Report, March 7, 1936, in ERC; Memorandum for Bayen in ERC; New York *Times,* November 17, 1935, November 27, 1935.
60. Hansberry Report, March 7, 1936, in ERC; *Journal and Guide,* January 25, 1936.
61. Chicago *Defender,* February 1, 1936; 884.51/49A, 50, Telegrams.
62. Hansberry Report, March 7, 1936, in ERC.

were traveling to Ethiopia during the conflict and since few ships carried supplies to or from Ethiopia, the main source of Shaw's operating income was American sympathizers. With Zaphiro's presence, not only had Shaw's influence diminished but his use of contributions was much more restricted. What is more, Zaphiro had especially identified himself with those African Americans whom, as the most vocal supporters of the cause, Shaw regarded as his own potential supporters.[63] The Pittsburgh *Courier* offered the opinion that "Zaphiro's action in virtually splitting with Consul-General Shaw and becoming president of the United Aid to Ethiopia in Harlem appears on the surface as a move to challenge Shaw and set up a twin 'Ethiopian Consulate' under all-colored direction in Harlem."[64]

Zaphiro thought there was another reason for Shaw's behavior. O'Ryan was planning for Shaw and American Aid for Ethiopia to operate an Ethiopian exhibit at the New York World's Fair from which the concessionaires, including themselves, would "step down as millionaires." Zaphiro argued that the Ethiopian government should operate the concession with the help of some African Americans; that would "smash" the scheme of Shaw and O'Ryan. The envoy requested that Hansberry get the Ethiopian Research Council to recommend him as Ethiopia's chief representative to the United States so as to disable Shaw's machinations.[65]

When Zaphiro returned to New York from Philadelphia, he sent a telegram requesting an urgent meeting with Steen, but Steen had Claude Lewis attend the meeting for him, because "I would trust no one else in New York."[66] Zaphiro repeated the recital he had made to Hansberry in Philadelphia, emphasizing Shaw's determination to stop the tours. Shaw was in Washington on March 6, he told Lewis, and probably had maneuvered to force Zaphiro out of the country. Lewis helped the envoy arrange a short trip to Washington to consult with Steen, Hansberry, and others. Hansberry had already invited him to meet council members and visit Howard University.[67]

On March 14, Hansberry and Steen had a lunch at Howard University to honor Zaphiro. The envoy took up the themes he had developed in talks across the country in the previous three months: that the bond of friend-

63. *Ibid.*; Memorandum for Bayen, in ERC.
64. Pittsburgh *Courier*, April 18, 1936.
65. Hansberry Report, March 7, 1936, in ERC.
66. William Steen to Dr. Julian Lewis, March 9, 1936, in ERC.
67. Dr. Julian Lewis to William Steen, March 11, 1936, in ERC.

ship between Ethiopian and "colored Americans" would deepen and that African Americans should not believe the "propaganda that the Ethiopians do not wish to be identified with the Black Race"; that together the Ethiopian Research Council, with its board of Americans of "African and Ethiopian descent," and the "native Ethiopians" in London, Paris, and Ethiopia had come to "represent a new and significant departure in international cooperation"; and that the Ethiopian government appreciated the "keen and sympathetic interest" the American people had manifested in the Ethiopian cause.[68] The envoy made no other formal appearance in Washington and did not attempt to raise funds. Instead he conducted consultations with officers of the council designed to give him a clearer vision of the organization, of African Americans, and of the conditions bearing on the Ethiopian cause in the United States. During the visit, Zaphiro was inducted as an associate member of the council.[69]

Secretary of State Hull had already sent a cable to the United States legation in Ethiopia setting out Shaw's criticism of Zaphiro. On March 12, William Phillips, as acting secretary, told the legation that Shaw, having learned Zaphiro was accusing him of being a traitor to Ethiopia, had ordered the envoy to return to London. Before leaving, Zaphiro was honored at a banquet by a number of friends and colleagues, including Donawa, Jones, King, Lewis, Powell, Savory, T. Arnold Hill, Cyril Phillips, Arthur Schomburg, Ray Williams, and a few others. Their party was a thank-you and a send-off.[70]

At the final conference Lewis had with the envoy they discussed, among other things, possibilities for radio communication between Ethiopia and African America. The envoy promised to pursue the idea on his return to Addis Ababa. Later, Savory, Powell, Schomburg, and a few others joined Lewis to bid Zaphiro farewell at Cunard Pier.[71]

68. News Release, Department of Public Information, Howard University, March 27, 1936. Present at the luncheon were Richard Hurst Hill, representing Mordecai Johnson, president of Howard University; Emmett J. Scott, university secretary; Walter G. Daniel, university librarian; Ralph J. Bunche, professor of political science and a member of the council; James V. Herring, director of the art gallery and a member of the council; Ruth Jackson, a faculty member of the social work department; Lucy D. Slowe, dean of women; E. P. Davis, dean of the College of Liberal Arts; and William Steen. William Leo Hansberry presided.
69. Ibid.
70. Dr. Julian Lewis to William Steen, March 19, 1936, in ERC.
71. Ibid.

Within a couple of weeks, Zaphiro wrote to Steen from London that he had reported to Martin, and he suggested that Steen share his opinions with the minister. He also revealed that he would be going to Addis Ababa with a report and suggestions from Martin, who favored appointing an older minister in the United States, with Zaphiro as consul to build on his experience with Americans. The envoy was pleased with that plan and spoke of delivering in Addis Ababa the letters Steen had written to Bayen.[72]

Zaphiro's comportment in the United States confirmed that both the envoy and official Ethiopia identified unequivocably with black Americans, that blacks made significant financial contributions to American Aid for Ethiopia and other white-led groups but garnered very little recognition for their efforts, and that the rift between Shaw and African Americans had deepened.

The animus between Shaw and Zaphiro, which brought to a head a number of incidents involving the consul, the several fund-raising organizations, and African Americans, convinced blacks perhaps more than anything else that they needed more direct links with the Ethiopian government. Several African-American leaders embarked on plans to dispatch a delegation to confer in London with Bayen, Martin, and the emperor.[73]

72. Lij Tasfaye Zaphiro to William Steen, March 30, 1936, in ERC.
73. The emperor acknowledged Ethiopia's debt to African Americans in his autobiography, translated by Ezkiel Gebissa as *My Life and Ethiopia's Progress,* ed. Harold Marcus (2 vols; East Lansing, Mich., forthcoming 1994). The acknowledgment is in Chapter 4 of Volume II.

Emperor Menelik II
From A History of Modern Ethiopia, 1857–1974, *by Bahru Zewde (Athens, Ohio, and Addis Ababa, 1991), 112. Used by permission of Bahru Zewde.*

Empress Zauditu Menelik
S. N. Mirgaoff, © National Geographic Society. Used by permission.

Emperor Haile Sellassie
Courtesy of Moorland-Spingarn Research Center, Howard University

Haile Sellassie and boys at court
Courtesy of Malaku Bayen, Jr.

Malaku Bayen
Courtesy of Malaku Bayen, Jr.

William M. Steen
Courtesy of William M. Steen

Mignon Ford, her sons Abiya (Abraham) and Yosef, and two of her adopted Ethiopian daughters, Ihitabezahu Manaze and Elizabeth.
Courtesy of Abiya (Abraham) Ford

Hubert ("The Black Eagle") Julian
By permission of Photographs and Prints Division, Schomburg Center for Research in Black Culture, New York Public Library, Astor, Lenox and Tilden Foundations.

Ethiopian Research Council reception at Howard University, August 14, 1936. First row: William Leo Hansberry, second from left; Lij Tasfaye Zaphiro, third from left. Second row: Ralph Bunche, far left; William M. Steen, far right.

Courtesy of William M. Steen

African Americans in Addis Ababa. Kneeling, left to right: Andrew Howard Hester, Edward Eugene Jones, Edgar F. Love. Standing, left to right: David Talbot, Thurlow Evans Tibbs, James William Cheeks, the Reverend Mr. Hamilton (Sudan), John Robinson, and Edgar D. Draper.
Courtesy of James William Cheeks

African-American pilots in Addis Ababa. Left to right: Edward Eugene Jones, James William Cheeks, Andrew Howard Hester, and John Robinson.
Courtesy of James William Cheeks

V

Italian-American Reactions

After the invasion and occupation of Ethiopia, Americans of Italian descent sided preponderantly with Italy and wanted the United States to do nothing that might hurt Italy's prospects. As early as August, 1935, fourteen Italian-American organizations in Connecticut submitted a petition to President Roosevelt stressing their devotion to Italy and their interest in preserving the "race of their extraction"; they also declared their opposition to the "coercive measures against" Italy that some Americans championed, and they called for the "strict neutrality" of the United States.[1] They noted that Italian Americans constituted a "considerable portion of the citizens of the United States" and that there was a "traditional affinity of interests" between Italy and the United States. Later that month the *Voice of Italy* published an open letter criticizing the New York *Times* for the "unfair attitude" it evinced when it gave greater emphasis to an article by the American Friends of Ethiopia than to one by the American League for Italy.[2]

When the war began, many Italian Americans held mass meetings, avowed their loyalty to Italy, and contributed money, food, and clothing to the cause. Reports emanated from New York City, Philadelphia, and Chicago—cities with sizable Italian-American populations—of war chests to which people had given their gold rings and watches, cigarette lighters, and crucifixes, as well as copper postcards by the hundreds.[3] The Com-

---

1. 765.84/877, Italian-American Societies, August 7, 1935.

2. *Voice of Italy,* August 24, 1935; 765.84/1738, Italo-Ethiopian Controversy, Conversation with Italian Ambassador, October 7, 1935.

3. New York *Times,* November 22, 1935, December 19, 1935, April 25, 1935, May 25, 1936, May 26, 1936.

mittee of One Thousand donated $14,000 to the Italian government from a collection at a rally at Madison Square Garden, and Generoso Pope, the owner of *Il Progresso Italo-Americano,* the Italian-language daily with the largest circulation in the United States, reported to another rally there that he had sent a check for $100,000 to Italy. The New York branch of the Federation of Italian World War Veterans raised $226,847, and the branch in Providence raised $7,026. In June, 1936, the Department of State heard that an Italian organization in New York announced the "sending of a seventh remittance of $100,000 to Italy."[4]

Italian Americans also responded with manpower. When Mussolini appealed for volunteers, scores of Italian Americans applied at consular offices in the United States. The Italian embassy in Washington, D.C., reportedly confronted hundreds of applications to serve in behalf of the "fatherland." But the ambassador, Augusto Rossi, announced that the embassy could accept no applications from American citizens.[5] Although the American government warned that residents and citizens who enlisted for military service in the war risked fines, imprisonment, and loss of citizenship, some Italian Americans did enlist. Despite Rossi's stance, over a hundred "reservists" sailed for duty in October, 1935, and in December an additional seventy-five, including an ambulance unit of Italian-American doctors, left for Italy. At about the same time, newspapers in Rome reported that five hundred American volunteers were training in Italy.[6]

Nevertheless, there was a diversity among Italian Americans about how to respond to the war. Luigi Criscuolo, a prominent Italian-born investment banker and publicist who had become an American citizen, had seen the Italian division he set up for the Liberty Loan Committee during World War I raise over $800,000 for the war effort. After the war, he promoted the Italy America Society, founded in New York in 1918. In 1921, the king of Italy decorated him for his work with the society.[7] Criscuolo frequently favored the Department of State with unsolicited advice

---

4. 765.84/4649, June 14, 1936; New York *Times,* December 19, 1935, June 14, 1936; *Voice of Ethiopia,* May 17, 1941.

5. *Voice of Ethiopia,* August 24, 1935; 765.841/1738, Italo-Ethiopian Controversy, October 7, 1935; New York *Times,* October 4, 1935, October 5, 1935, October 6, 1935, June 14, 1936.

6. New York *Times,* July 21, 1935, September 16, 1935, October 4, 1935, October 5, 1935, October 6, 1935, October 20, 1935, October 26, 1935, December 1, 1935, December 8, 1935, June 14, 1936.

7. 701.6511/685, Luigi Criscuolo to secretary of state, March 29, 1931.

and wrote articles and pamphlets on public issues. He forthrightly supported Mussolini in the 1920s, and although he later objected to some of the practices of the *duce,* he continued to align himself with Italy. But in 1931 he wrote to the secretary of state that "under present conditions in the so-called 'Italian colonies' here, it is unhealthy for any honest American resident or citizen to express views against the Fascist dictatorship in Italy because of the presence of active Fascist workers."[8] Still, notwithstanding his concern over the coercive forces acting upon Italian-American opinion, he did not falter in his own support of Italy's actions.

During the ominous summer of 1935, just prior to the invasion of Ethiopia, Criscuolo urged calm. He counseled American neutrality and ventured his hope "that Americans, and particularly Americans of African origin, would not allow themselves to be carried away by hysteria based on misinformation." He asked, "Why stir up a mass of bad blood between the white and black races in this country before there is any real reason for extreme action?" Observing that there were several pro-Ethiopian committees in the United States, he acknowledged that a movement was afoot to balance them with a pro-Italy committee.[9] That committee called itself the American League for Italy when it was founded in 1935 for the stated purpose of giving the "American public the facts about Italy's political aims and aspirations." Criscuolo, its chairman, connected Italy's behavior in 1935 to its harrowing position after World War I, when it was debilitated by the enormous debts it had incurred supporting the Allies in 1914. According to Criscuolo, Italy was "embarking on the Ethiopian venture" to compensate "for what the Allies failed to do" in the postwar period. He wrote to President Roosevelt on behalf of the League to recommend convening a conference of England, France, the United States, and Italy with a view toward canceling Italy's ruinous debts and sharing the colonies controlled by England and France. His reasoning was that Italy simply had no means of discharging what it owed and that it should be "compensated for what the Allies neglected to do in the past," when, at the Paris Peace Conference, in 1919, they failed to concede it the colonies that it needed and deserved.[10]

In acknowledging receipt of the proposal, the Department of State

8. Ibid.
9. 765.84/453, Criscuolo Urges Calm in Ethiopian Dispute, July 9, 1935.
10. 765.84/959, Luigi Criscuolo to President Roosevelt, August 24, 1935; 765.84/3455, January 8, 1936.

commended the group's "interest in seeking a means to prevent any outbreak of hostilities between Italy and Ethiopia." In 1936, after Italy had occupied Ethiopia, Criscuolo told President Roosevelt that Italian Americans saw no reason "for refusal of recognition [of Ethiopia's status as an Italian colony] on the part of the United States as an accomplished fact."[11] The American government did not heed that thinking.

The United Italian Association, which was formed "to do for our loved fatherland that which as individuals we cannot do," also served as a mouthpiece for Italian-American sentiment. It appealed for donations to send to Rome. Its executive secretary, Angelo K. Verdi, orated in a handbill, "Our brothers in Italy are ready to give their lives. . . . The world challenges us, unite with us for the safety of Italy. Long Live Italy."[12] The Italian Historical Society published pamphlets and organized lectures—some of which the Italian government financed—characterizing Ethiopians as backward, slave traders, and aggressors against Italy. The society also attempted to instigate divisions among African Americans by trying to revitalize the rumor of Ethiopian resentment toward black Americans.[13] The Friends of Italy and the Unione Italiana d'America lobbied Congress and the Department of State not to pass more stringent neutrality legislation. The pressure they applied was in the same vein as Criscuolo's warning to the National Democratic Committee that "in view of the impending presidential elections," it should be aware that Italian Americans might decline to vote for Roosevelt if he took an "unfair attitude towards Italy."[14]

Pope, who became a propagandist for Mussolini's government in *Il Progresso,* maintained direct contact with Rome until 1941. He also had significant influence in the Democratic party. His alliances with Tammany Hall led President Roosevelt to appoint him chairman of the Italian division of the Democratic National Committee in 1936. Because the Demo-

---

11. 765.84/4530, Criscuolo to President Roosevelt, May 28, 1936, August 24, 1935.

12. Angelo K. Verdi, handbill (flyer), November 22, 1935.

13. *The Italian Historical Society* (Pamphlet; New York, 1935), 9–10; John Patrick Diggins, "Mussolini's Italy: The View From America" (Ph.D. dissertation, University of Southern California, 1964), 274–75.

14. Diggins, "Mussolini's Italy," 276; 765.84/3455, Luigi Criscuolo to James Farley, May 28, 1936; Dwight Lee and George McReynolds, *Essay in History and International Relations* (Worcester, Mass., 1949). The political influence of the Italian Americans in Philadelphia became evident: the Republicans made electoral gains in that city when the Democrats supported sanctions against Italy. See Hugo V. Maile, *The Italian Vote in Philadelphia Between 1929 and 1946* (Philadelphia, 1950).

cratic party courted the ethnic vote, Roosevelt shrank from challenging Pope's pro-Fascist designs before the bombing of Pearl Harbor, in 1941, and after that, Pope began of his own volition to dissociate himself from Mussolini's policies. When Pope later condemned the Italian dictator, he had moved into complete harmony with the president's new policy of encouraging the American antifascists.[15]

The competing appeals in behalf of Ethiopia and Italy were singularly intense in New York City, where the nation's largest concentrations of African Americans and of Italian Americans lived in uneasy proximity. Physical clashes took place between them in the streets and elementary schools, Italian grocery stores were vandalized, and the heavyweight championship fight of Joe Louis and Primo Carnera became a proxy for frayed relations between the boxers' ethnic constituencies.

After a brawl between African Americans and Italian Americans on March 20, 1935, the NAACP sent a telegram to Mayor Fiorello La Guardia:

> NATIONAL ASSOCIATION FOR THE ADVANCEMENT OF COLORED PEOPLE URGES YOU TO APPOINT IMMEDIATELY A BI-RACIAL COMMISSION TO MAKE AN INDEPENDENT INVESTIGATION OF RIOTING IN HARLEM LAST NIGHT STOP COMMITTEE SHOULD HAVE OFFICIAL STATUS TO PERMIT THOROUGH AND IMPARTIAL INVESTIGATION INTO FUNDAMENTAL AS WELL AS IMMEDIATE CAUSES OF TROUBLE WITH RIGHT TO EXAMINE WITNESSES AND ALL PERTINENT RECORDS STOP WE SUGGEST THAT COMMISSION BE CHOSEN WITH DUE REGARD FOR FACT THAT LAST NIGHTS TROUBLE AND POSSIBLE FUTURE TROUBLE ARE ROOTED IN ECONOMIC DISTRESS OF NEGROES STOP IN NINETEEN NINETEEN AT TIME OF SERIOUS RACE RIOTS IN CHICAGO WASHINGTON ARKANSAS AND OMAHA WHEN THERE WAS TALK OF TROUBLE IN NEW YORK CITY A CITIZENS COMMITTEE APPOINTED AT THAT TIME DID NOTABLE WORK IN GETTING AT FACTS AND PREVENTING TROUBLE STOP THIS ASSOCIATION OF COURSE STANDS READY TO COOPERATE IN ANY WAY POSSIBLE.[16]

---

15. Philip V. Cannistraro, "Luigi Antonini and the Italian Anti-Fascist Movement in the United States, 1940–1943," *Journal of American Ethnic History*, V (1985).

16. In addition to Mayor La Guardia, the recipients of NAACP's telegrams supportive of Ethiopia were President Franklin Roosevelt, Secretary of State Cordell Hull, and Maxim

That offer of assistance did not prevent other clashes. After the defeat of Primo Carnera by Joe Louis on June 26, 1935, violence broke out between African Americans and Italian Americans. There were skirmishes in Jersey City on August 11 and in Brooklyn and Harlem on October 3.[17]

While African Americans and Italian Americans fought in the streets, their counterparts clashed in the political arena. New York's Mayor La Guardia, an Italian American, fueled the flames when he attended a pro-Italian rally in Madison Square Garden despite pleas from blacks and whites alike not to do so. When Justices Salvatore A. Cotillo and Ferdinand Pecora, of the New York State Supreme Court, and Representative William A. Sirovich joined him, many concluded that the mayor was not representing the entire community's interests. The insensitivity to African-American feelings reached its highest pitch when Sirovich said in his speech that "just as the Civil War freed the Negro in the United States, the Italians will free the Ethiopians."[18] Arnold Donawa, as secretary of Medcom, remonstrated to the mayor in a letter, "Whatever your personal feelings may be, by lending your distinguished presence at the Madison Square Garden to aid the Fascist cause of Italy, you have thrown the weight of your public office on the side of a country that has been declared by the world to be guilty of unwarranted aggression against a small and defenseless nation, Ethiopia, and have thereby earned the contempt of all fair-minded people."[19]

A few Italian Americans joined the Ethiopian cause. In August, 1935, a delegation of New York African Americans and Italian Americans, headed by Harry A. Maurer, of the Provisional Committee for the Defense of Ethiopia, submitted a petition to the Department of State urging nonbelligerent steps in aid of the Ethiopians. They called on Italy to stop preparing for war and asked the United States to deny loans to Italy. The delegation also submitted a petition to the Italian ambassador in Washington appealing for an end to war preparations and for a solution to be devised under the auspices of the League of Nations.[20]

Litvinov, president of the League of Nations Council. See NAACP, *Annual Report for 1935*, 39, 40.

17. New York *Herald Tribune*, June 26, 1935; New York *Times*, August 12, 1935; New York *Herald Tribune*, October 4, 1935.

18. New York *Times*, June 26, 1935, June 27, 1935; Philadelphia *Tribune*, December 26, 1935; Pittsburgh *Courier*, January 4, 1936.

19. Pittsburgh *Courier*, January 4, 1936.

20. New York *Times*, August 2, 1935; Diggins, "Mussolini's Italy," 277.

Comcomitant with these events was a diplomatic initative to get Ethiopia to surrender before defeat. Between the hostilities at Walwal in December, 1934, and the outbreak of war in October, 1935, Italy attempted to force concessions from the emperor. Sellassie, however, stood firm, counting on the League of Nations and the great powers to require compliance with the Kellogg-Briand Pact and prevent Italian aggression. Apart from the regular diplomatic channels with the United States, a few private American citizens also were disposed to helping Ethiopia seek relief. H. Murray Jacoby had stayed in close touch with the emperor's representatives, and in March, 1935, he notified the Department of State that he had received a telegram from the emperor soliciting his presence in Rome to help settle the dispute. Jacoby asserted that his plan was to urge the Ethiopians not to depend on either the Kellogg-Briand Pact or the League of Nations but to enter into direct negotiations with the Italians, and he sent a telegram to Ethiopia's foreign minister, Belaten Gheta Herouy, rehearsing his position:

> RESPECTFULLY REPEAT VIEW EXPRESSED MAKONNEN BAYEN MARCH DIRECT NEGOTIATION ONLY SOLUTION STOP RELIANCE LEAGUE KELLOGG PACT TOO UNCERTAIN REPEAT MY FORMULAR SALE STRATEGICALLY UNESSENTIAL LANDSTRETCHES FOR CASH PAYMENT PRECEDENT RUSSIAN JAPANESE RAIL TRANSACTION ALASKA VIRGIN ISLAND DEALS PLUS EXPLORATION CORPORATION MODELLED MESOPOTAMIA DEAL ETHIOPIA ENGLAND FRANCE ITALY STOCKHOLDERS THUS REENLISTING FRENCH BRITISH SUPPORT PLUS NEW INDEPENDENCE TREATY AUTOMATIC INVOCATION ARTICLE SIXTEEN LEAGUE COVENANT ANNEX SECTION F LOCARNO PACT PLUS CREATION INTERNATIONAL BOUNDARY POLICE UNDER NEUTRAL COMMISSIONER NET EFFECT SAFEGUARDING INDEPENDENCE PAYMENT PLUS INCOME EXPLORATION COMPANY AVAILABLE SCHOOLS HOSPITALS IMPROVEMENTS AVAILABLE MOMENTS NOTICE GO ROME ASSIST ELSEWHERE REGARDS[21]

Jacoby asked the Department of State if it had any objections to the approach his telegram summarized. There was some concern that Jacoby might be in violation of the Logan Act, which prohibited unauthorized

21. 765.84/5075, Memorandum of Conversation Between Wallace Murray, Paul Alling, and H. Murray Jacoby, October 5, 1936, Telegram.

negotiations by private individuals with foreign governments on matters in dispute with the United States. But since the United States was not a party in the Italian-Ethiopian conflict, the department's legal adviser concluded that there was nothing illegal. Within a few days, though, the Ethiopian government decided that Jacoby's role would not be necessary.[22]

About a year later, in March, 1936, Jacoby let the Department of State know that he had cabled Addis Ababa to urge direct negotiations.[23] What motivated him to insinuate himself into the matter is not clear. Perhaps he foresaw the collapse of the emperor's forces and was jockeying to broker the subsequent resolution. For Jacoby had a reputation of wanting to obtain business concessions. In any event, there seems to have been no follow-up to his initiative.

But he persisted. When he returned from a business trip to the Netherlands in September, 1936, in connection with which he visited the emperor in exile in England, he reported to the Department of State that he had the "very definite impression that the Emperor might now be willing to come to some arrangement with the Italians." He in fact believed that negotiations were already under way. He maintained that the Ethiopians were considering a plan of his according to which the emperor would abdicate and recognize the Italian conquest, the Italians would set aside an area in western Ethiopia that the emperor would govern with a commissioner appointed by the League of Nations, and an international force under neutral officers would prevent border conflicts involving the emperor's territory. Jacoby believed that his proposed "arrangement would not be altogether unsatisfactory" because the emperor would rule in a "definite territory" to which other Ethiopians could migrate.[24]

Since the implementation of his plan depended upon the Italian government, he had already made overtures to his friend Criscuolo, who he said was working with government figures in Rome. According to Jacoby, Criscuolo had conveyed to him that the Italian government recognized the enormous task of conquering and developing Ethiopia and therefore was attracted to his proposal as a way of cutting resistance short and providing a refuge for Ethiopians. Jacoby also relayed that Criscuolo thought that the establishment of a new Ethiopian state under the emperor would help

---

22. Dorothy Bayen recalled in an interview with the author on May 10, 1982, that her husband felt "let down" by Jacoby, a man he regarded as a friend of Ethiopia.

23. 884.01A/1, H. Murray Jacoby, March 6, 1935, 5, H. Murray Jacoby to Wallace Murray, March 25, 1935.

24. 765.84/5075, Memorandum of Conversation, October 5, 1936.

improve Italy's world image, especially in the United States, where there seemed to be a chance of easing its war debt by floating a loan. By Jacoby's account, Criscuolo thought that the Italian ambassador in Washington would propose a transaction whereby the United States government floated a bond issue in behalf of Italy, with sufficient proceeds to allow the Italians to set up a stock company to develop Ethiopia.[25]

Jacoby accepted this as a reasonable compromise since, although guerrilla warfare continued, Italy had defeated the legitimate Ethiopian government. He believed that the proposed settlement would help maintain peace in Europe by allowing Italy to return support to the Stresa front. Jacoby volunteered to serve as a "go-between" with the Ethiopians and Criscuolo, who he thought was in "close touch with Mr. Suvich," the new Italian ambassador in Washington.[26]

Although Wallace Murray, at the Department of State, made up his mind that he could not advise Jacoby and warned him to remember "in such negotiations that he was a private American citizen," the department exerted no effort to discourage him. It is arguable that Murray's response assumed that the negotiations would proceed. The department in any case sent a memorandum of the discussions to the American ambassadors in London and Rome.[27]

Jacoby continued to press his ideas on the emperor, who in October, 1936, wrote to express his thanks for the visit of September and suggested another to discuss resolving the crisis. But Jacoby, after exploring the prospects, wrote to Paul Alling, in the Department of State, that his talks "with our mutual acquaintance in New York [Criscuolo?] convinced myself, subrosa, and through high but unofficially friendly sources," that his proposal would have had a better chance when he first presented it. Because the military situation had shifted decisively in favor of Italy and because the position of the United States toward the belligerents was ambivalent, Rome had little motive to negotiate. Jacoby wrote to the emperor that a trip to London at that time would "serve no useful purpose." He sent copies of his correspondence with the emperor to the Department of State, which forwarded copies to the ambassadors in London and Rome.[28]

25. Ibid.
26. Ibid.
27. Ibid.
28. 765.84/5130, H. Murray Jacoby to Paul Alling, December 4, 1936, Haile Sellassie to H. Murray Jacoby, October 23, 1936, H. Murray Jacoby to Haile Sellassie, November, 1936.

Jacoby's friend and contact Criscuolo had earlier proposed to President Roosevelt that the Italian debt be canceled and Italy given a share of colonial territories. Jacoby's proposal would have accomplished both Criscuolo's goals. Dorothy Bayen recalled that Jacoby approached her husband to assist in persuading the emperor to abdicate in 1936. She recalled Bayen's great disappointment that a "friend" could propose such a plan.[29] Jacoby's "arrangement" amounted to abdication, for the emperor would have relinquished a major portion of his kingdom and, even in the part he retained, would have governed "with a commissioner."[30] That this proposal came from a person who had represented Ethiopia on a number of occasions and had served as a trusted adviser to Bayen no doubt accounted for the cool relations apparent between the two men when Bayen arrived in the United States as an envoy a few months later.

What impelled Jacoby may always be murky. He had several international ties, many of which he expanded after 1940, he was in close contact with the Italians through Criscuolo, and he maintained very close links to the Department of State. At least from 1930 he had sought to establish a business base in Ethiopia, and his proposal called for the formation of a corporation that would have been capable of extending his business interests. However one assesses his motives, the unavoidable conclusion is that his plan would not only have given Italy an earlier victory, it would also have subjected the emperor and his country to colonial rule.

A definitive assessment of the impact of the Italian-American reaction to Italy's aggression against Ethiopia is impossible, but evidently most Americans of Italian origin supported their "fatherland," spiritually, politically, and materially, without denying their American nationality. They resisted the claims of Ethiopia and its supporters and challenged African Americans on the issue. Like African Americans, Italian Americans demonstrated the powerful influence of heritage and identity. The critical difference between the two groups was their status in American society. The country included Italian Americans as an integral part of the political economy. They had substantial business assets and a strong presence in the labor unions, and their effect reached to the White House. Even before

---

29. Dorothy Bayen, interview with author, Washington, D.C., May 10, 1982.

30. For an account of French and Vatican proposals for the emperor to abdicate, see John H. Spencer, *Ethiopia at Bay: A Personal Account of the Haile Sellassie Years* (Algonac, Mich., 1984), 84.

they were well organized, they were sending hundreds of thousands of dollars to Italy. They were an attestation of the strong influence a diaspora community can have when it is committed, well organized, properly funded, and politically connected.

VI
African-American Envoys to England

In the face of defeat, Haile Sellassie went into exile. In May, 1936, he left the field of battle to dedicated guerrillas. The major European powers no doubt welcomed relief from the tense situation, especially at a time that war clouds were gathering over Spain and threatening other parts of Europe and, indeed, the Far East. But although defeated and without the support of influential nations, the emperor remained popular in the black world.

Shortly after Sellassie established himself in exile in England, rumors circulated that he planned to visit the United States to rally support for the Ethiopian cause. In reaction to the rumors and in order to increase the weight of African Americans with key Ethiopian officials, Dr. Phillip Savory and a number of other blacks in Harlem decided to sponsor a visit to England for an audience with the emperor. In preparation for the trip, Savory requested that Steen write a letter of introduction to Bayen apprising him of how things stood with the Ethiopian cause in the United States and including an assessment of Shaw's effectiveness as consul. Steen saw Savory's trip as an opportunity "to send some confidential information over to Bayen.... They [in Sellassie's entourage] don't know what is going on in Addis or any other place over there except what they read in the papers."[1]

Steen not only wrote an impressive letter of introduction for Savory and the Reverend William Imes, who along with Cyril Phillips joined the

---

1. William Steen to William Leo Hansberry, July 15, 1926, Dr. Phillip Savory to William Steen, July 16, 1936, both in ERC; William Steen, interview with author, February, 1982.

mission, but he also sent a number of extremely important documents to Bayen. The introductory letter explained that Savory had been treasurer of United Aid for Ethiopia and Medcom, chairman of the board of the Victory Mutual Life Insurance Company, of New York and Chicago, co-owner of the *Amsterdam News,* and chairman of the board of the Community Personal Finance Corporation. Steen also called him one of the most prominent physicians in New York.[2]

The letter identified Imes as the pastor of Saint James Presbyterian Church, of New York, the most "aggressive and intelligent" clergyman in Harlem, a member of the board of United Aid for Ethiopia, and the composer of a song to "His Imperial Majesty Haile Sellassie." Imes's church had sent money to Shaw, the consul general, to be transmitted to Ethiopia, and his church often held meetings to educate people about the Ethiopian cause.[3] Steen did not identify Phillips, whom Bayen had met during a previous visit to the United States.

Steen explained to Bayen that the Savory mission was in response not only to the rumored visit of Sellassie to the United States but also to African Americans' wish to learn how best to participate in efforts to "secure munitions and continue the war." Steen described Savory as "ready to serve as the medium through which His Majesty may contact the masses of Colored people of America and keep in touch with them . . . who will readily rise again to the cause." The mission, he said, also desired to find out how "financial aid can be sent so that it will reach His Majesty." Although personal funds financed the trip, Savory, Steen, and others regarded the mission as representing primarily United Aid for Ethiopia, the Ethiopian Research Council, and Medcom.[4]

The delegates made the trip in secret to ensure that no one opposing it derailed it. There was concern that Shaw might attempt to have the State Department deny passports if its purpose were known. Steen informed Savory, "It is absolutely essential that you and your party get away from New York without Shaw finding out or without any undue publicity. I personally know of a number of cases which Shaw has thwarted."[5] Of the seven documents Savory delivered to Bayen from Steen, one that especially

2. William Steen to Malaku Bayen, July 25, 1935, in ERC.
3. *Ibid.*
4. *Ibid.;* William Steen to Malaku Bayen, July 26, 1935, in ERC; William Steen, interviews with author, February, March, April, 1982.
5. Steen, interviews with author, February, March, April, 1982.

mattered to the delegation was a memorandum on Shaw, whose appointment as consul the council continued to take amiss.⁶ The document began with the comment that "the Council has made pointed objections" to Shaw "since his appointment [and] we have repeatedly urged the appointment of a native Ethiopian to represent the Emperor in the United States rather than a white man." Among the grievances and charges it went on to air were that Shaw had "bungled" efforts of the Ethiopian government to purchase two American bomber planes and had mishandled attempts to buy cartridges from the Remington Arms Company of America; that he had "lost all of the confidence of the American Negroes . . . when he ruthlessly crushed Robert Harris' Committee For Ethiopia, . . . the first organization to send medical supplies to Ethiopia"; that he had been the cause of contretemps he had had with Lij Tasfaye Zaphiro; that he had made "mistakes . . . concerning the new Ethiopian stamps" that were meant to raise funds for the cause; and that he had been unavailable to handle certain revenues collected. As a Parthian shot, the memorandum asserted that H. Murray Jacoby participated in the cause out "of his own financial interests and not particularly for any love which he may have had for Ethiopia."⁷

It is extremely difficult to gauge the merit of the accusations in the memorandum. Neither the bomber deal nor the purchase of cartridges was consummated, although there was no national prohibition against such sales at that time. The Boeing Aircraft Company, of Seattle, after negotiating intermittently for about a year decided not to proceed with the sale of the planes, because it "feared possible complications" resulting from the

---

6. Steen to Bayen, July 25, 1935, in ERC. The seven documents: (1) "United States Relations with Ethiopia Since the Fall of Addis Ababa," a summary based on press releases from the State Department and impressively accurate and detailed. (2) "The Proclamation of an Italian Empire and Its Implications," a copy of the complete text of the proclamation. (3) "Italian Military Operations in East Africa as of January 1, 1936," a report covering conditions of the water supply, roads, hospitals, and shipping facilities in Ethiopia and surveying the Italian troops stationed in East Africa—air, navy, and army—with a breakdown between "white and native." (4) "Organization of the Italian Medical Service in East Africa," a cataloging of hospitals, primarily in Ethiopia. (5) "Medical Supplies Available to Ethiopia from Canada." (6) "Movement of Italian Troops as of June 5, 1936," an accounting of movements from Italy as well as within Ethiopia. (7) "Memorandum for Dr. Malaku Bayen on the Activities of John H. Shaw, Ethiopian Consul General in New York City," a five-page recital of grievances and charges against Shaw.

7. Memorandum for Bayen, in ERC.

likelihood of war between Ethiopia and Italy.[8] Negotiations had gone on fitfully with Remington Arms for about eighteen months before Shaw's appointment as consul. The company and Shaw explained to Joseph C. Green, chief of the Office of Arms and Munitions Control of the Department of State, that "they had mutually agreed not to proceed with the transaction involving the purchase of five million cartridges by the Ethiopian Government." Green passed word along to the secretary of state that the company had told him confidentially that it had based its decision on the "attitude of Congress as revealed in the recent debates on neutrality legislation" and that it had retreated from the sale "in order to forestall possible criticism."[9]

The explanations do not absolve Shaw of "mishandling" the transactions. Both companies had been prepared to do business months before congressional or presidential decisions on neutrality. Moreover, a number of companies reached sales agreements with Italy before, during, and after passage of the neutrality legislation. Conceivably, through adroit maneuvering, the same might have been possible for Ethiopia. But however much or little the collapse of the deals owed to Shaw's ineffectiveness, it unquestionably convinced leaders of the Ethiopian Research Council that he was feckless.

Hansberry and Steen would have liked to see Shaw replaced, but inasmuch as the emperor was in exile, they did not want to open the issue of diplomatic recognition and authority. To sidestep the risk of losing Ethiopia's only representative in the United States, Steen tried simply to reduce Shaw's jurisdiction. He suggested advising the emperor to be cautious about letting Shaw handle visits to the United States and to instruct him to be more cooperative with United Aid for Ethiopia. Steen wanted the emperor clearly to identify himself with African Americans.

The most critical accusations against Shaw were those about Harris' Committee for Ethiopia and about the tensions with Zaphiro, for they had conspicuous racial implications. Imes complained to Martin that Shaw had shown no interest in mobilizing African Americans. Savory and his contingent sought to convince the emperor and Bayen that black Americans constituted the core of support for the cause and were the most loyal and that any mission trying to rally sympathy and funds in the United States had to

8. 884.248/39, Joseph C. Green, Memorandum, September 11, 1935.
9. 884.113/143, Joseph C. Green, Memorandum, September 6, 1935.

achieve rapport with African-American groups. Hansberry and Steen were careful not to propose exclusive attention to blacks, however, for they recognized that some whites were zealous in defending Ethiopia and that the potential for raising substantial funds was greater among whites. Still, they were convinced that a primary identification with African Americans would legitimate the assistance effort and benefit all sides.

Steen was also wary about how Hubert Julian's deprecations of Ethiopia might affect Savory's mission and any visit the emperor might make. He included an enclosure of Julian's "latest blast, which may possibly react against us, although I doubt it." Steen suspected that the Italians were supporting Julian to counter others' efforts to raise funds for Ethiopia.[10]

Having entrusted the delivery of the documents to Savory, Steen wrote separately to Bayen and reiterated that if Sellassie visited the United States, he should not be "taken completely into the hands of John Shaw . . . and the all-white groups," because he would "lose the last vestige of the loyal confidence which the Black People of America still have in him." For it was only black America, Steen contended, that gave "wholehearted support to Ethiopia throughout . . . and who will readily rise again to the cause if the Emperor so desires."[11]

Savory's mission went well. He met with the emperor and consulted with Bayen, Martin, and others. In a letter to Steen, he described Bayen as "very much pleased" to receive the "confidential data" and happy to present the delegation to Sellassie, who had been pressing Bayen, "Where are your American friends of whom you spoke?"[12] The emperor raised a number of questions: whether the delegation received publicity when it left the United States, whether African Americans would pay the expenses of a delegation of the emperor's in the United States, whether the United States government would object to or prevent the landing of the envoys, whether a non-interest-bearing bond could be floated without interference from the government.[13]

Savory addressed each point, evincing enthusiasm over the opportunity for African Americans to meet the challenge the visit would present. He recommended calling on Howard University alumni, who "are in every state of the Union and occupying varying positions of importance in the

---

10. William Steen to Dr. Phillip Savory, August 21, 1936, in ERC.
11. William Steen to Malaku Bayen, July 25, 1935, in ERC.
12. William Steen to William Leo Hansberry, August 25, 1936, in ERC.
13. Dr. Phillip Savory to William Steen, August 16, 1935, in ERC.

professional world," to "stage the most cooperative effort to raise money that has ever been put forward among our group in the U.S.A." If letters went "to various Howard Alumni Associations," Savory believed they would respond, "if not for the preservation and restoration of Ethiopia, then for the sake of an alumnus, Dr. Bayen, who has distinguished himself and further married an American girl." Together, he thought, the people associated with Howard, and the "groups working for the benefit of the Negro," and the Ethiopian Research Council, with members at Howard and in other organizations, "should not only be able to take care of such minor items as transportation and maintenance, but also coordinate their efforts as was never done before to bring in a few million dollars."[14]

Savory cabled his associate Dr. Cletis Powell to make inquiries at the State Department about admittance of the Ethiopian contingent into the United States; he also asked Steen to pursue that matter. He advised Bayen to leave the floating of a bond for the envoys to explore once they were in the country, and he assured the emperor that the delegation from America had shied from publicity and had received none.[15]

Impressed though Bayen was with Savory's plans for raising money, he hoped to do even more to forestall failure. He wondered about ways to make sure Americans would respond to the call and, if they did, that the funds would reach the emperor. Bayen was disturbed that the money already being raised was not getting to the emperor. He worried that the United States government would hobble fund raising. He wrote to Steen,

> It is most unfortunate for all the money that has been raised in the name of Ethiopia not to have reached His Majesty. . . . As you no doubt would realize, the money still can be used if there could be found a practical way of raising it, but I just have the fear that the American Government would put all the obstacles before any such proposition could be put to work. I wish you would give me your frank idea . . . as to the possible success of such a mission at this time. . . . If you really think it would be of material advantage to His Majesty, he is about to send me along. . . . I would want my mission to be particularly among the Negroes, if you think such a trip would be of especial advantage.[16]

14. *Ibid.*
15. *Ibid.*
16. Bayen to Steen, August 16, 1935, in ERC.

These were dark days for Sellassie. He had addressed the League of Nations on June 30, pointing out that the Ethiopian struggle was essentially a moral one that threatened the League itself. When the international body rejected his appeal for its good offices, a poem in the African-American journal *Opportunity* seemed to capture the sentiments of many:

> They could have stayed the iron hand of Might
> And fought for right, down to the earth's last man;
> But louder voices brayed into the night,
> So jackals ended what the League began.
> Now suave-voiced diplomats drone on and on;
> Geneva's air is rife with fear and hate;
> While at the council-table fights alone
> The fallen Emperor of a member State.
> Pile lies on wrong, and ring the curtain down
> Upon the closing scene of this last act;
> The King of Kings now yields his ancient crown
> To those who signed the Non-Aggression Pact,
> As weaker nations vanish one by one....
> Blow, bugles! Armageddon has begun![17]

Those lines captured the reality of a proud leader and a moral cause in defeat. And though the Savory visit had brought a ray of hope, other forces were intent on maintaining the status quo. At virtually the same time as the Savory mission, and about six weeks after the League's rebuff, the United States' ambassador in London, Robert W. Bingham, cabled the secretary of state that his sources said the emperor was contemplating a trip to the United States to raise funds. The State Department counseled the ambassador "to make every appropriate effort to dissuade the Emperor" and to stress that American interest was "wholly centered upon national elections next November." The idea was to convince the emperor that he would "receive scant attention" and would not be able to achieve his goal.[18]

A few days later, when Bingham met with Martin, his reaction to the minister's remark that people were importuning the emperor to visit the

---

17. Marcus B. Christian, "Selassie at Geneva," *Opportunity*, XVI (1938), 213.
18. 884.001, Selassie, 1/337, Telegram Received (389), August 5, 1936.

United States to raise money was to dwell on the American elections. Martin then broached the possibility of going himself but received no encouragement from the ambassador. Martin demonstrated in a letter he wrote Bingham after the meeting, though, that he was undeterred: "It has occurred to me that under our present critical position it will not only be unwise but dangerous for me to postpone my visit to America till November as very likely we will have been executed before then unless the necessary financial help is secured before long."[19] To Martin's request for permission to visit the United States, Bingham responded by inviting him for another visit in his office. Although the ambassador attempted to dissuade Martin from the trip, the Ethiopian minister maintained that his presence in the United States was imperative in order to get "certain sympathetic persons" to extend support. Once he conceded that any funds he collected would go toward continuing the armed struggle, Bingham declared that he would have to submit the matter to the government in Washington. Martin mentioned that if he was not able to go, the emperor's daughter would apply for a visa. Acquainted with Martin's determination to pursue the matter, Secretary of State Hull told Bingham that what Martin proposed "would be contrary to the spirit of our neutrality laws" and directed the ambassador to convey that "emphatically" to the minister. But Hull "confidentially" added that "the Department would not, for various reasons, consider it advisable to refuse visas to such individuals if they insist upon coming."[20]

Since Martin's discussions with Bingham occurred during August, when the Savory mission was conferring with the emperor's entourage, there can be little doubt that the "certain sympathetic persons" in the United States were African Americans. It is amazing there is no sign that Bingham or the State Department knew the Savory mission was in London. Probably that is because only a few members of the Ethiopian Research Council were aware of the mission until after it returned. Council officers, however, were abreast of the diplomatic exchanges between Bingham and the State Department and informed Savory of their content. Steen wrote to Savory that Dr. Arnold Donawa had gone to the State Department, as requested, and had learned that the matter of visas for the Ethiopian envoys would be left entirely "in the hands of the Consular represen-

19. 884.51/59, Robert W. Bingham to secretary of state, August 10, 1936.
20. *Ibid.*, August 10, 1936, August 18, 1936.

tative in London, unless, of course, pressure is brought to bear from this side." Steen had also acquired and sent to Savory a copy of a State Department memorandum on the case of Martin. Savory received as well a lengthy analysis that the State Department's legal adviser had submitted to buttress his conclusion that the proposed mission would not violate the provisions of the neutrality law and that there was no specific statutory authority for denying a visa to the Ethiopian envoys. The only grounds for denying entry would be that the visit would be contrary to the "public safety."[21]

Steen doubted that public safety would be invoked, because of the publicity it would generate. In addition, Donawa had let State Department officials know that "Negro voters would be interested in the treatment" accorded the case.[22] The implication was that the black vote, which was largely Democratic, could turn away from the party of the incumbent administration in the elections. Ironically, at the same time that the State Department was using the election to discourage the visit, the council was using it to cow the department into not blocking the trip. It was also of consequence that the president's neutrality proclamations of 1936 had been revoked on June 20 and that the United States, with an accredited official in Addis Ababa, had not recognized any change in the political status of the kingdom. The emperor, Martin, or any other Ethiopian official was entitled to a diplomatic visa. If the United States government wanted to keep the Ethiopians from coming, the only means that could avail was suasion.

Donawa's attendance at the Department of State on August 19 to inquire about visas seems to have given the department its first awareness of the African-American delegation in London, and even then it seems to have learned the scant minimum. Donawa, accompanied by James V. Herring, a council member and a professor of art at Howard University, disclosed to Wallace Murray that United Aid for Ethiopia had sent Savory, Imes, and Phillips to London to invite "some competent Ethiopian national to come" to the United States for "lecturing" on and "clarifying" the Ethiopian situation, and he showed Murray the cable in which Savory had made queries about procedures for securing a visa for the Ethiopians. Murray explained that the issuance of visas fell within the purview of

21. William Steen to Dr. Phillip Savory, August 20, 1936, in ERC.
22. *Ibid.*

American officials abroad. Obviously casting about to see how Savory's inquiry connected with the requests from the emperor and Martin, he asked if the council had a particular Ethiopian in mind. The answer he received was negative—that what it wanted was merely a knowledgeable "native-born Ethiopian." The State Department sent a summary of the discussion to Bingham marked, Confidential—For staff use only; Steen also sent a summary to Savory.[23]

In early September, Jacoby contributed to the effort to abort any plans the emperor had to visit the United States. He reported to the State Department that, since Bayen had told him Sellassie wanted to see him in London and since he could stop in London on a visit he was planning to the Netherlands, he expected the emperor would solicit his advice about royal participation in an American mission. Jacoby declared that he would discourage Sellassie from including himself on the grounds that the publicity would compromise the emperor's "dignity' and reduce the possibility of success. Paul Alling, of the State Department, was in accord with Jacoby's strategy.[24] On October 5, Jacoby could inform Alling that the emperor had decided against a visit. According to Jacoby, he had cautioned the emperor that his visit might ignite conflict between the "large Italian colonies in the United States" and Ethiopian sympathizers.[25] Although this appears to be the first time that official discussion touched on the possibility of such a confrontation, the chance of it was real. But it is unclear whether there was anything more tangible than Jacoby's need to strengthen his case against the emperor's trip that led him to bring it up.[26]

The Ethiopian Research Council continued its efforts to get some Ethiopian envoy to the United States. Howard Moore wrote Savory that "whoever comes, try to see that they are as dark as there is in London. No one of Zaphiro's color will do. They should speak English by all means."[27] Perhaps the council thought that Zaphiro's success had been limited by his light complexion. That belief could have arisen from the insistence in some quarters that Ethiopians were not black and had no reason to consider

23. 884.51/63, Memorandum, August 19; 884.51/63, Wallace Murray to William Phillips, August 20, 1936; Steen to Savory, August 20, 1936, in ERC.

24. 884.001, Selassie, 1/342, September 4, 1936, 353, September 8, 1936.

25. 765.84/5075, Memorandum of Conversation, October 5, 1936; 884.001, Selassie, 1/345, October 5, 1936, November 20, 1936.

26. For a discussion of Jacoby's interests in Ethiopia at this time, see above, p. 000.

27. Steen to Savory, August 20, 1936, in ERC.

themselves related to African Americans. Steen was soon able to inform Claude Lewis that the State Department had received a cable from the embassy in London communicating Martin's request of a visa for Bayen, his wife and child, and another Ethiopian. The department reportedly did not look favorably on fund raising by Ethiopian nationals but decided that it could not deny visas. Moore instructed Lewis to cable Savory, "State Department reluctant to give visas to Bayen and other party but will do so if they persist in demands notwithstanding what Embassy told Martin."[28] The council wanted Savory to shore up the Ethiopians' persistence, and he did. Since Mrs. Bayen and her son, Malaku, Jr., were American citizens, with United States passports, their right to reenter the country was assured in any event.

There was at least one non-African-American effort to get the emperor to the United States. The Reverend William Sheafe Chase, superintendent of the International Reform Federation, of Washington, D.C., notified the State Department that his representative in London, Edward Page Gaston, had extended an invitation to the emperor to attend a conference on the Ethiopian situation. Chase was disturbed by rumors that the department had already refused the emperor entry, but it explained that Sellassie had not applied for a visa. Although the department elaborated for Chase the reservations it had about a royal visit, he cabled Gaston that the emperor "would be visaed by the American Embassy." For him to have drawn that conclusion is puzzling unless he assumed that the department, by saying it was leaving the matter to the embassy, intended to imply that a visa would be forthcoming. When Gaston pursued the matter in London, however, Bingham reiterated the problems involved and Gaston decided not to press the issue.[29]

On August 28, Moore wrote Powell in a letter, Highly Confidential To Be Closely Guarded, that a source had learned authorization had come through for Bayen's visa but that the State Department objected to Ethiopians' raising "funds to continue the war," as Martin had uncircumspectly put it. There was no resistance, however, Moore went on, to canvassing for funds for the sick, wounded, and homeless. What is more, once funds were in hand, nothing could prevent their application to munitions "so long

28. Howard Moore to Claude Lewis, August 27, 1936, in ERC.
29. 884.001, Selassie, 1/338, Rev. William Sheafe Chase to Cordell Hull, September 4, 1936, 1/339, Rev. William Sheafe Chase to Cordell Hull September 9, 1936.

as we are not supposed to know that fact." Moore suggested cabling Savory: "Washington objects avowed purpose of mission solicitation funds continued warfare. Please change purpose solicitation funds for sick, wounded, homeless."[30] So delicate did Moore regard his message that he had it delivered to Powell by the "Council's confidential agent in New York because I do not know if anyone else opens mail that comes to your office."[31] Moore coached Claude Lewis, "You understand that if the Ethiopians raise funds here for the sick, etc., and they use the money for guns, we haven't a thing to do with that, so the law will be all wet in such a case. We must work fast in this matter because it is not yet certain just when they will leave."[32]

On August 31, Moore composed a five-page, single-spaced letter briefing Bayen on what to know, do, and have for the visit. He was to "avoid all references to continuing war" and stress his "purpose of raising funds for the sick, etc." Moore explained that "the Italians have done this frequently and consistently in this country and more than half a million dollars have been sent to Italy in the past six months." Bayen was to "come to the United States as an accredited representative of the Emperor himself, not Martin," because the ambassador's name had been "bandied around" by a number of people wanting to identify with official Ethiopia but that approach seemed to have "worn thin."[33] Moore counseled Bayen to bring a letter to the Pittsburgh *Courier,* which had been raising funds since May 1 and printing in the paper the names of contributors along with the statement that "the money is being held in trust until it is called for by the Emperor Haile Sellassie, or his authorized representative of Ethiopia, calls for this fund, it will be transmitted through the Ethiopian Consul General in this country, John H. Shaw. If the proper representative of Ethiopia fails to request the fund, or if it is discerned that it is not possible to use it to aid Ethiopia, every penny will be returned by The Courier to the persons contributing."[34] Moore suggested that the emperor or foreign minister instruct Shaw to receive the money and present it to Bayen, since the *Courier* was working "hand in hand with Shaw." Moore also urged Bayen to establish an address to receive funds directly by mail or to assume control of the consulate. The intent, he thought, should be to keep Shaw in the

30. Howard Moore to Dr. Cletis Powell, August 28, 1936, in ERC.
31. *Ibid.*
32. Howard Moore to Claude Lewis, August 28, 1936, in ERC.
33. Howard Moore to Malaku Bayen, August 31, 1936, in ERC.
34. *Ibid.;* Pittsburgh *Courier,* August 29, 1936.

background "except in such cases where he can be used to garner some funds." For not only was it necessary to ensure that the effort was black-run but there was also some reason to suppose Shaw duplicitous. Nevertheless Moore stressed that there "is to be no discrimination against any group . . . and . . . no personal animosities are to come into play, but . . . all groups are to cooperate to put over the program." That was a sensitive matter, since Shaw's race was still an issue and there remained a widespread preference for an Ethiopian or African American as consul general.[35]

To Bayen's question about a visit by the emperor, Moore replied that he was sure he could come in spite of any protest from Italy, since the United States had not recognized the Italian annexation of Ethiopia. Moore felt certain that the United Sates would "give adequate protection: anytime G-men can protect Roosevelt they can protect the Emperor." Moore ended his letter by repeating "that it will hardly do you or anyone else any good to come *unless you are coming as a representative of His Majesty.*" Stationery with the emperor's seal would be an asset for official correspondence, he added. Because Hubert Julian might publicly question whether Bayen represented the emperor, it would be essential to "have authorized credentials" and "be prepared for any eventuality."[36]

Moore followed up his highly relevant and perceptive advice to Bayen with a dispatch to Savory in which he covered some of the same ground and asked Savory to inform the press that the purpose of the mission was to collect funds for relief rather than for continuing the war. He mentioned that he had assured Bayen that the council would begin approaching some "of the 20 thousand alumni of Howard," and he urged Savory to reflect on the advisability of having Bayen start a new organization in order to minimize interorganizational antagonisms and at the same time allow for the affiliation of "any white group" interested in the cause. Moore admonished Savory against overoptimism. "A few millions, as you state, may be a little overestimated." Moore did not want the Ethiopians to have false expectations. On the other hand, he remained hopeful, provided that the emperor's ties with the campaign were close. That, he believed, would "revive the people on the [Ethiopian] question which is slowly dying."[37] Moore and Steen may have seen the drive as the last chance for African Americans to show their full support for the Ethiopian cause.

35. Moore to Bayen, August 31, 1936, in ERC.
36. *Ibid.*
37. Howard Moore to Dr. Phillip Savory, September 1, 1936, in ERC.

Word that the emperor was himself still planning to visit the United States continued to circulate and drew particular attention when the American ambassador in Rome conveyed the concerns that Count Galeazzo Ciano, the Italian minister for foreign affairs, had. The foreign minister identified Hansberry and Steen as leaders of a group determined to put the emperor to propaganda purposes, and the Ethiopian Research Council as sponsor of the envisaged mission. Willis Huggins, Ralph Bunche, and George M. Jones, as well as Herring and Lewis, were implicated, too, along with the Istmo-African Bureau of Panama, the Rising Sun Club of Philadelphia, the Peace Movement of Ethiopia, in Chicago, and the Medical Committee for the Defense of Ethiopia. It was Ciano's position that a visit by the emperor "would be most unfortunate."[38]

The State Department replied to the ambassador in Italy that, according to Jacoby, the emperor's trip would not occur and that "the persons mentioned in your telegram are not of great importance."[39] Little did the Department know of the role Hansberry, Steen, Savory, and their associates were playing in orchestrating Bayen's trip to the United States over State Department objections.

Savory devised an overall plan that called for a national organizer and intensive publicity in about fifty of the "colored papers, not including the *Chicago Defender, Pittsburgh Courier,* and the *Afro-American.*" Inasmuch as he felt that "professional jealousy" on the part of Robert Lee Vann, publisher of the Pittsburgh *Courier,* Carl Murphy, publisher of the *Afro-American,* and Robert Sengstacke Abbot, publisher of the Chicago *Defender,* might easily undermine their cooperation, he proposed having Bayen "handle Vann" through the letter the emperor would send regarding the *Courier's* fund raising, and having Hansberry, who was in Chicago then and had many contacts there, try to win Abbott's support. The *Afro-American* remained a problem, especially in view of the controversy in 1935 about Bayen's recruiting volunteers for the Ethiopian army. Savory also planned to court the support of black churches and a number of black leaders—including A. Phillip Randolph, of the Brotherhood of Sleeping Car Porters, Roy Wilkins, of the NAACP, and M. L. Gordon, of the Peace Movement—to help dispose of the hundred thousand autographed pho-

---

38. 884.001, Selassie, 1/349, William Phillips to Cordell Hull, November 20, 1936, 345; *Papers Relating to the Foreign Relations of the United States* (Washington, D.C., 1936), III.

39. 884.001, Selassie, 1/346, Telegram, November 21, 1936.

tographs of the emperor, to encourage the contribution of a day's pay to help Ethiopia, and to participate in floating a loan for the cause. He also suggested cooperation with fraternal and trade-union groups and with branches of the National Negro Congress to spark interest and increase the sale of photographs. Howard University alumni were to be prime prospects for contributions.[40]

"In order to avoid any trouble with the law, and to prevent any criticisms" if the United States recognized the "'annexation' of Ethiopia," Savory proposed the establishment of United Aid for People of African Descent (UAPAD), which was to function as a regular social organization but also encompass autonomous groups that could stage their own activities while participating in and contributing to the organization's central operation. All money from the sale of photographs was to go directly to Bayen; money from fund-raising entertainment was to help cover expenses, with a percentage earmarked for Bayen.[41]

According to plan, Haile Sellassie issued Bayen an official letter of appointment as "His Majesty's Special Envoy for the Western Hemisphere," thereby favoring him with a higher rank and a larger geographical area than Shaw enjoyed. The foreign minister instructed Shaw to transmit contributions to Bayen and to use his good offices as consul general to assist the campaign. Savory wrote to Steen, "Your influence helped to make our efforts successful."[42]

Rumors had surfaced that John Robinson and others were also planning to send a mission to see the emperor, but nothing seems to have come of that. Still, Steen remained concerned about possible conflicts and the need to organize Chicago, New York, and Philadelphia. He thought Philadelphia was the most unified, but he also believed that Savory's success as an emissary to the emperor under the partial auspices of United Aid for Ethiopia would help solidify competing groups. Steen wrote, "We must all present a unified front."[43]

The Savory mission was indeed a success, for it not only channeled vital information to Haile Sellassie and his entourage and secured the dispatch of the emperor's envoy, it deepened the sense of confidence and

40. Dr. Phillip Savory to William Steen, September 18, 1936, in ERC.
41. *Ibid.*
42. *Ibid.*
43. William Steen to Dr. Phillip Savory, September 20, 1936, Steen to William Leo Hansberry, September 20, 1936, both in ERC.

commitment among both African Americans and Ethiopians and assured direct, influential input by both groups. Moore and Steen demonstrated perception and meticulous attention to protocol and details and thereby became indispensable to the effort. The mission demonstrated to the "Chief [Hansberry] that there are intelligent forces in action which want a central guiding agency to coordinate the whole for the common good."[44]

Savory gave assurances that Medcom would "subordinate itself to work not as leader of organizations but on par with others, white or black." His main concern was to help Ethiopia obtain the money necessary to get the "planes and munitions necessary to bring our people back into their rightful possession. . . . Success in this venture will enable Negroes to find themselves to a greater extent in America and to cooperate to solve our problems at home."[45] It is not without significance that Hansberry, Steen, and Savory were willing to settle for secondary leadership roles. Nor is there cause to minimize the statements of Steen, Savory and others that they welcomed participation with other groups, black and white. Although they wanted to assure a means of effective black expression and support, they rejected exclusivity. Through them the Bayen mission to the United States had great potential at a very uncertain time.

44. *Ibid.*
45. 884.001, Selassie, 1/346, Telegram, November 21, 1936.

VII

The Emperor's Special Envoy for the Western Hemisphere

The Savory mission had led to the appointment of an Ethiopian, Bayen, to supervise the emperor's fund raising and promote Ethiopia's general interests in the Americas. Bayen's title of special envoy for the Western Hemisphere, by surpassing that of Shaw, was critical for fund raising and accommodated a point that mattered to African Americans. That the envoy had a medical degree from Howard University, was a founder of the Ethiopian Research Council, had developed close personal contacts with a number of African-American leaders in the pro-Ethiopian cause, and was married to an African American deeply committed to Ethiopian and African-American interests engendered an optimism that the Ethiopian–African-American connection would not only nurture support for the struggle against Italy's aggression but also reinforce pan-African links generally.

Never before had blacks in the United States been in such a favorable position to exercise influence on a foreign representative in this country and, by virtue of that, possibly to exert influence on American foreign policy. It is uncertain how many African Americans fully recognized the great potential the situation afforded and were prepared to capitalize on it. Hansberry, Steen, and the members of the Savory mission understood what was opening before them, but would African Americans be able to devise and implement plans appropriate to the task?

On September 23, 1936, Bayen, Mrs. Bayen, and their son, Malaku, Jr., arrived in New York City, where they were met by Savory and his wife, Imes, Charles Mackey, Cyril Phillips, and Claude Lewis, among others. That was a historic moment, marking the first result of a mission designed and carried out entirely by African Americans for the purpose of challenging aggression a European power was embarked on in Africa with the support, or at least the acquiescence, of the most powerful countries of the world. Bayen was not officially recognized by the American government, but diplomatic recognition had not been sought. What was important at the time was that the envoy represented the emperor and was going to work closely with black Americans for Ethiopia's liberation.

But it was not long before the rude reality that black people in the United States faced asserted itself, prefiguring the magnitude of the task of establishing a viable black power base in the United States. The management of the Hotel Delano, in New York, despite reconfirmed reservations, denied rooms to the Bayens. The Delano had catered a number of black-sponsored affairs, but residence by blacks was apparently a different matter. Savory was among those who attempted to resolve the problem with the management on the spot but failed. The NAACP, the International Labor Defense, the *Amsterdam News,* and the *Daily Worker* became involved, but after hours of irresolution, the Bayens went to the Savorys' home. Later they found lodging at the Hotel Rex.[1] The incident quickly attracted public and official attention. The New York *American* carried the headline "Hotel Here Bars Selassie's Cousin"; the New York *World-Telegram,* "Snub to Prince Deplored." The All Peoples party, led by Donald J. Phillips, condemned the incident and called on President Roosevelt to issue a statement censuring the hotel, insisting on an apology, and asking for a "withdrawal [of] this unheard of discrimination against a friendly envoy." Secretary of State Hull replied with an expression of "sincere regret" but explained that since Bayen had not been accredited in a *diplomatic capacity,* the federal government had "no authority to intervene." The secretary did, however, refer the matter to New York's Mayor Fiorello La Guardia.[2]

Ignacious E. Lawlor, executive secretary of All Harlem Independent Political Action, renamed the All Peoples party, an organization of representatives of trade unions and relief and civic societies, wrote to the Hotel Delano, branding the incident an "intolerable insult" and calling for an

   1. 033.8411/85, A. R. Burr to R. C. Bannerman, September 28, 1936; Claude Lewis to William Steen, September 23, 1936, in ERC.
   2. 033.8411/84, Cyril Phillips to President Roosevelt, September 26, 1936, Cordell Hull to Cyril Phillips, telegram, September 26, 1936, Cordell Hull to Fiorello La Guardia, September 26, 1936; New York *American,* September 26, 1936; New York *World-Telegram,* September 28, 1936; New York *Times,* September 28, 1936; *Amsterdam News,* October 3, 1936.

apology to Bayen. The hotel explained, unconvincingly, that it had not been able to provide the "two connecting rooms" that "appeared" to be required. Wallace Murray, of the State Department, regarded the All Peoples party's telegram and the department's letter to Mayor La Guardia as "quite in order."[3]

Steen and Hansberry were naturally resentful over the Delano affair but did not want it to cloud Bayen's arrival and mission. Steen had informed Savory that Hansberry and the Rising Sun Club in Philadelphia "did not like the idea of a white hotel at all." Hansberry had observed, "Personally, I think Bayen's headquarters as well as stopping place should be uptown *with the Blacks*. Financial as well as propaganda reasons would seem to favor such a course." But Steen counseled that the matter be dropped and that spokesmen "say as little about it in the papers . . . as possible." He was especially concerned that the incident might eclipse the immediate issue and that the Communist party might capitalize on it to increase its appeal to black members.[4]

Although the Bayens were familiar with racism in the United States, their experience at the Delano was a crude reminder that the situation had not changed during their stay abroad and that color or racial discrimination was not restricted to American blacks. The Bayens' black hosts and friends had to be distressed that they lacked the power either to guarantee the respect of their Ethiopian guests or to respond effectively when that respect was violated, but they were at least vindicated in their view that all black people in the United States were first of all, no matter what their nationality, black and subject to racial discrimination. Since that was the primary basis of the call for unity, Bayen could proceed directly with the mission at hand.

Less than a week after his arrival, he addressed a gathering of approximately three thousand Harlemites at the Rockland Palace, well known as a center for militant black rallies. Sponsored by United Aid for Ethiopia and Peoples of African Descent, the rally began with the singing of "We'll Sing Ethiopia," the lyrics of which Imes had written, with the music by

---

3. 033.8411/85, Burr to Bannerman, September 28, 1936, Ignacious E. Lawlor to Hotel Delano, September 25, 1936.

4. William Steen to Claude Lewis, September 24, 1936, William Steen to Malaku Bayen, September 24, 1936, William Steen to Dr. Phillip Savory, September 24, 1936, Claude Lewis to William Steen, September 26, 1936, all in ERC; 033.8411/87, Wallace Murray to secretary of state, September 28, 1936.

Luckeyeth Roberts. Bayen, in his address, praised Colonel Robinson and others like him for their work in Ethiopia, and the thrust of his remarks was that Ethiopia would not surrender. He appealed for assistance while recognizing that the United States was a neutral power. Imes, Savory, and Phillips also spoke, and a collection was taken.[5]

Bayen remained in demand as a speaker on Ethiopia, but the financial collections were insufficient to cover expenses, not to mention support for war-related relief. He therefore turned his greater hopes to other projects. From the very beginning, though, he and his hosts differed over procedures for raising and distributing funds. In a letter to Hansberry, Steen expressed disappointment that Bayen did not want to charge an admission fee to his lectures and insisted on keeping overhead to a minimum. Steen realized that, without remuneration, few people would invest their time for long in planning and running the pro-Ethiopian programs. He also stressed the need for advertising. What Steen proposed was a sharing of realized amounts with host groups—churches, social clubs, fraternities, and the like—which would organize, advertise, and generally supervise meetings, lectures, and rallies. He suggested prizes for persons who sold the most tickets, and in general he advocated building in incentives for supporters. Bayen, at least initially, wanted everyone to be admitted without cost, hoping that that would inspire them to work harder and contribute money at collection time. He believed that blacks should support their "brothers" without remuneration. Steen viewed Bayen as having "false pride" in not wanting to commercialize the emperor and make him appear "hard up."[6] Steen's realism came from his involvement in fund raising and his familiarity with its constituency.

Bayen's preferences prevailed. He had brought some hundred thousand autographed photographs of the emperor from London and a number of Ethiopian stamps. After consulting with others, he launched the Haile Sellassie Fund to support refugee and other war-related relief programs. House-to-house canvassing was part of the drive, but the most effective part was the distribution of Ethiopian stamps. Local merchants were enlisted to distribute stamps with each purchase, and the *Voice of Ethiopia* carried a directory of cooperating businesses. The stamps were re-

---

5. Claude Lewis to William Steen, October 9, 1936, in ERC; *Amsterdam News*, October 3, 1936; Malaku Bayen, *The March of Black Men* (New York, 1939), 7.
6. William Steen to William Leo Hansberry, October 2, 1936, in ERC.

deemable for an autographed photograph of the emperor. When the drive began in Harlem in December, 1936, it met with a good deal of enthusiasm. The example of Mildred Houston, who collected 1,672 stamps in two weeks, was especially encouraging. Nonetheless, the drive did not catch on in other localities and had only limited success in Harlem.[7] Poor organization and advertisement, too few committed volunteers, and plain hard times prevented the project from achieving all it aimed for.

There was also a mail-in campaign. Persons who sent a check for a dollar or more received a photograph of the emperor and an Ethiopian seal. The meager information available about this drive suggests that it had some appeal. Bayen soon established two bank accounts. Contributions given exclusively for pacific purposes went into an account for Ethiopian refugees, many of whom were in Jerusalem and in Djibouti, Sudan, Kenya, Somaliland, and neighboring countries. Other contributions went into a separate account "to carry on the struggle against the Italian conquest of Ethiopia." When Jacoby apprised the State Department of those arrangements, it asked him to impress on Bayen the obligation to comply with federal regulations regarding fund raising. The department was uneasy about the funds going "to carry on the struggle." But Jacoby predicted that the problem would resolve itself when Bayen became discouraged over the small amounts coming in.[8]

Bayen did become frustrated, but he understood that hard economic realities prevented the great majority of African Americans from matching their sentiments with money. He continued his appeals, acknowledging the constant but small flow of income. He expressed deep disappointment, however, at the trickle of contributions from white Americans who professed sympathy with the cause. He was greatly chagrined that people like Jacoby, Shaw, and Henry A. Lardner, with business connections in Ethiopia and their own wealth as well as wealthy friends, did not deliver support.

In a letter to President Roosevelt in December, 1937, Bayen explained,

7. *Ibid.*; *Amsterdam News,* December 5, 1936, January 2, 1937, January 23, 1937; *New York Age,* December 19, 1938; William Randolph Scott, "Malaku Bayen: Ethiopian Emissary to Black America, 1936–1941," *Ethiopia Observer,* XV (1972), 136; *Voice of Ethiopia,* July 17, 1937.

8. 033.8411/88, Memorandum of Conversation Between Wallace Murray, George Alling, and H. Murray Jacoby, October 5, 1936.

We are here, having been sent by His Majesty Emperor Haile Selassie to seek aid for the Ethiopian refugees. We have met with very little success so far.

We know that it might not be to the best interests of the country for you to take a hand in our unfortunate affair, but I am sure Mrs. Roosevelt could do something about it if she sees fit. We have thirteen thousand refugees at the present time, scattered over the territories adjacent to Ethiopia and in other countries; in Djibouti, Berbera, Aden, Mombasa, Khartoum, Port Said, Cairo, Jerusalem, Paris and London. Even the Emperor himself is hard pressed because he is not able to render much aid to his refugees.[9]

The letter was acknowledged but neither of the Roosevelts seems to have lent assistance.

Even in England, the emperor was in difficult financial straits. Accordingly, Bayen explored all avenues of support he considered open. Often discouraged, he never gave up hope. He continued to believe that Americans of financial means would respond to his call for humanitarian assistance. His problems worsened as friction developed between him and some of his close friends. United Aid for Ethiopia had covered the envoy's expenses at the Hotel Rex but had expected to recoup some of its outlay from funds to be raised later. Bayen, however, seems to have decided that all revenues would be committed directly to the Ethiopian cause. That resulted in disagreement, because much of the UAE money came from the initiative of Savory and even out of his personal assets.[10]

Hansberry and Steen were disillusioned when Bayen decided to hold in abeyance the appeal they had drafted to Howard University faculty, students, and alumni.[11] At least part of the problem seems to have stemmed from the Ethiopian Research Council's lack of organizational structure and funds comparable to those of the New York group, which was also more aggressive politically and had Bayen's ear. In the short run, particularly, the New York group had an advantage that was damaging to the

---

9. 884.001, Selassie 1/356, Malaku Bayen to President Roosevelt, December 24, 1937.
10. Steen to Hansberry, October 2, 1936, in ERC; Bayen, *The March of Black Men*, 8.
11. William Steen to William Leo Hansberry, October 9, 1936, February 7, 1937, both in ERC.

cause, since the group in Washington had the intellectual capacity, the dedication, and the appeal that might have provided a stronger base and an extension of Bayen's movement into a wider sector of the black middle class, especially around Howard University. As it was, the Washington group, while continuing to support the cause, did not function with the enthusiasm that had buoyed its activities from 1934 to 1936. Bayen no doubt concluded that Savory's associates had greater financial potential, and therefore he pursued his objectives and developed a cadre in New York.

Bayen, from the beginning of his efforts to raise funds, had considered with his friends the possibility of organizing a new group. Steen had been behind such a suggestion to Savory prior to Bayen's appointment as envoy.[12] But several leaders warned against launching an organization that would consume time and money and could possibly antagonize competing groups. Consequently, the decision had been to initiate programs with a view toward attracting a wide spectrum of Americans and to delay forming any new organization. Within a few months, however, Bayen had come to appreciate how an umbrella organization with the stamp of approval of the emperor would bring greater harmony and cooperation to the movement. Zaphiro and some African Americans had attempted something along that line when they founded UAE, but Zaphiro did not have the emperor's sanction and did not remain in the country.

There had been cooperation among several pro-Ethiopian groups after the crisis erupted at Walwal in 1934. The Menelik Club, which a small group of African Americans had organized to stimulate support for Ethiopia, had helped sponsor several activities, and Savory later incorporated it into United Aid for Peoples of African Descent. The thinking was that the new organization's name would minimize the chances of investigation by the FBI and not leave African Americans stranded if the United States decided to recognize Italy's occupation of Ethiopia. Steen decided that "the new name is indeed a wise move" in appropriately including both Africa and its diaspora.[13] UAPAD was a loose confederation in which individual groups retained autonomy in their affairs but sent money to, and participated in the efforts of, the central office. Savory, however, was unable to win the wholehearted support of the affiliating organizations, partly be-

12. William Steen to Dr. Phillip Savory, September 1, 1936, in ERC.

13. Dr. Phillip Savory to William Steen, September 18, 1936, William Steen to Dr. Phillip Savory, September 30, 1936, both in ERC; *Voice of Ethiopia*, July 19, 1941.

cause they envied his dominating presence and financial clout in the cause and wanted to preserve their own contours.

Bayen had the advantage of being a newcomer on the scene with the support of the emperor and several African-American leaders. After prolonged consultation with a number of African Americans, he on August 25, 1937, founded the Ethiopian World Federation (EWF) to advance his long-held ideals: "Yes, the two factors that were in my mind as early as 1921 when I was worrying over the safety of our independence from European imperialism, these two thoughts, the solidarity of the Black race, and the undying determination of our people at home to be free, have become realities and offer the greatest assurance of the perpetuation of Ethiopia's independence."[14] Bayen, that is, envisioned the EWF as an entity with branches throughout the world to fight for the interests of Ethiopia and black people everywhere.

Although Bayen was well known and had the emperor's backing, he chose not to head the new federation. He wanted its leadership vested in an African American, to whom he was willing to give the full support of his position as the emperor's envoy. Bayen hoped to demonstrate that the EWF, though embracing members of other organizations, was a new group prepared to welcome the support of a wider constituency. He cast his support for a lesser-known but respected minister, the Reverend Lorenzo H. King, pastor of Saint Mark's Methodist Episcopal Church, in New York. Bayen became first vice-president to King, and executive director.[15] That arrangement allowed him greater flexibility to travel and speak to groups, to raise funds, and launch membership drives, while King attended to daily administration.

New York City was home to the international headquarters of the federation and also to its first branch, New York Local No. 1. Within two years the branches numbered nineteen, of which Local No. 1 was the most active and the largest. Officials of the central office participated regularly in the New York branch, and the activities of one often seemed to coincide with those of the other. Frequently, the regular weekly meetings, on Friday and Sunday evenings, heard Bayen or King present an address or appeal to which the other branches looked for policy guidelines. Much of the ac-

---

14. Bayen, *The March of Black Men*, 8; *Voice of Ethiopia*, June 25, 1938, September 9, 1937, October 7, 1937, December 16, 1937.

15. *Voice of Ethiopia*, July 1, 1939, October 19, 1940, July 12, 1941.

tivity at the central office involved the local branch, which provided significant voluntary support for the headquarters.

Branch meetings were both inspirational and substantive. In the New York branch, a meeting typically began with a prayer, which was followed by the singing of "Ethiopia Awaken," a song by Arnold J. Ford that the federation adopted as its anthem. Bayen, King, Warren Harrigan, Charles Watts, or a guest speaker would address in an inspirational vein the need for black unity and the prospects for black redemption in Africa and abroad. There would normally follow committee reports on practical concerns like programs, memberships, and fund raising. Frequently the meeting would include music by the regular choir, the juvenile unit, or a uniformed marching band. On some occasions a discussion of black writers was part of the format.[16]

Because Local No. 1 was in the preeminent international city of the United States, visitors of renown from throughout the black world could often speak or perform on short notice. In addition, a number of African-American residents of New York who had lived in Ethiopia participated regularly in branch affairs. Colonel Robinson, besides appearing frequently as a speaker, served as head of the marching unit and of more than one athletic group. Eudora Paris chaired meetings, sang solos, and directed the choir. Dr. John West was an occasional speaker and led discussions on Ethiopian affairs. Hattie Edwards Koffie visited a number of meetings, and Daniel Robert Alexander spoke to the group after he was forced from Ethiopia by the Italian invasion.[17] All provided links to Ethiopia through their experiences and continued contacts.

The president of the Chicago branch, another extremely active local, was Harry Broome, who with his wife, Pearle, had spent several years traveling in the southern United States to rally support for the Ethiopian cause. They corresponded regularly with Steen, provided him with information, and requested data and materials. Their popularity in the Chicago area imparted good momentum to their chapter. In addition to the Broomes, the local's leadership, including Henry Emery, Will Kirkman, Frank Lynch, and Lydia Simon, sponsored the Bantu College of African

16. *Ibid.,* September 30, 1939, October 7, 1939, December 23, 1939, June 7, 1940, July 19, 1941, *et al.*

17. *Ibid.,* August 5, 1939, September 9, 1939, October 7, 1939, December 16, 1939, January 27, 1940, January 18, 1941, August 9, 1941.

Languages and a series of lectures, films, exhibits, and stage performances on Ethiopia and Africa generally. The Chicago branch received praise from the New York office.[18]

From the beginning, Bayen's principles shaped the federation. In addition to emphasizing black unity, he frequently stated that "the philosophy of the Federation is to instill in the minds of the Black people of the world that the word Black is not to be considered in any way dishonorable but rather an honor and dignity because of the past history of the Race." Bayen was altogether persuaded that with a thorough knowledge of the African heritage, black people would affirm their pride and dignity. He consequently maintained that blacks must write their own history.[19] He was already committed to black solidarity and pan-Africanism when he arrived in the United States in 1921. The succeeding course of events, especially the Italo-Ethiopian War, intensified his commitment. In addition, time and maturity, as well as exposure to pro-African ideas among African Americans, sharpened his perception of black solidarity. He has written that it was his "belief in Race Solidarity" that caused him to enroll at Howard University and to marry an African American in 1931.[20]

In the absence of the text of Bayen's speeches, it is risky to attempt to analyze his philosophy. But one point is both conspicuous and arresting: nowhere in his book *The March of Black Men* and nowhere else in the available correspondence or other materials from before 1940 is there even a passing mention of Marcus Garvey. That may seem strange in light of Bayen's preoccupation with black solidarity and his presence in the United States during the latter part of the Garvey era. But Bayen was in high school until the mid-1920s, and after that an undergraduate student and less outspoken politically. What is more, during the late 1920s and early 1930s he represented his country in Washington, since it had no official envoy to the United States. Given that the United States had deported Garvey in 1927, any alignment Bayen saw between his and Garvey's ideas would have required guarded expression. After that period, Bayen cultivated close relations with the Department of State and would have found it imprudent to articulate an enthusiasm for Garvey. In any case, Bayen

---

18. *Ibid.*, June 25, 1938, January 8, 1939, June 3, 1939, July 8, 1939, May 24, 1941, July 12, 1941, July 26, 1941.
19. *Ibid.*, June 25, 1938, April 29, 1939.
20. Bayen, *The March of Black Men*, 6.

was always careful not to entangle himself in controversies he regarded as divisive of the black community.

By 1940, however, Bayen had on several occasions not only praised Garvey but credited the Universal Negro Improvement Association with laying the basis for the Ethiopian World Federation. How and why Bayen arrived at acknowledging Garvey's merits may never be known, but it could have been partly the result of his association with the many Garveyites who held important positions in the federation, or of the reading of Garvey's works. But Bayen and Garvey shared some views from the beginning—regarding black pride and solidarity, self-help and economic development. Moreover, Bayen greatly admired and was impressed by the Yale-trained historian William Ferris, who had been the editor of Garvey's *Negro World* before becoming an editorial adviser to the *Voice of Ethiopia* (*VOE*),[21] the federation's official publication. Bayen's principal means of disseminating his views, as well as information and appeals, was through that organ, first published in January, 1937, as a "Paper for the Vast Universal Black Commonwealth and Friends of Ethiopia Everywhere." Fittingly, the *VOE*'s slogan was Ethiopia Is Stretching Forth Her Hands unto God.[22]

Dr. Gilbert Balfour Bovell, a fellow student of Bayen's at Howard University's medical school and a founding member of the Ethiopian Research Council, served as editor of the paper for a few months. Although no explanation survives in the documents for the change in editorship, it is reasonable to assume that Bovell's responsibilities as a practicing physician kept him from devoting full time to editing. Moreover, Bayen probably reassessed the paper's possible utility to the federation, and for the promotion of his philosophy. Within a few months, Bayen himself became editor; his wife, Dorothy, became business manager of the publication, and later international secretary of the federation.[23]

Bayen made a conscious effort throughout his tenure as editor to nourish a rapport between Ethiopia and communities of African descent in the diaspora, and he thereby to a great extent pinned the hopes of his country's war efforts on black people. He made that choice in spite of the limited material support he had received from blacks and in the face of the European powers' and the United States' rejection of the premise of equality for blacks when they at first acquiesced in Italy's conquest of Ethiopia.

21. *Voice of Ethiopia*, January 27, 1940, February 17, 1940.
22. Bayen, *The March of Black Men*, 7; *Voice of Ethiopia*, April 2, 1938.
23. *Voice of Ethiopia*, July 17, 1937, July 6, 1940.

The *VOE* sold for five cents a copy, with an annual subscription costing two dollars in the United States and three dollars overseas. The paper carried appeals for individual memberships in the federation and for the establishment of branches throughout the world. The assumption was that the black world would be sufficiently interested in the publication and the organization to sustain them, and given the four-year life of the paper and the still-active life of the organization, that assumption seems to have been sound.

The federation and the *VOE* played a signal role in the development of black and African consciousness and unity, especially in the United States. Slogans were an integral part of the appeal that the paper made in its articles, reports, editorials, and special features, and particularly in its one-liners at the bottom of the page. The "History Makers" section focused on the black heritage and on black personalities throughout the world, though African Americans gained the greatest attention. The federation filled to a degree the void left by Garvey's deportation, the *VOE* carrying on the work of the *Negro World*. The paper lent its energy to the redefinition of African people. It made clear its unequivocal opposition to the term *Negro*, which it found insulting and a device to divide black people. The federation and the paper adopted the term *black*, for its "clearer reference" to a universal African connection than *Negro* had, which they regarded as a European creation. Blacks were also identified as Ethiopians. "We are no more West Indian and American Black people, but true Ethiopians under Bayen," the *VOE* proclaimed. "Black men, Ethiopia is yours." Among the most popular slogans were Black Men Let Us Get Together and Save Ethiopia, and No Black Man Shall Shed His Blood for Europe Until Ethiopia Is Free. The appeal to freedom was a constant: It Is Better to Die Free Than Live in Slavery, and Ethiopia Must Remain Free. The editor was always concerned that a long struggle against Italy could diminish support for the cause. One appeal read, Remember the Ethiopians Are Still Fighting—Give Them a Chance.[24]

Bayen wrote, "We are out to create a United States of Africa." The pan-African perspective was reinforced by articles on the history and culture of Ethiopia and Haiti, and of blacks in the United States, the Caribbean, and Africa. Some branches of the federation, notably those in Manhattan and Brooklyn, offered regular classes on Amharic and Ethiopian

---

24. *Ibid.*, March 19, 1938, April 29, 1939, June 24, 1939, July 15, 1939, July 29, 1939, *et al.*

history. Quizzes on black history appeared regularly in *VOE,* along with pieces on black notables like Henri Christophe and Pierre Toussaint L'Ouverture, of Haiti, Emperor Menelik, of Ethiopia, and Paul Laurence Dunbar and Richard Wright, of the United States. Reviews of the books of black authors like W. E. B. Du Bois, Joel A. Rogers, and Akiki Nyabongo were featured. George Padmore and Nnamdi Azikiwe contributed special articles, and the dean of African-American history, Carter G. Woodson, praised the paper.[25]

Ferris, author of *The African Abroad,* wrote scholarly pieces on African history and critical comments on contemporary issues. His work had a high intellectual quality and included particularly thorough coverage of the federation's activities. Indeed, Ferris was just the kind of black intellectual the *VOE* had made an appeal for support. He continued his relationship with the paper until his death in 1941.[26]

Articles specifically about Ethiopia carried the greatest urgency, however, not only because Ethiopianism had historical resonance for blacks but also because the very existence of Ethiopia as a free nation had been undermined. Although the federation appealed to the United States government to withhold recognition of Italy's occupation, the organization's major emphasis was on mobilizing black consciousness, which it viewed as critical to increasing support for the war effort. Blacks needed "a Flag and a country," according to the *VOE,* and Ethiopia was it. Italy was threatening to destroy the only indigenous national government in Africa, and it was up to the black world to defend the African heritage. Having fought on the Ethiopian side at the outbreak of the war, John Robinson ignited enthusiasm when he said he was "still willing to risk [his] life for Ethiopia."[27]

25. *Ibid.,* March 19, 1938, May 6, 1939, June 10, 1939, July 8, 1939, February 3, 1940, May 24, 1940, July 19, 1941.

26. *Ibid.,* April 27, 1940, April 26, 1941, May 17, 1941, May 24, 1941, June 14, 1941, July 26, 1941, August 30, 1941.

27. 865D/01/551, Ethiopian World Federation to President Roosevelt, November 16, 1938; *Voice of Ethiopia,* May 6, 1939. Robinson established an aviation fund in Chicago, where he subsequently formed the John C. Robinson National Air College to train pilots and mechanics and handle charter air services. See John Robinson to Claude Barnett, July 1, 1936, Claude Barnett to Scipio A. Jones, July 6, 1936, Claude Barnett to Dr. Phillip Savory, July 8, 1936, Dr. Phillip Savory to Claude Barnett, February 9, 1937, Webster to Civil Aeronautics Authority, January 4, 1939, all in Barnett Papers, Chicago Historical Society (Microfilm at Moorland-Spingarn Research Center, Howard University).

As a result of the strong appeal of the *VOE* and the efforts of Malaku Bayen, Dorothy Bayen, and their allies, locals sprang up and were sustained outside Manhattan, Brooklyn, and Chicago, with three in Philadelphia, two in Baltimore, and others in Buffalo, Detroit, Evanston, Kansas City, Nashville, and St. Louis, as well as in Okmulgee, Stone Bluff, and Tulsa, Oklahoma. Financial contributions arrived from groups without clear identification as chapters in Los Angeles, San Francisco, and Seattle, and in Portland, Oregon. By 1941, there were at least twenty-seven chapters, including seven overseas.[28]

Dependent on blacks in the United States for financial support, the federation also followed and endorsed efforts in behalf of civil rights as part of the general struggle toward justice for blacks. It presented speakers and held discussions on topics ranging from self-help to lynchings to discrimination in education, housing, employment, and public accommodations. Among the popular speakers at Local No. 1 were the Harlem political activist and bookstore owner Richard Moore, the attorneys Hope Stevens and Vernal Williams, the trade unionists Arthur Reid and Ashley L. Totten, the Ugandan educator and pan-Africanist Ernest Kalibala, the historian of blacks Des Graves, and the historian of ancient Africa Charles Siefert.

Branches throughout the United States called for justice in the Scottsboro case and in a number of lesser-known local infringements on the rights of blacks. Branches supported labor and NAACP causes, especially the collecting of names on antilynching petitions. Clergymen were prominent participants in all the branches.

The *VOE* carried information on branches abroad. Jamaica was a particularly fertile ground for Ethiopianism, for it was the birthplace of Marcus Garvey, who returned there after his deportation from the United States in 1927. He did not succeed in reunifying his movement, however, and he moved on to England. But a group of Jamaicans continued to profess their commitment to Garveyism. For many Garveyites, the crowning of Ras Tafari "King of Kings," or Emperor Haile Sellassie, in 1930 was a revelation. Garveyites in Jamaica recalled that in 1916, before going to the United States, Garvey had enjoined, "Look to Africa for the crowning of a Black King; he shall be the redeemer." The coronation of Haile Sellassie thus appeared to fulfill a prophecy, and it functioned to inspire the move-

---

28. *Voice of Ethiopia*, August 9, 1941. See below, p. 000.

ment, which, adopting the emperor's earlier name, Ras Tafari, called itself Rastafarian. Rastas, as the adherents were popularly known, hailed Haile Sellassie as God and as redeemer of all black people.[29] Jamaica's Ethiopianism received a good deal of impetus from the EWF's objectives, slogans, and support for the emperor. On July 23, 1939, an estimated eight hundred Jamaicans witnessed the unveiling of a charter of the federation. C. P. Jackson was president of the chapter, S. A. Reid vice-president, and A. Gordon secretary. Participants in the inaugural program included Alexander Bustamante, a labor leader, and Mrs. Morris-Knibb, a councillor. The guest speaker, whose address followed the singing of "Ethiopia Awaken," was Amy Jacques Garvey. She, along with a number of the other speakers, praised her husband's work, called for "nationhood," and pledged dedication to "Right, Justice and Independence of Ethiopians at home and abroad"—a clear reference to freedom for all African people.[30]

The branch in Tela, Spanish Honduras, received its charter on November 1, 1939. D. H. Dyer was listed as organizer, C. H. Buchner as chairman, and I. H. Fearen as secretary. After the singing of the anthem, Buchner enlarged upon how Garvey had "worked to prepare the race for nationhood." Four days later, the ceremony of unveiling a charter took place in Havana. "Ethiopia Awaken" was the anthem; the president was a man named Mullins and the vice-president Cyril O. Scott. W. E. Barnes, G. Ithfill, and L. Levey were listed as members.[31]

The international influence of the federation may be gauged by the number of mentions of it in foreign newspapers. The Saint Kitts *Union Messenger* reproduced the federation's protest against the European "sell out" of Ethiopia. In Africa, the Nigerian publisher of the *West African Pilot*, Nnamdi Azikiwe, wrote, "The people in this part of the world are all proud of your heroic efforts to educate Americans." The *VOE* acknowledged in an editorial that there had been good response from its readers and that some of its articles had been reprinted in the *Comet*, in Nigeria, the *Union Messenger*, in Saint Kitts, and *The People*, in Trinidad, as well as in the *Florida News*.[32]

It is also possible to get a sense of the scope and influence of both the

---

29. Leonard Barrett, *The Rastafarians* (Boston, 1977), 82–86.
30. *Voice of Ethiopia*, August 19, 1939.
31. Ibid., November 5, 1939, November 11, 1939, December 9, 1939.
32. Ibid., May 13, 1939, October 14, 1939, March 2, 1940.

organization and its newspaper by examining the letters to the editor in the *VOE* and the sections that acknowledged contributions. On top of the letters received from readers in the United States, there were letters from Jerusalem and Panama, Jamaica, Honduras, Venezuela, Nigeria, Egypt, Ethiopia, and Sudan. Most of the correspondents expressed satisfaction with the *VOE* and the federation. L. D. Kemp, president of the Federation of the Workers Protection Association in Belize, reported that the *VOE* and Joel A. Rogers' publications were widely read by Hondurans. From Jerusalem came an appeal for assistance for Ethiopians who had been in exile with the emperor but had remained when he moved to England. Other appeals for assistance to refugees came from Egypt, Brazil, Kenya, and Sudan.[33]

The response of overseas groups to the federation's refugee fund also provides a measure of the group's influence. During nine months of 1939, financial contributions were acknowledged from British Guiana and Cuba, and from Bocas del Toro and Gamboa, Panama; San Andrés Island, Colombia; Westmoreland, Jamaica; and Maracaibo and Logunillas, Venezuela.[34] Research into other periods will no doubt verify an even greater international influence for both the federation and the *VOE*.

As important as the pan-African appeal abroad was, the primary target remained American blacks, because of their numbers and relative affluence. One incentive to wide distribution of the paper in the United States was the Boosters Club, which honored salespersons who regularly reported sales of a hundred or more copies of the *VOE* weekly. The top salesperson in 1938 was Annie I. V. Roker, of Miami, who sold 140 copies or more for several weeks. Hubbard Corio-El and Ella Nesbitt, of New York, sold between a hundred and two hundred copies for several weeks. Pictures of Roker and Corio-El appeared in the *VOE*. It is virtually impossible to arrive at any meaningful estimate of overall circulation, however. Occasional references to sales appear in letters to the editor, but those seldom give specific numbers over any extended period of time, except for Herbert McCabe, who between March, 1937, and March, 1938, distributed 3,765 copies in the Virgin Islands.[35]

33. *Ibid.*, September 23, 1939, October 4, 1939, July 13, 1939, August 17, 1940.

34. *Ibid.*, August 5, 1939, August 26, 1939, September 9, 1939, September 30, 1939, October 28, 1939, November 18, 1939, January 27, 1940, March 16, 1940, November 23, 1940, June 1, 1940, June 29, 1940.

35. *Ibid.*, March 26, 1938, April 2, 1938, March 8, 1941.

All the federation's fund-raising activities were advertised in the *VOE*, and the names of many contributors appeared there. In addition, from time to time there was a directory of businesses participating in the stamp campaign, meant as advice on "where to spend and help." No compilation of amounts collected appeared in any of the issues examined for the present study, however. Still, the acknowledgments of contributions and the accounts of how they were spent corroborate the general idea that most contributions were to the food-and-clothing committee of the refugee fund. There was one report that seven barrels of supplies of food and clothing were sent to refugees in Aden and Djibouti.[36] Several former members of the federation recall that a number of shipments of supplies went to refugees.

The first international convention of the federation ran from July 19 to July 23, 1939, in New York City. The dates permitted the emperor's birthday, on July 22, to be part of the festivities. According to King, the president, the conference had the objective of promoting an "understanding between the leaders of our people throughout the world." He underscored the federation's aims of achieving justice for Ethiopia and its people and of obtaining better conditions for blacks worldwide. The leaders of the organization wanted to rally worldwide support for its cause, clarify its objectives and activities, ratify its constitution, elect officers, and generally define its future direction.[37]

The preliminary program listed among the conference speakers C. L. R. James, a Trinidadian author and pan-Africanist, and A. Phillip Randolph, the president of the Pullman Sleeping Car Porters, which had only recently gained recognition as a trade union, but the final program did not include either James or Randolph. Totten, secretary of the Sleeping Car Porters, replaced Randolph, but James seems not to have been represented—possibly because of the expense involved and the difficulties that the increased international tensions were causing for international travel. The other conference speakers included Bayen, Imes, Kalibala, King, Savory, and Stevens, in addition to Arthur Reid and Vernal Williams. Also speaking were Henry C. Craft, executive secretary of the YMCA; Archbishop William Ernest; Crystal Bird Fauset, a Pennsylvania state representative; Dr. Charles A. Petioni, of Harlem; Augusta Savage, an artist; Mrs. Ferrol B.

36. *Ibid.*, May 13, 1939.
37. *Ibid.*, July 1, 1939, July 8, 1939, July 15, 1939, July 22, 1939, July 29, 1939.

Smoot, a community organizer; Finley Wilson, grand exalted ruler, and Richard E. Warner, exalted ruler, of the Elks (IBPOE); and Max Yergan, of the International Committee on African Affairs.[38] The full program involved both plenary sessions and discussion groups focusing on problems relating to Ethiopia and Africans more broadly.

According to the *VOE*, the emperor's birthday ball, at the Renaissance Casino, attracted several black socialites, and on the final day of the conference, a grand parade, coordinated by Colonel Robinson, wound from the federation's auditorium, at 142nd Street and Eighth Avenue, to Saint Mark's Methodist Church, at 138th Street and Edgecombe Avenue, where there was a special service in honor of the emperor. The speakers at the service, besides Imes, King, and Wilson, were Lij Araya Abebe, Bishop James W. Brown, and Akiki Nyabongo. Afterward, a capacity audience watched a film about the Ethiopian war in the federation's auditorium, at no admission charge.[39]

Organizations that participated in the convention included the African Orthodox Church, the American League of African Descent, the Better Harlem Welfare Association, the Community Progressive "Negro" Painters, the Daughters of Israel, the Divine House of Prayer, the Harlem Labor Union, the Pyramid Institute, led by Mrs. Seth Sahara, the Royal Order of Ethiopian Hebrews, headed by Rabbi W. A. Matthews, Saint James Presbyterian Church, the military units of the UNIA, headed by Major Hines, the Universal African Union, and the Harlem branch of the YMCA.[40]

In the absence of minutes from the conference, the *VOE* must serve as its only record, but the paper gave very limited coverage. Editorially the *VOE* wrote, "There was every indication that hope in the heart of the Blacks is reviving. . . . The whole Black world is coming to see the value and necessity of the program of the Ethiopian World Federation." The editor detected unity: "The Black Commonwealth is gradually moving as a unit." Some of the delegates "crossed the ocean; others have come thousands of miles to attend this gathering." He was convinced that the delegates "felt the spirit and really sensed the purpose of this organization. . . . Locals of the Ethiopian World Federation, the Order is Forward March."[41]

38. *Ibid.*
39. *Ibid.*, July 29, 1939.
40. *Ibid.*
41. *Ibid.*

Bayen wrote in the *VOE* that the delegates "turned out in great numbers as Harlem had never seen before." Ethiopian flags were on display throughout that part of the city, and Bayen felt that the conference was "put over big." The lasting impression, even to this day among survivors, is that the conference was very well attended and had great impact. So great was the impact that Bayen announced plans to hold the next year's conference in Madison Square Garden.[42] The emperor sent his compliments, which arrived after the meeting ended: "It is gratifying to learn that people throughout the world are rising to the aid of Ethiopia and her sufferers. . . . The splendid cooperation you are giving to Dr. Bayen, our messenger of good will in the western hemisphere, . . . is greatly appreciated. . . . We have not given up hope."[43] Princess Tsahai, the emperor's daughter, cabled the women of the EWF, "On behalf of the women of Ethiopia, I wish to express our gratitude. . . . Let us persevere strong in the belief that Justice will be rendered to Ethiopia."[44]

With the emperor's public endorsement, sales of the *VOE* reportedly increased significantly. Letters to the editor increased in volume, and six months after the conference the editor introduced a section "News of the Black Commonwealth," which carried items from Africa, the Caribbean, South America, India, Europe, the United States, and Canada. The network was expanding. The high level of unity and enthusiasm that the conference generated was a significant achievement, particularly in view of the surveillance of the meeting by local and federal authorities and the infighting that had developed over fund raising.

Bayen's health was beginning to decline, however. On several occasions the *VOE* had reported that illness prevented him from fulfilling engagements. In May, 1940, he died. That was a serious loss to the federation, for he had become a symbol and a source of inspiration, as well as a perceptive and diligent leader. His memory was honored at a rally in New York, and a new Philadelphia branch took his name.[45]

Bayen's dream of having the EWF conference in Madison Square Garden in 1940 was not fulfilled. Still, attendance at the second annual conference, in July, seems to have been encouraging. The *VOE* expressed pride

42. Ibid.
43. *Voice of Ethiopia*, August 5, 1939.
44. Ibid.
45. *Voice of Ethiopia*, August 12, 1939, October 28, 1939, March 23, 1940, May 11, 1940, May 18, 1940, June 21, 1941, August 9, 1941.

over the election of Finley Wilson as president to replace King, who had gone to Miami as bishop; there was also satisfaction in Imes's acceptance of the post of first vice-president. Both the new officers had already established a national following and were known as dynamic leaders. Wilson's base among the Elks and Imes's among Methodists suggested that both would rally new members and chart new directions for the organization after the loss of its founder. Others elected in July, 1940, were Dorothy Bayen as executive secretary, Matthew Gardner as organizer, Warren Harrigan as second vice-president, Lij Araya Abebe as treasurer, and Sydney Dalrymple, Ella Mae Hopkins, and Eudora Paris as members of the executive council.[46]

When the conference ended, the *VOE* related that many delegates had traveled "several hundred miles" to participate. It judged the gathering a success. Once again a huge parade coordinated by Colonel Robinson was a highlight.[47] The federation had lost its founder but not its spirit and determination.

The federation reached a turning point when the Allies began to force the Italians from Ethiopia and the emperor returned to Sudan with plans to have Ethiopians join with British troops to bolster the Ethiopian guerrillas. The federation sounded a note of optimism and called on all its branches to reinvigorate their membership drives and raise the funds Ethiopia would need for reconstruction. The leaders saw the role of the federation as even more critical than before, since the emperor would require enormous inflows of supplies, money, and trained manpower. The *VOE* pleaded for contributions in bold print throughout the month of August.

The more aggressive pursuit of funds enabled the federation to announce the opening of supplementary offices on West 125th Street, in Harlem. The *VOE*'s quarters stayed at the old address, and the new office concentrated on fund raising for refugees. Apparently for the first time, the group took direct and concrete steps to develop an international fundraising effort in cooperation with nonmembers. The advisory board of nonmembers appointed to assist included Randolph, Shaw, and Adam Clayton Powell in New York; Dr. W. H. Jernagin and Mary E. Terrell in Washington, D.C.; Bishop King in Atlanta; E. Sylvia Pankhurst in England; Lij Andargue Massai in Aden; Michael Dei-Anang in the Gold Coast; Richard

---

46. *Ibid.*, July 27, 1940, August 3, 1940.
47. *Ibid.*, August 3, 1940.

Rathbee in South Africa; and Nyabongo in Uganda.[48] The inclusion of Shaw was of particular significance, since he remained Ethiopia's consul general. Pankhurst enhanced the cause's international standing. She had been in contact with Ethiopians and African Americans throughout the struggle. The greater inclusivity in the federation's alliances seemed to presage better effectiveness just as Ethiopian victory was at hand.

On May 25, 1941, the EWF sponsored a victory parade and a mass rally to celebrate the emperor's return to the throne. Speakers for the occasion were Shaw, Wilson, Judge Heuston, Myles Paige, and James Watson.[49] It seemed that 1941 would be a harvest year. The *VOE* estimated that some five thousand would participate at the third annual convention, in July. The paper carried more announcements than it had for the two earlier conferences. In a full-page advertisement on July 19, it announced the convention would mark the inception of a refugee fund drive for fifty thousand dollars. Similar notices continued up to the conference.

Although reports of the proceedings are scanty, there was in some respects better coverage than in previous years. A Cuban delegate attended, and the membership rolls showed ten thousand members. The branches had increased to twenty-seven, with the twenty-seventh local, in Philadelphia, the one named in honor of Bayen.[50]

Wilson was reelected president, and Lucious L. Delaney became first vice-president, Dalrymple second vice-president, Heuston treasurer, Wilfred E. Lewin executive secretary, Gardner international organizer, and the Reverend G. M. Blackett chaplain. Angeline Blocker, Rosalind Jackson, and David A. Montague were elected to the executive council. All were from Manhattan and Brooklyn except for Montague, who was from Chicago.[51]

The participating organizations included the American Society for Peace Mobilization, the Ethiopian Welfare Foundation of Brooklyn, the IBPOE, the Independent Order of Odd Fellows, the International Workers' Order, the National Negro Congress, the Royal Order of Ethiopian Hebrews, and the UNIA. In addition to speeches by federation leaders, there were addresses by Arthur Reid, Vernal Williams, and Kingsley Ozumba

---

48. *Ibid.*, April 5, 1941.
49. *Ibid.*, May 24, 1941, June 7, 1941.
50. *Ibid.*, August 9, 1941.
51. *Ibid.*

Mbadiwe, a Nigerian student.[52] There were no published reports of the amount of money raised at the convention.

But although 1941 was a banner year for Ethiopia, the federation, and all those who had labored for the defeat of the Italians and the restoration of the emperor to the throne, the favorable turn of events cast into question the raison d'être of the federation and other pro-Ethiopian groups. So much of the EWF's time, energy, and money had been absorbed by the war and its consequences, including the refugee problem, that the leadership had not laid the basis for continuing in peacetime. The ideal of racial solidarity could attract support, but in the EWF that ideal's ties had been so closely with the Italian-Ethiopian crisis that other organizations working for racial solidarity had the edge once the crisis had passed. In addition, World War II was monopolizing Europe's attention, and within a few months that of the United States. Other international matters got lost in the call for *national* solidarity against fascism. The war also provided employment for many blacks. As a result, the federation's membership declined and the organization seemed on the brink of dissolution. The sense of African identity that it had galvanized continued, however, and fueled the freedom movements in Africa and the diaspora in later years. The assumption of Ethiopian names, the development of study groups to teach African languages and cultures, and the campaign to replace the term *Negro* with *African, black,* or *Ethiopian* were precursors of the militant resurgence of the civil-rights movement in the United States in the 1960s and 1970s. Partly because the federation had profited from the work of the Ethiopian Research Council and extended the process of pan-African consciousness and cooperation, it did not die but remains active today in several communities in the Americas. The paths the council and the federation cleared also led to African-American participation in the postwar development of Ethiopia.

52. *Ibid.*

VIII

African Americans in the Reconstruction of Ethiopia

The emperor returned to Ethiopia with the help of British and Commonwealth forces, some Sudanese soldiers, and hundreds of Ethiopian exiles. Hastily organized and trained, the troops joined battle in support of the guerrilla forces that had resisted the Italians throughout the occupation. Victory came of cooperation, and for a second time in less than fifty years, Ethiopia triumphed over Italy.

Shortly after the emperor returned in February, 1941, he set out to restore his authority by appointing ministers, in spite of opposition from the British military governor, General Philip Mitchell. In January, 1942, Britain and Ethiopia signed the Anglo-Ethiopian Agreement, which recognized Ethiopian independence and provided for a division of responsibilities. Britain obtained control over financial matters, as well as consultation rights concerning the appointment of the emperor's advisers. Thus, although Ethiopia secured recognition of its independence and had responsibility for the day-to-day operation of the government, its sovereignty was limited by British supervision in military and foreign affairs. The agreement of 1942, in force for two years, was a source of considerable friction between the two countries throughout its life.

Restiveness over the pact's terms led Sellassie to seek assistance from the United States, which was reassessing its Near Eastern policy and its communications network with countries farther east. The State Department regarded Ethiopia as a potentially significant link in that expanding network of relations. The time was propitious, therefore, for both Ethiopia and the United States to explore collaborative possibilities.[1]

---

1. For an excellent account of the relationship between the national interests of Britain, the United States, and Ethiopia during this period, see Harold Marcus, *Ethiopia, Great Britain, and the United States, 1941–1974* (Berkeley and Los Angeles, 1983).

Against that background, the emperor appointed his top official in the ministry of finance, the vice-minister Yilma Deressa, chief delegate to the United Nations Conference on Food and Agriculture, at Hot Springs, Virginia, from May 18 to June 3, 1943. The emperor charged Deressa to deliver to the State Department a request for a loan, two airplanes, and some general military equipment. The emperor and his government were concerned about continuing unrest in several parts of the country, as well as about the general need to establish direct and speedy communication throughout the nation. Disarming and demobilizing guerrilla forces was difficult not only because news of the Italian defeat reached some regions slowly but also because factions who opposed the emperor saw an opportunity to act accordingly. The displacement of Ethiopians by the war was still a serious problem requiring resettlement expenditures and aggravating the unemployment crisis. Medical and social needs of all kinds waited to be addressed. Disruptions of banking, agriculture, and internal and external trade contributed to the serious shortages of food and supplies. The educational system had to be reestablished. The regular army—infantry, artillery, engineers, transport, ordnance, and supply—included only about eight thousand men; there was no air force or navy. Deressa's mission, therefore, had as much of a connection with Ethiopia's need for economic development as with its desire to reduce Britain's sway.[2]

But Deressa had another agenda too. He informed the State Department that he planned to recruit teachers and technicians on his own. The department was willing to assist him regarding his recruits' passports, visas, and travel arrangements, and he began meeting with African Americans he might engage.[3] He could do that free of the State Department, since he had quarters in Carver Hall, a dormitory at Howard University that black dignitaries often used, since they could not have obtained lodging in

---

2. 884.00/543, 544, Memorandum by Adviser on Political Relations, January 11, 1943; 884.00/545, Current Events, Ethiopia, Military Observer, East Africa, April 19, 1943; 884.001, Haile Selassie 10-1744, Report of Audience with the Emperor, October 17, 1944; 884.51/66, Berle to Pierson, August 4, 1943; 884.24/142, Cy Caldwell to secretary of state, September 29, 1943; 884.24/107, Memorandum, May 15, 1943; 884.24/129, Yilma Deressa to Cordell Hull, August 14, 1943; 884.51/66, Berle to Pierson, August 4, 1943, Berle to secretary of the treasury, August 4, 1943; Marcus, *Ethiopia, Great Britain, and the United States*, 18–21. Deressa signed a Lend-Lease agreement on August 9, 1943.

3. 884.01A/9-02943, Paul Alling to R. B. Shipley, September 9, 1943; 884.01A/46, Wallace Murray to Besosa, August 17, 1943; *Papers Relating to the Foreign Relations of the United States* (Washington, D.C., 1943), IV, 112; 884.24/142a, secretary of state to vice-minister of finance, August 12, 1943.

racially segregated Washington. Hansberry had made arrangements for several black Americans to meet Deressa at the dormitory. William M. Steen approached the Ethiopian delegate to be considered for a teaching position in Ethiopia. Steen was well recommended—as a student of Ethiopian history under Hansberry, a friend and colleague of the late Malaku Bayen, a founder of the Ethiopian Research Council, and a longtime supporter of pro-Ethiopian causes. Deressa interviewed and offered positions to other African Americans as well, including James William Cheeks, of Oxford, Ohio; Edgar D. Draper, of Baltimore; Andrew Howard Hester, of Villa Ridge, Illinois; Edward Eugene Jones, of Chicago; Joseph Muldrow, of Sumter, South Carolina; David Talbot, of British Guiana (Guyana); Thurlow Evans Tibbs, of Washington, D.C.; and Obdulio Vazquez-Delgado, of San Juan, Puerto Rico. John Robinson, who had served as a pilot for Ethiopia during the war with Italy, also received an appointment. Among those offered positions who seem not to have gone to Ethiopia were Thomas Edward Watson, Lloyd G. Wheeler, and several women: Mabel Beckles, E. M. Foley, and Dorothy I. Height.[4]

Before Deressa returned to Ethiopia, he named John W. Finger, at five hundred dollars a month, to act as a recruitment agent in the United States until an embassy could be established. Finger, a lawyer with experience in banking, finance, and real estate, had extensive contacts and wanted to establish an export-import business in Ethiopia. He continued to recruit and perform other services for Deressa and Ethiopia even after the embassy was open.[5]

By December, 1943, the African Americans began arriving in Addis Ababa. Draper, along with Hiley A. Hill and Edgar F. Love, joined the faculty at the Ras Makonnen School, in Harrar Province; Love became headmaster. Vazquez-Delgado was instructor in electricity at the Arts School in Addis Ababa. Steen was director of the English section of the Press and Propaganda Department of the Ministry of the Pen, a position a British subject had held until his contract was terminated. Steen, whose appointment began on February 19, 1944, became editor of the English-

---

4. 884.49/9, William Steen to Paul Alling, July 12, 1943, Paul Alling to William Steen, July 19, 1943; 884.01A/46, Besosa to Paul Alling, July 12, 1943, Murray to Besosa, August 17, 1943; 884.01A/9-2943, Paul Alling to Shipley, September 29, 1943; James William Cheeks, David Talbot, Thurlow Evans Tibbs, Edgar D. Draper, and William Steen, interviews with author, 1981–84.

5. 884.01A/7-544, Paul Alling to Cy Caldwell, July 22, 1944; 884.796/22, J. A. Hanley to Clark, November 22, 1943; 884.796/22, A Report by K. C. Lauter, October 13, 1943.

language weekly newspaper the *Ethiopian Herald* by virtue of his directorship and supervised the English-language radio broadcast for the government's station in Addis Ababa.[6]

The *Ethiopian Herald*, a four-page paper, had first appeared on July 3, 1943, under the editorship of Ian H. Simpson and was one of the few foreign-language newspapers in the country at the time. It published articles of local interest, items from the Reuter's news service, and stories from the foreign embassies. It was a popular source of information for the Ethiopian elite and foreign readers. Steen contributed articles about the war and the status of Ethiopia and Eritrea. He also edited the *Ethiopian Review*, an illustrated monthly that carried more specialized articles, commentaries, and scholarly pieces. Three of Hansberry's early articles, for example, appeared in the *Ethiopian Review* as installments of "Ethiopia in the Middle Ages." By April, 1944, Talbot had succeeded Steen as editor; Talbot wrote several books on Ethiopia while in that position. The English-language broadcasts for which Steen was responsible included musical programs, talks by and about dignitaries, and rebroadcasts of British Broadcasting Corporation news.[7]

On January 2, 1944, seven more African Americans sailed from New Orleans for Ethiopia. Five of them were airplane technicians with five to ten years' experience in civil aeronautics programs in the United States. The leader of the group, Robinson, was a pilot. Cheeks, Jones, and Muldrow were mechanics; Hester, a pilot, was also a specialist in parachutes and business administration. A radio technician, Vazquez-Delgado, was already in Addis Ababa. With that team in place, C. W. Lewis, of the Division of Near Eastern Affairs in the State Department, supported Ethiopia's request for two additional light aircraft under the Lend-Lease program. The United States Munitions Assignment Board had already allocated two aircraft to the country. Together, the four planes were intended to improve the country's communications and security capability.[8]

---

6. 884.01A/64, Cy Caldwell to secretary of state, December 28, 1943; 884.01A/72, Cy Caldwell to secretary of state, March 13, 1944; Draper, Steen, and Tibbs, interviews with author, 1981–84.

7. 884.01A/72, Employment of American Citizens by the Ethiopian Government, March 13, 1944; *Ethiopian Herald*, July 3, 1943, August, 1943, February 12, 1944, February 26, 1944, September, 1944, October, 1944, April, 1945. Talbot's books include *Contemporary Ethiopia* (New York, 1952) and *Haile Selassie I: Silver Jubilee* (The Hague, 1955).

8. 884.796/3-2144, John W. Finger to Claude Lewis, March 21, 1944; 884.24/177A, Memorandum; 884.24/177A, Villard to Stone, March 21, 1944; James William Cheeks,

Robinson and his team were accompanied to Ethiopia by Tibbs, who went as a schoolteacher, and by Talbot. The group sailed by freighter to Capetown and went on to Durban by train. Talbot and Tibbs both recalled racial discrimination on the train and in the stations. They continued their trip by freighter to Mombasa, Kenya, where they awaited the completion of arrangements for the final stage of travel. During their approximately three weeks in Mombasa, they again faced racial discrimination. Unable to secure desirable hotel accommodations, they stayed at a British military camp. On March 30, 1944, they left by truck from Nairobi for Addis Ababa.[9]

On April 19, they arrived in Addis Ababa exhausted and ill from a difficult trip over rugged roads and through sometimes dense woods. Their reception by Ethiopians seems to have been cordial. Cheeks later wrote that they were "introduced to the generous Ethiopian hospitality."[10]

The team quickly found that there were no operable airplanes in the country. While waiting for some to arrive from the United States, the technicians were assigned to the Orma Garage and Workshops, an industrial complex in Addis Ababa, with Robinson as the administrator. Hester served as office manager, Jones supervised the machine shop, Muldrow was in charge of engine rebuilding, and Cheeks worked as personnel and supply officer. The total work force consisted of seven to eight hundred Ethiopian, Italian, and other mechanics, drivers, technicians, and general shopworkers. The plant's job was to maintain government cars and trucks, provide office furniture for public operations, and build roads. A particular responsibility was the maintenance of the emperor's vehicles.[11]

The Brood, as the African Americans referred to themselves, organized aviation classes at the garage, but when the planes arrived, the training was transferred to the Addis Ababa airport. Throughout the program, there remained a shortage of proper training planes and equipment; there was also the frustration of students who lacked a technical background.

"The Brown Condor and the Brood," *Journal of the Ethiopian Students in North America*, III (1962), 9.

9. 884.01A/1-544, Arrival of American Pilot-Mechanics Engaged by the Ethiopian Government, July 5, 1944; 884.20/69, Enclosure No. 1, Memorandum by George F. Bogardus (Enclosure No. 2 includes the name, passport number, birthplace, and date for each member of the group); Cheeks, "The Brown Condor," 9; Steen, Talbot, Tibbs, interviews with author, 1981–84.

10. Cheeks, "The Brown Condor," 9.

11. *Ibid.*, 9–10; Cheeks, telephone interviews with author, 1981–82.

By November 2, 1944, the two airplanes Ethiopia requested under the Lend-Lease plan had arrived. Both were twin-engine Cessnas. The arrangement was for Captain Ernest Hulme and Technical Sergeant M. Oberhelman, who delivered the second plane, to spend up to thirty days instructing Ethiopian pilots and mechanics on the operation and maintenance of the aircraft, but in fact they trained the African-American pilots and mechanics, who then trained Ethiopians. Miska Babitscheff, the director of air transport, and two other Ethiopians were identified as pilots who "could probably operate" the airplanes, although they had not had any recent experience in flying. But when Babitscheff was appointed secretary to the Ethiopian embassy in Moscow, Robinson replaced him as director, thereby becoming head of the Ethiopian air force. He and the other African-American pilots and mechanics continued to work at the garage while in training on the Cessna planes.[12]

At the end of the training period, Hulme decided that only Robinson was qualified to fly the aircraft. The other African-American pilots did not qualify, he said, and did "not have United States licenses as pilots." In addition, he held that the Ethiopians who appeared for training were not "sufficiently advanced to benefit by instruction."[13] Hulme's conclusions raised questions, especially at the American embassy, about the background of the African-American technicians. Robinson's use of the title of colonel also drew scrutiny. Lieutenant Colonel Daniel S. Cotter, American commanding officer for the Eritrea Base Command, made inquiries of Robinson, who replied that he did not have an American commission, rank, or number but that a "non-official organization in the United States" had awarded him the title of colonel. Robinson also explained that Jones, Hester, Cheeks, and he had been released as instructors by the United States Army Air Force Technical Training Command for work at the request of the Ethiopian government. Muldrow had been released from a defense plant in Detroit.[14] The question of rank and qualifications does not seem to have gone beyond that.

In December, Robinson established a pilot's school to train Ethiopi-

12. 884.248/11-1444, Delivery of Aircraft to Ethiopian Government, November 14, 1944.

13. 884.248/12-1244, Training of Pilots Employed by the Ethiopian Government, December 12, 1944, with Enclosures.

14. 884.248/11-1444, Delivery of Aircraft to Ethiopian Government, November 14, 1944, p. 2, Enclosure No. 2; 884.248/11-1444, John Robinson to Daniel S. Cotter, September 12, 1944.

ans. Within a couple of years he and his team had trained over eighty cadets, several of whom became colonels in the Ethiopian air force. One of them, Abera Wolde Mariam, was among the original recruits in 1944 and became the first to complete the program, in 1949. Subsequently, Abera became a major general and as chief of the Ethiopian air force was responsible for over two hundred planes.[15]

A number of the cadets Robinson and his team trained became the first Ethiopian pilots for Ethiopian Air Lines, which Trans World Airlines managed. Among those pilots were Captains Assefa Ayele, Girma Bedane, and Alemayo Obebe.[16] But by 1947, Robinson's position at the training school had become less to his taste, although the sequence of events that led to that is not clear. The emperor had purchased several planes from Sweden and later appointed a Swede, Carl Gustaf von Rosen, to direct the training of pilots. Robinson was retained as an instructor, but the new order of authority was especially embarrassing for him, since he and Rosen had been famous rivals during the Italo-Ethiopian war, when they both flew for the emperor. The pretext that Swedish planes required a Swedish director did not placate Robinson. When the strained relations between the two men exploded in a physical fight that sent Rosen to the hospital and Robinson to court, the testimony revealed that Robinson had been in a number of similar conflicts, and he was dismissed from the school.[17]

Nevertheless, Robinson remained the most popular African American, if not American, in Ethiopia. He had the reputation of being the spokesman for African Americans in the country, which was reinforced when he announced that thirty additional technicians would arrive. Rumor also linked him to a supposed plan to bring in some twenty black American women with experience in aircraft factory work. The rumors around him no doubt provided the context for an American intelligence report that the British in Addis Ababa were worried by increases in the arrival of African Americans.[18]

15. General Abera Wolde Mariam, Captain Adamo, interview with author, Addis Ababa, March 19, 1983. General Abera had only recently been released from prison, where he had been confined for ten years because of his role in Haile Sellassie's administration.

16. *Ibid.*; James William Cheeks, unpublished manuscript.

17. General Abera Wolde Mariam, Captain Adamo, interviews with author, Addis Ababa, March 19–20, 1983.

18. 884.01A/1-544, Memorandum of Conversation with Colonel Francis T. Colby, June 15, 1944; 884.4061/6-2844, Claude Lewis to Cy Caldwell, June 28, 1944; 884.4061/

Caldwell later wrote that the British in Ethiopia were "not particularly disturbed by the arrival of the American Negroes," but the crux is in the modifier "not particularly." The British maintained a rigid color bar in eastern and southern Africa, where many of the British residents in Ethiopia had earlier lived, becoming accustomed to racial preference. African Americans in Ethiopia had on occasion betrayed their resentment of the British in their actions. In one case, Muldrow struck an American, K. C. Lauter, who he thought was British. Robinson later ascribed the problem partly to the treatment his team had experienced in South Africa and Kenya.[19]

But the friction between Ethiopian officials and British authorities also rubbed off on the African Americans. Since neither the emperor nor the Ethiopians regarded their country as occupied enemy territory, they resented the authority the British had assumed after the Italians withdrew. Relations between the two powers deteriorated further when the British military left with many of the supplies and much of the equipment the Italians had abandoned. Moreover, the 1942 agreement between Great Britain and Ethiopia stipulated that British advisers were to hold key positions in all ministries of the government. The close British supervision over Ethiopia, especially in external relations such as trade and foreign assistance, added to the complications Ethiopia had with the United States. The State Department expressed its embarrassment to the Ethiopian minister in Washington, Blatta Ephrem T. Medhem, that Ethiopia had not informed the British in advance concerning the group of African Americans about to begin working for the government. But the minister argued that consultation was necessary only for advisers, not teachers and airplane technicians. The department reiterated, however, that it felt a "considerable amount of embarrassment" and suggested that the minister consult with his government about the matter.[20]

Within a context that included Ethiopian resentment regarding the

---

6-2844, Office of Strategic Services Situation Report, June 17, 1944; Mignon Ford, Talbot, interviews with author, Addis Ababa, March 20, 1983.

19. 884.4016/7-1744, Cy Caldwell to Claude Lewis, July 17, 1944; 884.01A/1-544, Arrival of American Pilot-Mechanics Engaged by the Ethiopian Government, July 5, 1944.

20. *Papers Relating to the Foreign Relations of the United States* (Washington, D.C., 1943), IV, 89, 90, 97, 104; 884.00/543, Memorandum by Wallace Murray, January 11, 1943; 884.01A/68, Embarrassment Caused American and British Officials in Ethiopia, February 16, 1944.

policy and actions of Britain, British and American sensitivity over the lack of consultation about the arrival of African-American technicians, and the tradition of the British color bar, the concern the British in Ethiopia may have had about the possibility of a significant influx of black Americans taking positions formerly held by them was understandable. The African-American technicians found themselves in the unenviable position of being at the center of international tensions for the easing of which they might seem expendable.

The tensions, however, subsided without significant consequences. Most of the African-American technicians returned to the United States at the expiration of their contracts, in 1946. Robinson and Talbot remained. Robinson served off and on as an adviser to the Ministry of War until his accidental death in a plane crash in 1954. He is buried in Addis Ababa. Talbot continued his work with government publications and broadcasting in addition to supervising the American Institute, the elementary and secondary school he and Robinson had founded in Addis Ababa in 1946. With the overthrow of the emperor in 1974, Talbot had to retire, and the American Institute was nationalized. Talbot died in 1988, and he too is buried in Addis Ababa.[21]

Although the African-American technicians confronted problems of adjustment similar to those the settlers of the 1930s had known, there were also important differences. Because the new group came as trained technicians, they were sojourners and not primarily permanent settlers. In addition, they benefited from the established network among Ethiopians and African Americans that had developed during the 1920s and 1930s as a result of the Ethiopian missions to the United States, the settlers of the 1930s, a couple of whom had remained during the war, the Ethiopian Research Council, the Ethiopian World Federation, and the host of other groups supportive of the war against Italy. Most significant, the technicians were plainly contributing to the development of the country.

Still, some Ethiopians regarded the black Americans as too "European in habits and outlook," while others probably envied their educational and economic status. The African Americans sometimes reacted to Ethiopians with impatience and condescension. Both sides were behaving normally, in tune with their different cultural backgrounds. Azaj Workneh Martin and

21. General Abera Wolde Mariam, Captain Adamo, Talbot, Ford, interviews with author, Addis Ababa, March, 1983.

his family, however, became friendly hosts and helped smooth relations between the groups. Tibbs recalled that after his father's death, he felt like an "adopted son of the Martins'." Cheeks and Steen had similar recollections about the Martins and about friendship with other Ethiopians. Talbot remembered that on at least one occasion Robinson led a group of blacks to discuss relations between Ethiopians and African Americans with the emperor, who was sympathetic and understanding and sought to ease the rigors of adjustment. Mignon Innis Ford, the early settler who did not leave Ethiopia during the war and still resides there, has commented that she raised her family among Ethiopians as Ethiopians. Her two sons were educated there and grew up speaking Amharic. Both sons, Abiya and Yosef, recall growing up with an identity as Ethiopians; today they are at home among African Americans and Ethiopians in the United States.[22]

Although Mignon Ford's husband, Arnold Josiah Ford, died in 1935 and most of the other African-American settlers returned to the United States on the eve of the Italo-Ethiopian War, she and Albertha Thomas remained in the country. In December, 1941, the two of them founded the Beit Ouriel School, for Ethiopian boys and girls; in 1943, the name was changed to Princess Zennebe Worq School. That, the first coeducational school in the country, began with ten students, including Ford's two sons, but by 1943 the enrollment had reached eighty, twenty-five of whom were boarders. By 1945, the physical facilities could not accommodate the number of students applying for admission. It was then that Her Majesty the late Empress Menen donated the larger premises in Addis Ababa where the school stands today.[23] By 1966, the school had extended training from the elementary level through the secondary. It had an enrollment of 580, of whom 120 were boarders. The number of teachers had climbed from two to sixteen. Throughout the school's history as a private institution, about 40 percent of the students were orphans who attended free of charge; the others either paid or received government scholarships. The school also generated income through the staging of plays, the sale of student crafts, and the solicitation of donations. The government of Mengistu Mariam nationalized the school in 1975, ending after thirty-four years its service

22. Steen, Talbot, Tibbs, Ford, and Ford's sons, Abiya (Abraham) and Yosef, interviews with author in Washington, D.C., and Addis Ababa, 1983–84.
23. Princess Zennebe Worq School Silver Jubilee Program (N.p., n.d.), 1–12; Ford, Talbot, interviews with author, Addis Ababa, March 29, 1983.

under private auspices. During the time of private operation it educated a number of Ethiopians who went on to achieve distinction in government and private service.[24]

Ford, frustrated by her seemingly unsuccessful struggle to retain her property under the new regime, returned to the United States in 1984, intending to remain. But Ethiopia had become home for her and the place of many of her friends. She is again in Ethiopia, where she is the sole living link to the African-American settlers of the 1930s. Talbot, who died in Addis Ababa in 1988, was the last of the African-American technicians in the country. Ford, Talbot, and those who accompanied them to Ethiopia helped develop that country, reinforced an identity between Ethiopians and African Americans, and demonstrated the relevance of black skills for African development.

The relationship of African Americans with Ethiopia continued with the establishment of the repatriated settlement at Shashimana by members of the Ethiopian World Federation in the late 1940s, the enrollment of larger numbers of Ethiopian students in African-American colleges and universities, and more recently, the interaction in the United States between African Americans and refugee Ethiopians who have joined the diaspora.

24. Ford, interview with author, Addis Ababa, March 29, 1983; interviews over a number of years with other Ethiopians inside and outside Ethiopia.

CONCLUSION

The historical appeal of Ethiopia, both classical and modern, sharpened as Ethiopians and African Americans encountered each other in the twentieth century. The initial stage of their encounter occurred between 1897 and 1930, when several African Americans visited Ethiopia for commercial and political purposes; at least two of them became permanent settlers there. The official visits of Ethiopian delegations to the United States in 1919, 1927, and the 1930s afforded an opportunity for a number of group meetings and solidified earlier contacts. The period from 1930 to 1944 saw the emigration of several African Americans, primarily from Barbados and the United States, to Ethiopia as permanent settlers and the sojourn of several advisers and technicians. The ensuing encounters between Ethiopians and African Americans tested the extent of their shared identity and afforded opportunities for collaboration in their mutual interest.

If Ethiopians had been or had regarded themselves as Caucasians, as prevailing European and American views held, the foundation of Ethiopianism would have been shattered and descendant Africans would no longer have been able to point with pride to Ethiopia as an ancient and great African civilization that maintained its independence during the partition of Africa, defeated the Italians in 1896, joined the League of Nations in 1923, and was a model fit for inspiring freedom movements throughout the world of African peoples. Although Liberia was black and had been independent since 1847, it, by being the much later creation of black and white Americans, was not indigenous. Ethiopia was the anchor to which continental and diaspora Africans pinned much of their pan-African aspiration. It was essential, therefore, especially for African Americans, to affirm a shared identity between Ethiopians and other Africans.

Ironically, affirmation of a common identity came from an undesired quarter when, in 1919, a New York restaurant refused to serve an official Ethiopian delegation because it was black. As disheartening as it was for black Americans to acknowledge their powerlessness in that situation, the incident underscored the common social bind of all African people, at least in the United States. Additional assurances about the pan-African awareness of Ethiopians came from the statements and actions of Haile Sellassie, Malaku Bayen, Ato Kantiba Gabrou, Azaj Workneh Martin, Tecle-Hawariate, and Lij Tasfaye Zaphiro and from the official government invitations for black immigration to Ethiopia. The evidence is that Ethiopians not only identified with African Americans but wanted them to join in the development of their country.

But questions persisted through the Italo-Ethiopian War. White observers were quick to deny any connection between Ethiopians and diaspora Africans. Some based their views on the writings of C. G. Seligman, the English anthropologist who ascribed the ancient Nile Valley civilizations, which included Ethiopia, to the Hamites, whom he defined as belonging to the same "branch of mankind as whites." With a stroke of the pen, Ethiopians became white, and blacks were removed from any meaningful role in history.

Carleton Coon, a popular American anthropologist, visited Ethiopia in 1935 and wrote that African Americans should remember "that the Ethiopians do not consider themselves to be Negroes." Coon was no doubt unaware that many African Americans also rejected the Negro label at the same time that they accepted identification with continental and diaspora Africans. But statements like those by Seligman and Coon created and reinforced ambivalence and encouraged distortions about the identity of African descendants abroad. Even State Department officials, whose official capacity it was to represent all citizens and project a positive national image, demonstrated their low regard for black Americans by referring to them in derogatory terms and promoting the view that Ethiopians did not identify with them.

That background made the Italo-Ethiopian War a particular landmark in the history of African people by virtue of the way the war pitted an aggressive European imperial power against a much weaker, unoffending African country. It came to stand for the overall unequal struggle between Africa and Europe, between blacks and whites, thereby consolidating feelings of African identity. Just as Africans in the Gold Coast, Nigeria, Sierra

Leone, and elsewhere on the continent perceived the Ethiopian struggle as part of their own liberation, African descendants in the Americas viewed it as an opportunity for a collaborative effort for racial dignity and freedom.

Although Africans and black Americans had for many years articulated their common identity, the Italo-Ethiopian War occasioned the first concurrence of the protestations of identity with a major concrete issue around which to rally, a large and internationally receptive constituency, and the means to act. That was behind the proliferation in the United States, Jamaica, Trinidad, Panama, Barbados, and other areas of the Caribbean of protest movements and demonstrations against Italy, behind the recruitment, volunteer, and fund-raising efforts in support of Ethiopia, behind the bold initiatives in private diplomacy, behind the building of an international network, and behind the involvement of diaspora Africans in the reconstruction of postwar Ethiopia.

The Ethiopian Research Council was the impetus for a movement that succeeded in harnessing the resulting sentiments and energies and culminated in the establishment of the Ethiopian World Federation by Malaku Bayen in New York in 1937. Much of the appeal of the federation stemmed from Bayen's Ethiopian nationality, his experience of having worked with and been taught by black Americans, and his marriage to a black American; he had conspicuous attachments with black America. His appointment as Haile Sellassie's envoy in the United States during the Italian occupation of Ethiopia could only enhance his appeal.

In addition to raising funds and collecting supplies for the war, the federation and its *Voice of Ethiopia* greatly expanded the pan-African constituency and significantly deepened the black consciousness of diaspora Africans in the Americas. The evidence for this is in the adoption of African, especially Ethiopian, names by black Americans, the introduction of courses on African history and languages by social and church groups, and the avid reading of news and publications about Africa. The federation and the *VOE* skillfully related African issues to American civil rights. The Ethiopian Research Council and the EWF attracted intellectuals as well as rank-and-file blacks in a movement that heightened pride in the African heritage and encouraged hope for the future.

Those remarkable developments were not limited to the United States but included the blacks of several Caribbean countries. Aided by the earlier works of W. E. B. Du Bois and Marcus Garvey in particular, in spite of their suppression, blacks in the United States forged links with groups from Cuba, Jamaica, Panama, and Trinidad to South America and England. Blacks at all economic levels manifested a deep consciousness of Africa and vigorously supported the Ethiopian cause. Never before had they so seriously considered fighting in Africa, nor had they ever before undertaken so dramatic an adventure in private diplomacy as they did during the Italo-Ethiopian War. The delegation to the emperor represented a signal effort that achieved the short-term goal of securing a representative who answered the criteria African Americans set, and the long-range consequences of the venture illustrated the potential for black American influence in private and public diplomacy.

At the same time it is evident that, notwithstanding Hansberry's and Steen's statements to the contrary, expansion of the constituency for the Ethiopian cause received too little attention. Particularly lamentable was the failure to press for Bayen's official accreditation as envoy. Although the United States government was not likely to give public endorsement to the pro-Ethiopian effort, it conceivably might have been maneuvered into sanctioning the cause by engaging in discussions with Bayen and others as representatives of a government the country still recognized. After all, Italy continued to maintain its embassy in Washington and had direct contacts with the government and with supporters of Italy in the United States up to the break of diplomatic relations on the eve of World War II. Although the council and the federation involved Africans and their descendants from several regions of the Western diaspora, they failed to cultivate and sustain across national borders a cadre of effective leaders who could establish a mechanism to assure consistent concentration on a broad range of issues of high priority. Historically, single-issue black and white organizations, especially internationally oriented ones, have lost their vitality soon after achieving their short-term objectives. There were two junctures at which stronger and more effective leadership might have made a difference: at the launching of the federation and after Bayen's death. As commendable as Bayen's decision was not to head the federation so that an African American could, the leadership he was capable of offering in 1937, when the organization was founded, might have brought greater unity to the movement, especially between the branches in Washington and New York. Moreover, Bayen had contacts that he never really tapped: State Department officials, businessmen, and academics he knew from his student days. They could have provided access not only to greater funding but to political decision makers as well.

Conclusion

The African-American tradition of reliance on the clergy for political leadership led to the selection of the Reverend William Imes and Bishop Lorenzo H. King for influential positions. Both men commanded respect and brought support from their congregations, but their energies were too widely diffused among organizations and issues for them to give the federation their best. Their preoccupations extended to such causes as antilynching, voting rights, employment opportunities, and assistance to victims of the depression generally, and they had to allocate limited church resources to competing needs. In addition, religious leaders and their congregations usually avoided affiliation with organizations having visible connections to Garveyites and Communists. Although Garveyites exerted considerable influence in the federation, neither it nor the Ethiopian Research Council was an organization with hard-line commitments to Garvey. Still, for many African Americans the strong emphasis on black identity and initiative, and the high profile of Garveyites, were a deterrent: a preferable future seemed to many blacks to lie in a less assertive blackness.

Communists were much less of a factor in the federation and the movement, even if some of them were extremely vocal and visible at rallies. Their impact was too slight to warrant the anxiety the United States government and the press aroused by publicizing a supposed Communist infiltration of black groups. Federation leaders, like other African-American leaders, were aware of Communist inroads into their organizations, but they also knew that racism existed in the party and were alienated when the American Communist party did not denounce the Soviet Union's sale of oil and war-related supplies to Mussolini. Blacks were prepared to protect the integrity of their organization. But when party members tried to win black support through a visible participation in pro-Ethiopian demonstrations, many church followers and others turned away.

That clerics like Imes and King identified with the federation and made their churches available for some of the rallies is impressive, but they were less successful in aligning the wider religious community with the movement. Even so, black churches and their members contributed to many fund-raising and public-relations efforts in behalf of Ethiopia.

The pro-Ethiopian movement was virtually limited to the English-speaking diaspora. In spite of the diligence of some others, the greatest response came from Barbadians, Jamaicans, Trinidadians, English-speaking Panamanians and Hondurans, and blacks in England and the United States. The reasons are clear. First, the most successful imperial power during the slave trade and colonial eras was England, which acquired what became the most populous regions in Africa and the Americas, thereby assuring the predominance of the English language. And within that community of English speakers, the blacks of the United States have played the major pan-African role.

Although blacks in the United States experienced the most blatant racial discrimination and oppression, underpinned as it was by legislation and court decisions that ensured the development of a rigid system of segregation, the same system allowed for the evolution of autonomous black socioeconomic and political institutions that provided both a national and an international perspective on, and a means to confront, racism and colonialism. African Americans in the United States, therefore, became the most openly and threateningly race-conscious community in the black world. A deep sense of black consciousness and the existence of separate and autonomous institutions, a sizable informed and articulate class, aggressive efforts to include blacks from Africa and the diaspora, and a significant degree of mobility and freedom to organize at home and abroad, as well as the emergence of the United States to economic and political dominance in international affairs—all these conditions contributed to making American blacks the critical players not only in the pro-Ethiopian campaign but also in the development of black world networks with divers aims.

Many blacks contributed to both black and white groups that sent supplies and money to Ethiopia, and there is no way to determine the total amount. Still, the financial assistance to Ethiopia from all sources fell far short of what the leaders had expected. But for the most part, blacks could not afford more. They certainly lacked the economic and political clout to affect major decisions in the way the Italian Americans could. The world depression sapped their power, too. Blacks by themselves simply could not mobilize the enormous financial and material resources required to accomplish the high goals they had set, and white Americans were unwilling to do so.

The laws of the United States forbade citizens from participating in foreign wars against friends of the United States, but those laws were far more rigidly enforced in the case of Ethiopia than in the case of Spain. Moreover, derogatory references to African Americans as "darkies" and unfavorable comparisons of them with Ethiopians not only showed the personal insensitivity of American officials but also betrayed a government role in attempts at preventing meaningful links with Africans. There were also special efforts to discourage black Americans from visiting Ethiopia even when laws and policies did not require dissuasion. In the end, the persistence of African Americans and the receptivity of Ethiopians prevailed and led to effective cooperation in the postwar reconstruction of Ethiopia.

Of greater consequence for African Americans, Ethiopians, and other Africans in the pro-Ethiopian era were the affirmation of a shared identity, the resolution to collaborate, and the development of an international constituency spanning the United States, the Caribbean, Europe, and Africa that together filled the vacuum resulting from the lull in pan-African initiatives between the 1920s and 1945. Out of that seedbed emerged leaders for the black nationalist and pan-African movements. The developments of the 1930s and 1940s have a place as important forerunners of the resurgence of the nationalist and pan-Africanist pursuit of independence in Africa and the Caribbean during the 1950s and afterward. In the United States, especially, the movement deepened the sense of African identity, quickened the pace of the civil-rights movement, and demonstrated the potential for African-American influence on, and participation in, international affairs.

APPENDIX A

Ethiopian World Federation Locals
A Partial List

New York City, Local No. 1, Haile Selassie Local

Liz Araya Abebe, treasurer
Ivy Arno
Augustine Bastian
Dorothy Bayen
Malaku Bayen
Mr. Biggins
G. M. Blackett
Mrs. Blackstone
A. Blocher
G. Balfour Bovell
Robert Brown
Eddie Mae Cochran
Alva Doyle
O. A. Edet, secretary
Elaine Gale
Victor C. Gasper
Oliver Green, vice-president
Warren Harrigan
J. Hibbert
Wilfred Hibbert
Merrill James
Rosalind Jackson, treasurer
Lorenzo H. King
Hattie Edwards Koffie
Wilfred Lewin, vice-president
Mr. McBain
Herbert McCabe
Morris Mattavous
Ella Nesbitt
Eudora Paris, vice-president
Lewis Paul, vice-president
Gloria Plummer
Lloyd Plummer
Robert Pratt
Arthur Reid
John Robinson (also a member of the Chicago local)
Nathan Russell, secretary
Clara Selman, secretary
John Simons
Lelia Strachn, secretary, juvenile group
Doris Thompson, president, juvenile group
Charles Watts
Louise Williams
Vernal Williams, president
John Zebulum

APPENDIX A

North Philadelphia, Local No. 2

Mr. Brunso
Mamie Butler
L. Donner
Evelyn Emanuel
Bessie Harkness
Fannie Harris
Helen Jacobs
Harvey Johnson
Philip Johnson
Sarah Johnson
Emmett Jones, president
E. D. Kennedy, president

Frank Knight, president
Caesar Moore, president
Mr. Porter
C. Racketts
Jerry R. Ruffin
Mr. Simpson
William Sprowal
Mrs. Surtanna
George Thompson
Charles Williams, vice-president
Rodie Wydeman

Chicago

Melobin Banfield
Harry Broome, president
Pearle Broome
Rev. Samuel Brown
Henry Emery, treasurer
Harvey Fagin
James A. Garfield
Rev. J. Jones
Will Kirkman, vice-president
M. B. Lamb
Frank Lynch, vice-president

D. A. Montague
S. J. K. Morris
John Robinson (also a member of
    Local No. 1, New York City)
Lidia Simon, secretary
Rev. Wesley Spearman, vice-
    president
Rev. Peter Vaughn, vice-president
William Walker
W. Woodrad
Modecia Woodward

Brooklyn

Sidney H. Dalrymple, president
Mr. Dorn, vice-president
Edna Guy
Dr. Matilda Johnson, vice-
    president

Canon Miller
Alice Storey, secretary

Baltimore

Theodore Allen
John Brown
Rosa Bryant
Maggie Crometee, vice-president
Olive DeLyons, president
John Holliday, president
Alethia Jackson
Walter Jackson
William Jackson
William Mason
Mamie Moore
Cler Pyles
Anna Ragler
Pearl Smith
Mrs. S. R. Smith, president
Leon Tibbs
Fred Walters, vice-president
Charles Williams
Gertrude Williams
James Wright

Buffalo

Mrs. John Battle
Robert Browne
Matthew Gardner
Mrs. Harris
George Harris
Virginia Pye
Mrs. Swindle
Mrs. Thomas
M. York

Detroit

Henry W. Tigget, president

Evanston, Illinois

Mr. H. H. Hogan

Gary, Indiana

C. A. Carter, vice-president
M. M. Cook, secretary
Rev. M. L. Johnson, vice-president
John Mayer
W. M. Sneed, president
George B. Williams

APPENDIX A

Kansas City, Missouri

Robert L. Johnson, president

Nashville

H. W. Newell

Okmulgee, Oklahoma

Rev. F. R. Baker   Joe Nettles
Mr. Lattimer, president   Rev. J. S. Sykes

St. Louis

Joseph Junepher, vice-president

Tulsa

Julius C. Hill, secretary
Miss Algereta Jackson
Mr. N. C. Lewis, president

Wichita, Kansas

J. S. Thompson, president
Rev. G. B. Winston

Bocas del Toro, Panama

Oscar Clachar   J. S. Rankine, organizer
Daniel Garvey   Nathaniel Small
Zack Grant   Uriah H. Walker
Sam Machone, president

Ethiopian World Federation Locals

British Guiana

Robert H. Schwartz

Colon, Canal Zone

F. M. Bright

Cristobal, Canal Zone

I. Blackett
L. Blackett
Stedfast N. Bright

Miss A. Brown
Mr. Deniston
Mr. S. Paddy

Dominican Republic

Anthony Bastian

Gatum, Canal Zone

John Rennie

Havana

W. E. Barnes
W. S. Gillard
Miss G. Ithfill
L. Levey

A. Mullins
C. Mullins, president
Cyril O. Scott

Kingston, Jamaica

S. Garrick
A. Gordon, secretary

C. P. Jackson, president
S. A. Reid, vice-president

APPENDIX A

Maracaibo and Logunillas, Venezuela

Alfred B. Murray, president

Westmoreland, Jamaica

Louis A. Atkins

These lists are compiled from various issues of the *Voice of Ethiopia*. No years were indicated for terms of office.

APPENDIX B

Aviation Cadets Trained by John Robinson's Team

1. Abraha Kelet
2. Assefa Gebresilase
3. Taye Tarea
4. Gelan Urgessa
5. Guetacheou Tarekegne
6. Chanalew Belai
7. Mengheshia Yilma
8. Getachew Tarekenny
9. Ambaye Alemayehu
10. Mamo Admassu
11. Asefa Ayele
12. Elias Abate
13. Teferi Woldeamak
14. Berrhe Jakob
15. Asefa Teklezion
16. Amanuel Tesfamikel
17. Membere Woldetensaye
18. Mengesha Seyfe
19. Makonin Wondim
20. Okbit Debessay
21. Bataye Debassay
22. Ameha Zionkifle
23. Chefeke Teketay
24. Merkorios Haile
25. Gizaw Gedle Giorgis
26. Yohanis Haile
27. Yeheyis Gabre Selasse
28. Ehdego Andegiorgis
29. Gugsa Habtemekael
30. Mulageta Ababe
31. Menasse Belachou
32. Zerefu Zerudu
33. Larkow Markas
34. Zedeke Begashet
35. Agzau Gebrehanna
36. Tedla Desta
37. Kelilachew Tekle
38. Hawariat Taye
39. Metcha Getachew
40. Kenfere Zegeye
41. Worku Abraha
42. Abera Tadesse
43. Aleme Bekele
44. Efrem Asafaw
45. Wolde Mikael
46. Girma Bedane
47. Negashe Woldemikael
48. Alem Ayehu Abebe
49. Tesfaye Mankere
50. Lt. Tesfaye Tamarat
51. Fikeru Samuel
52. Dachew Admasu

APPENDIX B

53. Kassa Feleke
54. Fresenbet Amede
55. Yeshetala Tasse
56. Shemelis Tekle
57. Bekele Makuria
58. Chanyalew Belay
59. Beyene Shonne
60. Yohanis Bekele
61. Tasse Zewge
62. Tesome Yeshe
63. Seyum Melesa
64. Gadasa Guma
65. Sagay Saifu
66. Bekele Efrem
67. Ayell Agnaffr
68. Ashenafi Seshu
69. Mekael Sahlemariam
70. Ketema Tessema
71. Deressa Mamede
72. Melion Hailemariam
73. Zewge Selew
74. Abera Wolde Mariam
75. Asfaw Boru
76. Geressu Degagu
77. Dawit Gedle
78. Chefeke Teketay
79. Moge Aldi
80. Asafa Woldemikael
81. Makonen Hialoua
82. Assafa Temtim
83. Habtemikel Wolde Kidan

This list has been provided by James William Cheeks. The order of names is that of his roster.

BIBLIOGRAPHICAL NOTE

Recommended books on the general history of Ethiopia include *Ethiopia: A Comprehensive Bibliography*, by Paulos Mikias (Boston, 1989); *A History of Modern Ethiopia, 1857–1974*, by Bahru Zewde (Athens, Ohio, and Addis Ababa, 1991); *Ethiopia and the Red Sea: The Rise and Decline of the Solomonic Dynasty and Muslim-European Rivalry in the Region*, by Mordecai Abir (London, 1980); *Ethiopia: Power and Protest—Peasant Revolts in the Twentieth Century*, by Gebru Tareke (New York, 1991); and *The Ethiopian Royal Chronicles*, by Richard Pankhurst (Addis Ababa and London, 1967). William Leo Hansberry's contribution is included in Joseph E. Harris' *Pillars in Ethiopian History: The William Leo Hansberry African History Notebook* (Washington, D.C., 1974). *Ethiopia at Bay: A Personal Account of the Haile Sellassie Years*, by John H. Spencer (Algonac, Mich., 1984), is a good biographical study with segments pertaining to the Italo-Ethiopian War. *Haile Sellassie I: The Formative Years, 1892–1936*, by Harold Marcus (Berkeley and Los Angeles, 1987), is a probing biography that sets the stage for understanding the era of the Italo-Ethiopian War; Marcus' *Ethiopia, Great Britain, and the United States, 1941–1974* (Berkeley and Los Angeles, 1983) is a penetrating analysis of national interests and their relevance to Ethiopia from the postwar period to the fall of Sellassie.

The best single volume on the intellectual currents of Ethiopianism is Mutero Chirenje's *Ethiopianism and Afro-Americans in Southern Africa, 1883–1916* (Baton Rouge, 1987). St. Clair Drake's two volumes *Black Folk Here and There* (Los Angeles, 1986–90) relate Ethiopianism to aspects of the history of African peoples around the world since antiquity. The literature on the Italo-Ethiopian War itself is much more limited. Standard books include *The Ethiopian War, 1935–1941*, by Angelo del Boca, and translated by P. D. Cummins (Chicago, 1969); *The War in Abyssinia*, by Pietro Badoglio (London, 1937); *The Coming of the Italian-Ethiopian War*, by George W. Baer (Cambridge, Mass., 1967); *The United States and the Italo-Ethiopian Crisis*, by Brice Harris (Stanford, Calif., 1964); *The Abyssinian Crisis*, by F. Hardie (London, 1974); and *Ethiopia Under Mussolini: Fascism and the Colonial Experience*, by Alberto Sbacchi (London, 1985). For reactions of continental Africans to the war, see S. K. B. Asante's *The Pan-African Protest: West Africa and the Italo-Ethiopian Crisis, 1934–1941* (London, 1977). Accounts of the African diaspora's reactions to the war are largely limited to a few articles, master's theses, and doctoral dissertations, primarily by William Randolph Scott, Stanley Ross, and Brian L. Friday, all of whom are cited in the text. Scott's book relating to the subject is scheduled for publication too late for me to have consulted it. William A. Schack gives a valuable overview of black Americans who were in Ethiopia early, in "Ethiopia and Afro-Americans: Some Historical Notes, 1920–1970," *Phylon*, XXXV (1974).

The Black Eagle: Colonel Hubert Julian, as Told to John Bulloch (London, 1964) and *The Black Eagle*, by John Peer Nugent (New York, 1971), provide a sense, although exaggerated, of the activities of the most colorful African American to involve himself with Ethiopia. David Talbot's books *Contemporary Ethiopia* (New York, 1952) and *Haile Selassie I: Silver Jubilee* (The Hague, 1955) are useful indices of the perspective of an African American who migrated to Ethiopia, remained there, and became an adviser to the emperor and his government. Malaku Bayen's *The March of Black Men* (New York, 1939) presents an Ethiopian's outlook upon his country, its relationship to the diaspora, and pan-African activities in the United States.

The *Voice of Ethiopia*, the journal published by the Ethiopian World Federation, is held in bound volumes in the Library of Congress. Readily available, it is perhaps the most valuable surviving source for the events the present volume addresses.

INDEX

Abbot, Robert Sengstacke, 117
Abebe, Lij Araya, 137, 139
Aberra, Kidane Mariam, 32
Abyssinian Baptist Church, 64, 80
Addams, Jane, 52
Advocate, 35–36
African, as term, 141
African Americans: and emigration to Ethiopia, 2–3, 5–7, 11–18, 150, 153; and identification with Ethiopians, 4–5, 7, 11, 153–54; press of, 4–5, 7, 117; racial classification of, 5; as technicians, 9, 31, 33, 56–57, 145, 147, 150; and black unity, 12, 39, 51, 131, 134, 155, 158; and Ethiopian Research Council, 28; and enlistment for Italo-Ethiopian War, 38–39, 41–42, 54; and letters to President Roosevelt, 41–42; *black* as term for, 44; and Spanish Civil War, 60–61; and international affairs, 64–65, 120; connection of, with Ethiopia, 65, 78, 79, 82–83, 107–108, 119, 120; and John H. Shaw, 77–84, 106–108; and Italian Americans, 97–98; and postwar Ethiopia, 141, 143–44; and Great Britain, 148–50; relationships of, with Ethiopians, 150–52; and pan-Africanism, 155–56; and leadership, 157. *See also* Fund raising; Racial discrimination
African diaspora, 1, 44, 130, 153–55, 157–58
African Legion, 49
African Orthodox Church, 137
African Patriotic League, 48
African peoples, 1, 19, 131, 141, 154–55
Afro-American, 46, 117
Afro-American Producers' and Consumers' League, 48
Afro–West Indian League, 37
Airplanes, 145–47. *See also* Aviation training program
Albert, Samuel, 39
Alexander, Daniel Robert, 2, 16, 128
All Harlem Independent Political Action, 121
All Peoples party, 121, 122
Alling, Paul, 101, 113
American Aid for Ethiopia: and fund raising, 71, 74, 75, 78, 80; racial mix in, 73; and African Americans, 81, 84; and New York World's Fair, 82
American Civil Rights Association, 48

INDEX

American Committee on the Ethiopian Crisis, 77
American Conference of Rabbis, 70
American Friends of Ethiopia, 93
American Institute, 150
American Jewish League, 12
American League Against War and Fascism, 64
American League for Italy, 93, 95–96
American League of African Descent, 137
American Pro-Falasha Committee, 66
American Red Cross: and African Americans in Ethiopia, 18; and use of Red Cross flag, 67–68; and fund raising, 71, 74, 75, 76, 78
American Society for Peace Mobilization, 140
Amsterdam News, 105, 121
Andrews, Orhardo, 41
Anglo-Ethiopian Agreement, 142
ANP, 56, 57, 79
Arms and ammunition, 64, 69–70, 73, 106–107, 114–15
Ashe, C. Malcolm, 47
Associated Negro Publishers (ANP), 56, 57, 79
Association for Ethiopia's Independence, 43
Auberson, Jacques, 31
Aurienoth Club, 11
Aviation training program, 54–55, 147–48, 167–68
Ayele, Assefa, 148
Azikiwe, Nnamdi, 35, 132, 134

Babitscheff, Miska, 147
Bagre, Ayela, 33
Bantu College of African Languages, 128–29
Barnes, W. E., 134

Barnett, Claude, 23, 56, 57, 79
Bayen, Dorothy: and H. Murray Jacoby, 102; visa for, 114; visit of, to U.S., 120; and *Voice of Ethiopia*, 130; and Ethiopian World Federation, 133, 139
Bayen, Malaku: and African-American emigration, 6; influence of, 8; Addison E. Southard's attitude toward, 9; and U.S. economic aid, 9; and Ras Desta Demtu, 11; as student at Howard University, 22–23, 120; and Ethiopian Research Council, 23, 25, 76, 77, 120; and racial discrimination, 30, 121–22; and Sufi Abdul Hamid, 38; as liaison with African Americans, 46, 84, as speaker on Ethiopia, 46, 122–23, 136; and State Department, 46, 129; and aviation training program, 54–55; and Hubert Julian, 54–55, 60; and African-American technicians, 56–57; and foreign advisers, 59; and secret code, 68; and fund raising, 77–78, 109, 115–16, 118, 120, 126; and H. Murray Jacoby, 102, 113; and Phillip Savory mission, 104, 105, 107, 108; and visas, 114; and Haile Sellassie's proposed U.S. visit, 115, 116; as envoy to U.S., 119, 120–27, 156; and President Roosevelt, 124–25; and Ethiopian World Federation, 127–30, 133, 138, 155; and Marcus Garvey, 129–30; philosophy of, 129–30; death of, 138; and pan-Africanism, 154; and leadership, 156
Bayen, Malaku, Jr., 114, 120

172

Beckford, Lawrence, 17
Beckles, Mabel, 144
Bedane, Girma, 148
Beit Ouriel School, 151
Belgium, 3
Beth B'nai Abraham, 11
Better Harlem Welfare Association, 137
Bingham, Robert W., 110–11, 113, 114
Black Eagle. *See* Julian, Hubert
Black nationalist movements, 159
Black unity: and Marcus Garvey, 12, 39, 51, 131, 134, 155; and Ethiopian World Federation, 129, 131, 138; and African Americans, 131, 158. *See also* Pan-Africanism
Blackett, G. M., 140
Blackman, 37
Blacks, as term, 44, 131, 141. *See also* African Americans; African diaspora; African peoples; Pan-Africanism
Blocker, Angeline, 140
Boeing Aircraft Company, 106–107
Bono, Emilio de, 21
Booker T. Washington Memorial Association, 27
Boosters Club, 135
Bovell, Gilbert Balfour, 23, 130
The Brood, 146
Broome, Harry, 39, 128
Broome, Pearle, 39, 128
Brotherhood of Sleeping Car Porters, 117, 136
Brown, James W., 137
Brown Condor. *See* Robinson, John
Bruner, J. Van, 52, 53
Buchner, C. H., 134
Buck, Sam, 41–42
Bunche, Ralph, 23–24, 76, 117
Bustamante, Alexander, 134

Caldwell, Cy, 47, 149
Canada, 76
Carnera, Primo, 97, 98
Carr, Wilbur J., 15
Caucasians, 1, 153. *See also* White Americans
Chase, William Sheafe, 114
Cheeks, James William, 144, 145, 146, 147, 151
Chicago, 128
Chicago *Defender*, 117
Chicago Society for the Aid of Ethiopia, 73
Christophe, Henri, 132
Churches, 157
Ciano, Galeazzo, 117
Coles, Joseph C., 43
Colson, Everett A., 9, 31
Comet, 134
Comintern, 61
Comité d'Action Ethiopienne, 25
Commercial Trading Company, 63
Committee for Ethiopia: and fund raising, 24, 75; and petition to League of Nations, 64; objectives of, 66–67; and Ethiopian Research Council, 77; and John H. Shaw, 106, 107
Committee of One Thousand, 93–94
Committee on the Ethiopian Crisis, 70, 74
Communist party, 64, 122
Communists, 157
Community Personal Finance Corporation, 105
Community Progressive "Negro" Painters, 137
Conseil de Recherche d'Ethiopie, 25
Cook, Andrew, 26
Coolidge, Calvin, 3
Coon, Carleton, 42, 154

INDEX

Corio-El, Hubbard, 135
Cotillo, Salvatore A., 98
Cotter, Daniel S., 147
Cowan, F. A., 16–17
Craft, Henry C., 136
Crawford, Anthony, 63
Criscuolo, Luigi, 94–96, 100–101, 102
Crisis, 37

Daily Worker, 121
Dalrymple, Sydney, 139, 140
Daniels, Samuel, 48, 49–51
Daughters of Israel, 137
Davis, Benjamin O., 43
Davis, Walter J., 44–45
Debs, Eugene, 61
Dei-Anang, Michael, 139
Delaney, Lucious L., 140
Delano, Hotel, 121–22
Democratic party, 21, 96–97
Demtu, Ras Desta, 10
Deressa, Yilma, 143–44
Detroit Committee for Aid to Ethiopia, 43
Diaspora. *See* African diaspora
Diaz, John A., 43
Digest, 25
Diouf, Galandou, 65
Discrimination. *See* Racial discrimination
Divine House of Prayer, 137
Donawa, Arnold, 72–73, 83, 98, 111–12
Dove, Karl, 1
Drake, St. Clair, 20
Draper, Edgar D., 144
Du Bois, W. E. B., 19, 62, 132, 155
Dunbar, Paul Laurence, 132
Dyer, D. H., 134

Eaton, James Y., 52, 53
Edwards, Ulyses S., 52, 53
Elks, 63, 137, 140
Ellis, William Henry, 2–3, 5
Emery, Henry, 128
Emmanuel, Tamrat, 12
Engert, C. Van H., 81
England. *See* Great Britain
Ernest, William, 136
Erwin, David D., 17
Essien-Udom, E. U., 7
Ethiopia: racial identity of people of, 1–2, 5, 113–14, 153, 154; and African-American emigration, 2–3, 5–7, 11–18; and defeat of Italy, 2, 19; and Great Britain, 3, 142, 149–50; missions of, to U.S., 3–11, 120–27; relations of, with U.S., 3, 9, 21–22, 142; and African-American relations, 4, 150–52; African Americans' connection with, 4–5, 7, 11, 65, 78, 79, 82–83, 107–108, 119, 120, 153–54; and racial discrimination, 4–5; and foreigners, 8, 30–32, 59; and African-American technicians, 9, 31, 33, 56–57, 145, 147, 150; and Judaism, 11; as symbol of black liberation, 19–20; and western influences, 28–29, 32; and social class, 32; and League of Nations, 34; commercial opportunities in, 40; recruitment movements of, 49–54; and aviation, 54–55, 145–48, 167–68; arms for, 64, 69–70, 73, 106–107, 114–15; and white Americans, 108, 124, 158; and African diaspora, 130, 153; and *Voice of Ethiopia*, 131; recon-

174

struction of, 143; and leadership, 156–57. *See also* Fund raising; Haile Sellassie; Italo-Ethiopian War
Ethiopia Relief Fund Committee, 35
Ethiopian, as term, 141
Ethiopian Air Lines, 148
Ethiopian Defense Committee, 28
Ethiopian Emergency Medical Aid, 78
Ethiopian Guild of the Latter-Day Garveyites, 48
Ethiopian Herald, 145
Ethiopian Missionaries to Abyssinia, 7
Ethiopian Pacifist Movement, 48
Ethiopian Red Cross, 68, 69, 71, 72, 74
Ethiopian Research Council: formation of, 20–23, 120, 130; leadership of, 22–25; affiliates of, 25–28; publications of, 25–26; correspondence of, 26–27; and Italo-Ethiopian War, 38–41, 150; and fund raising, 66, 75, 78–79, 82, 83, 109, 117, 125–26; and Committee for Ethiopia, 68; and arms for Ethiopia, 69–70; and Medical Committee for the Defense of Ethiopia, 72; and Phillip Savory mission, 105, 111; and John H. Shaw, 107; and efforts to get Ethiopian envoy to U.S., 113; and Ethiopian World Federation, 141; and pan-Africanism, 155; and Garvey, 157
Ethiopian Review, 145
Ethiopian stamps, 69, 106, 123–24, 136
Ethiopian Welfare Foundation of Brooklyn, 140
Ethiopian World Federation (EWF): formation of, 57, 127; branches of, 128–29, 131–34, 161–66; and black unity, 129, 131, 138; publications of, 130–32; and black consciousness, 132; and civil rights, 133; international influence of, 134–35; and African Americans, 135; conventions of, 136–39, 140–41; and fund raising, 136, 139; decline of, 141; and Italo-Ethiopian War, 150; and settlement at Shashimana, 152; and pan-Africanism, 155; and Communists, 157
Eyessus, Afeword Gebre, 29

Falashas, 11
Fauset, Crystal Bird, 136
FBI, 47–54, 59–60
FEA, 65–66, 71
Fearen, I. H., 134
Federal Bureau of Investigation (FBI), 47–54, 59–60
Federal Council of Churches, 70
Federal Council of Churches of Christ in America, 70
Federal Emergency Relief Administration, 18
Federal Reserve Bank, 9
Federation of Italian World War Veterans, 94
Federation of the Workers Protection Association, 135
Ferguson, Dutton, 47
Ferris, William, 130, 132
Finger, John W., 144
Florida News, 134
Foley, E. M., 144
Ford, Abiya, 13, 151
Ford, Arnold Josiah, 11–14, 16, 27, 128, 151

INDEX

Ford, James W., 64
Ford, Mignon Innis, 13, 14, 151, 152
Ford, Yosef, 13, 151
France, 3, 29, 34, 54–55
Friends of Ethiopia, 28, 37
Friends of Ethiopia in America (FEA), 65–66, 71
Friends of Italy, 96
Fund raising: for medical supplies, 24, 67–73, 76, 78, 80; coordination of, 26–27, 74–75, 81, 118, 120, 126–27; and photographs of Haile Sellassie, 26, 48, 117–18, 123–24; and African Americans, 63–84, 107–108, 116, 124; incentives for, 65; and Ethiopian stamps, 69, 106, 123–24, 136; and neutrality laws, 70–71, 74, 76; and racial issues, 70, 71, 73, 75, 76, 79–80, 116, 119; conflict among groups regarding, 73–74, 76, 78, 80, 125–26; and white Americans, 80, 84, 108, 124, 158; and Italian Americans, 93–94, 115; and United States, 109; for arms and ammunition, 114–15; purpose of, 114–15, 116; and mail-in campaign, 124; for refugee fund, 136, 139

Gabrou, Ato Kantiba: and mission to U.S., 4, 23; and African-American emigration, 5–6, 9, 12, 13, 16; and pan-Africanism, 154
Gardner, Matthew, 139, 140
Garvey, Amy Jacques, 37, 64, 66, 134
Garvey, Marcus: and black unity, 12, 39, 51, 131, 134, 155; and Malaku Bayen, 129–30; and Jamaica, 133
Garvey movement, 14, 48, 133, 157

Gary, Alvin C., 24
Gaston, Edward Page, 114
Geneva Disarmament Conference, 21
Giorgis, Wolde, 33
Goldstein, Sidney E., 70
Good Samaritans, 52
Gordon, A., 134
Gordon, M. L., 17, 117
Gratien, Candace, 65
Graves, Des, 133
Grayson, Cary T., 71
Graziani, Rodolfo, 33
Great Britain: and Ethiopian relations, 3, 142, 149–50; and Italo-Ethiopian War, 34–35; and Haile Sellassie, 104; Phillip Savory mission in, 104–12; and African-American recruitment, 148–49; and African diaspora, 158
Green, Joseph C., 107
Green, Lige, 39

Haile, Makonnen, 23
Haile Sellassie: and relations with U.S., 3, 9, 142; and African-American emigration, 6; coronation of, 7, 10, 12, 133–34; and attitudes toward foreigners, 8; photographs of, 26, 48, 117–18, 123–24; and Young Ethiopian Movement, 30–31; and western influence, 33; and enlistment, 44; exile of, 60, 104, 125; and fund raising, 67, 115; and Italy, 99; and Phillip Savory mission, 104–109, 118–19; proposed visit of, to U.S., 108, 110–14, 116–17; and League of Nations, 110; and Malaku Bayen, 118; and Rastafarians, 133–34; endorsement of *Voice of Ethiopia* by, 138; return of, to Ethiopia, 140,

176

142; and reconstruction of Ethiopia, 143; and pan-Africanism, 154
Haile Sellassie Fund, 123
Haiti, 131
Hall, Joseph, 8
Halpert, Frank de, 31
Hamid, Sufi Abdul, 38, 48, 49
Hamitic Africans, 1, 154
Hampton, Bernard, 52
Hansberry, William Leo: and Ethiopian Research Council, 22, 24, 25, 69, 78–79, 82; and pro-Ethiopian effort, 23, 156; and fund raising, 27, 80, 81, 117, 120, 125; and Arnold Donawa, 72; and hospital field unit, 76, 78; and John H. Shaw, 107–108; and Phillip Savory mission, 119; and Malaku Bayen mission, 122, 123; and Yilma Deressa, 144
Harlem, 10, 47–49, 63–64, 80, 124
Harlem Labor Union, 137
Harrigan, Warren, 128, 139
Harris, Fannie, 27
Harris, Robert F. S.: and Ethiopian Research Council, 24, 25, 77; and fund raising, 66–70, 75; and medical supplies, 71, 76; and John H. Shaw, 74, 77, 80, 106
Havana, 134
Hawkins, T. H., 49
Hayes, Arthur P., 11, 43
Haynes, George E., 70, 71
Height, Dorothy I., 144
Helping Hand Finance Corporation, 63
Herouy, Belaten Gheta, 75, 99
Herring, James V., 112, 117
Hester, Andrew Howard, 144, 145, 146, 147

Heuston, Judge, 140
Hicks, Mae, 39
Hill, Hiley A., 144
Hill, T. Arnold, 83
Hines, Major, 137
Hitler, Adolf, 21
Hoare-Laval compromise, 34
Homes, Dan, 41
Hopkins, Ella Mae, 139
Hospital field unit, 76, 78
Hotel Delano, 121–22
Houston, Mildred, 124
Howard University: demonstrations at, 10, 52; and Malaku Bayen, 22–23, 120; and William Leo Hansberry, 22; volunteers from, 76, 143; and Lij Tafaye Zaphiro, 82–83; and fund raising, 108–109, 116, 118, 125–26
Huggins, Willis: and Ras Desta Demtu, 11; and Ethiopian Research Council, 25, 77; and Friends of Ethiopia, 28; and Hubert Julian, 58; and fund raising, 64–66, 79, 80; and Haile Sellassie's proposed visit to U.S., 117
Hull, Cordell: and African-American emigration, 17–18, 43–44; and Italo-Ethiopian War, 64; and fund raising, 81, 83; and visas, 111; and racial discrimination, 121
Hulme, Ernest, 147

IBPOE. *See* Elks
Imes, William: and Phillip Savory mission, 104–105, 112; and John H. Shaw, 107; and Malaku Bayen mission, 120, 122–23; and Ethiopian World Federation, 136–37, 139, 157
Independent Order of Odd Fellows, 140

INDEX

International African Friends of Abyssinia, 65–66
International African Progressive Association, 44–45
International Black League, 48, 49
International Committee of the Red Cross, 71
International Committee on African Affairs, 137
International Council of Women of Darker Races, 27
International Friends of Abyssinia, 66
International Labor Defense, 48, 121
International Reform Federation, 114
International Workers' Order, 140
Isham, Walter, 52–53
Istmo-African Bureau, 25, 26, 27, 117
Italian Americans: and Italo-Ethiopian War, 21; and fund raising, 93–94, 115; and African Americans, 97–98; and social status, 102–103; and Haile Sellassie's proposed visit to U.S., 113; power of, 158
Italian Historical Society, 96
Italo-Ethiopian Treaty of Friendship, Conciliation, and Arbitration of 1928, p. 21
Italo-Ethiopian War: and African-American settlements, 14; and Walwal incident, 18, 20–22, 27, 46, 99, 126; and Ethiopian Research Council, 20–21; and President Roosevelt, 21, 41–42; and Great Britain, 34–35; and pan-Africanism, 34–35; protests against, 35–38, 47–51; African-American enlistment in, 41–45; and FBI, 47–51; Italian-American response to, 93–103; and Malaku Bayen, 129; and United States, 130; ending of, 142; and African diaspora, 154; and African identity, 154–55. *See also* African Americans; Fund raising; Italian Americans
Italy, 2, 19, 101, 156
Italy America Society, 94
Ithfill, G., 134

Jackson, Aron, 13
Jackson, C. P., 134
Jackson, Henry, 25
Jackson, Lola, 47
Jackson, Rosalind, 140
Jackson, William A., 8
Jacoby, H. Murray: and Ras Desta Demtu, 10–11; and Ethiopian Red Cross, 71; and John H. Shaw, 74; and State Department, 99–102; complaints against, 106; and Haile Sellassie's proposed visit to U.S., 113, 117; and fund raising, 124
Jacoby, Mrs., 10–11
Jamaica, 36, 133–34
James, C. L. R., 136
Jernagin, W. H., 139
Jews, 11, 70
Johannes, Engueda, 23
Johnson, Joseph Green, 39–40
Johnson, Mordecai, 76, 78
Johnson, Walter, 42
Jones, Edward Eugene, 144, 145, 146, 147
Jones, Emmett, 13
Jones, George M., 24, 78, 81, 83, 117
Jones, J. J., 72
Jones, Thomas Jesse, 70
Jordan, William, 48
Julian, Hubert, 8, 54–56, 57–60, 108, 116

Juliano, Huberto Fauntleroyana. *See* Julian, Hubert

Kalibala, Ernest, 133, 136
Kellogg-Briand Pact, 67, 99
Kemp, Ira, 48
Kemp, L. D., 135
Kimble, Henry, 42
King, A. L., 64, 83
King, Lorenzo H., 127–28, 136–37, 139, 157
Kirkman, Will, 128
Koffie, Hattie Edwards, 13, 17–18, 128
Kolmodin, Johannes, 31

La Guardia, Fiorello, 97, 98, 121, 122
Lambie, Thomas A., 70, 73
L'Amour pour la Patrie, 25
Lardner, Henry A., 74, 124
Lauter, K. C., 149
Law, Oliver, 61
Lawlor, Ignacious E., 121
Leadership, 156–57
League of Nations: and Ethiopia, 25, 34; and Willis Huggins, 64–65; and Kellogg-Briand Pact, 67, 99; sanctions of, 76; and pro-Ethiopia Italian Americans, 98; and Haile Sellassie, 100, 110
League of Nations Society, 70
League of Struggle for Negro Rights, 63
Lend-Lease program, 145, 147
Levey, L., 134
Lewin, Wilfred E., 140
Lewis, C. W., 145
Lewis, Claude A. De. M.: and Ethiopian Research Council, 24, 25; and Lij Tasfaye Zaphiro, 82, 83; and Malaku Bayen mission, 114,

120; and fund raising, 115; and Haile Sellassie's proposed visit to U.S., 117
Lewis, Julian, 73
Liberia, 22, 153
Liberty Loan Committee, 94
Livingstone, Lewis, 16
Logan Act, 99
Louis, Joe, 97, 98
L'Ouverture, Pierre Toussaint, 132
Love, Edgar F., 144
Lynch, Frank, 128
Lynch, Mary, 13

McCabe, Herbert, 135
McClintock, James, 76, 79
Mackey, Charles, 120
Makonnen, Ras Tafari. *See* Haile Sellassie
Manamano, Ato Paulos, 10
Mariam, Abera Wolde, 148
Mariam, Mengistu, 151
Martin, Azaj Workneh: visit to U.S., 6–7, 8; and African-American emigration, 12, 22; and fund raising, 64, 65, 66, 69, 79, 107, 115; and Lij Tasfaye Zaphiro, 81, 84; and Phillip Savory mission, 108; and Haile Sellassie's proposed visit to U.S., 110–14; and relations between African Americans and Ethiopia, 150–51; and pan-Africanism, 154
Massai, Lij Andargue, 139
Matthews, W. A., 137
Maurer, Harry A., 98
Mayard, Constantin, 65
Mbadiwe, Kingsley Ozumba, 140–41
Medcom. *See* Medical Committee for the Defense of Ethiopia
Medhem, Blatta Ephrem T., 149

179

INDEX

Medical Committee for the Defense of Ethiopia (Medcom): and Ethiopian Research Council, 25; and fund raising, 72–73, 119; and secret code, 77; and Italian Americans, 98; and Phillip Savory, 105; and Haile Sellassie's proposed visit to U.S., 117
Medical supplies, 24, 67–73, 76, 78, 80
Medical volunteers, 70–72, 76, 78
Mends, Alfred, 36
Menelik, Emperor, 2–3, 29, 132
Menelik, Zauditu, 8
Menelik Club, 126
Menen, Empress, 151
Mills, Thomas, 47
Mitchell, Philip, 142
Mitchell, Randolph, 45
Montague, David A., 140
Moore, Howard: and Ethiopian Research Council, 23, 68, 72; and fund raising, 69, 75, 76, 77–78, 115; and Haile Sellassie's proposed visit to U.S., 113–14, 116; and Phillip Savory mission, 119
Moore, Richard, 133
Morris-Knibbs, Mrs., 134
Moulton, C. C., 27–28
Muldrow, Joseph, 144, 145, 146, 147, 149
Murphy, Carl, 117
Murray, Wallace, 74, 101, 112–13, 122
Mussolini, Benito, 21, 28, 60, 64, 94–97

NAACP, 37–38, 97, 117, 121
Nadou, Dadjamatch, 3–4, 5
Nathan, Ernest, 47
National Association for the Advancement of Colored People (NAACP), 37–38, 97, 117, 121

National Committee for Ethiopia, 75
National Democratic Club, 5
National Democratic Committee, 96
National Ethiopian Week, 66
National Geographic, 16
National Negro Congress, 27, 118, 140
Near Eastern Foundation, 70
Negro, as term, 131, 141
Negro Welfare Social and Cultural Association, 28, 37
Negro World, 37, 130, 131
Nelson, Shellie, 43
Nemours, General de, 65
Nesbitt, Ella, 135
Neutrality laws: and enlistment, 40, 51, 158–59; and fund raising, 70–71, 74, 76; and Italian Americans, 95; and arms, 107; and visas, 111–12
New Statesman and Nation, 36
New York City, 12, 15, 97, 127–29
New York *American*, 121
New York *Evening Journal*, 50
New York *Times*, 5, 50, 67, 93
New York World's Fair, 82
New York *World-Telegram*, 121
Newspapers. *See* Press coverage
Nyabongo, Akiki, 132, 137, 140

Obebe, Alemayo, 148
Oberhelman, M., 147
Oldham, G. Ashton, 66
Opportunity, 110
O'Ryan, John, 81, 82
Osborn, Herbert, 47

Pacific Movement of Philadelphia, 38
Pacific Movement of the Eastern World, 17
Padmore, George, 66, 132
Paige, Myles, 140

180

Pan-African Congress of 1919, p. 19
Pan-African Reconstruction Association (PARA), 48, 50–51
Pan-Africanism: and Ethiopia, 19–20, 153; and Italo-Ethiopian War, 34–35; and Malaku Bayen, 120; and Ethiopian World Federation, 131, 141; movements of, 159. *See also* Black unity
Panama, 27–28
Panama American, 28
Panama Star and Herald, 28
Pankhurst, E. Sylvia, 139, 140
PARA, 48, 50–51
Paris, Eudora, 13, 128, 139
Park, James L., 10
Parrish, Frank, 53
Payne, John, 66
Peace Movement of Ethiopia, 25, 117
Pecora, Ferdinand, 98
The People, 36, 134
Perkins, W. P., 42
Petiono, Charles A., 136
Phelps-Stokes Fund, 70
Philadelphia Committee for the Defense of Ethiopia, 27
Phillips, Cyril, 83, 104–105, 112, 120, 123
Phillips, Donald J., 121
Phillips, William, 83
Pilots, training of, 54–55, 147–48, 167–68
Pioneer Lumber Company, 17
Pioneer Shoemaking Company, 17
Pioneering Club, 25, 26, 27, 28
Pioneers of Aethiopia, 16–17
Pittsburgh *Courier*: and fund raising, 27, 65–66, 73, 115, 117; and enlistment, 45; and Lij Tasfaye Zaphiro, 82
Plain Talk, 36
Pope, Generoso, 94, 96–97

Powell, Adam Clayton, 64, 66, 83, 139
Powell, Cletis, 109, 114, 115
Press coverage: and racial discrimination, 5, 121; and Ethiopia, 16, 145; and fund raising, 27, 65–66, 67, 73, 115, 117; and C. C. Moulton, 28; and Italo-Ethiopian War, 35–36, 73; and enlistment, 45, 50–53; and black journalists, 75; and Italian Americans, 93, 94; and Malaku Bayen mission, 117, 121; and Ethiopian World Federation, 134, 140.
Price, Cyril, 8
Princess Zennebe Worq School, 151
Il Progresso Italo-Americano, 94, 96
Prominent Lagos Women's Society, 35
Provisional Committee for the Defense of Ethiopia, 63, 64, 72–73, 98
Pyramid Institute, 137

Racial classifications, 1–2, 5
Racial discrimination: and Ethiopian missions, 4–5, 10; and State Department, 10, 154; and Ethiopians' education, 29–30; and Malaku Bayen, 30, 121–22; and African Americans, 146, 158
Randall, H., 42
Randolph, A. Phillip, 117, 136, 139
Ras Makonnen School, 144
Ras Tafari, 133, 134
Rastafarian movement, 134
Rathbee, Richard, 139–40
Red Cross, 70, 71. *See also* American Red Cross; Ethiopian Red Cross
Red Cross flag, 67–68
Redding, Cleveland, 7
Refugee fund of Ethiopian World Federation, 136, 139
Reid, Arthur, 133, 136, 140
Reid, S. A., 134

INDEX

Remington Arms Company of America, 106, 107
Rising Sun clubs, 13, 25, 26–27, 117, 122
Rivoire, Denis de, 1
Roberts, Luckeyeth, 123
Robeson, Paul, 59
Robinson, John: and Italo-Ethiopian War, 54, 56–57, 123, 132; and Haile Sellassie, 118; and Ethiopian World Federation, 128, 137, 139; and Ethiopian reconstruction, 144–47, 150; and training of pilots, 147–48, 167–68
Rogers, Joel A., 64, 132, 135
Roker, Annie I. V., 135
Romney, Charles T., 48
Roosevelt, Eleanor, 125
Roosevelt, Franklin Delano: and African-American emigration, 17, 18; and Italo-Ethiopian War, 21, 41–42; and Spain, 62; and Ethiopian fund raising, 67; and Italian Americans, 93, 95–97; and Italian debt, 102; and Malaku Bayen, 121, 124–25
Rosen, Carl Gustaf von, 148
Ross, Emory, 70
Ross, Harry, 47
Rossi, Augusto, 94
Royal Order of Ethiopian Hebrews, 137, 140

Sahara, Mrs. Seth, 137
Said, Ismael Mohammad, 66
Saint James Presbyterian Church, 105, 137
Sandeford, Thomas, 13
Savage, Augusta, 136
Save the Children Fund, 66
Savory, Phillip: and fund raising, 81, 115, 116, 118, 125, 126–27; and Lij Tasfaye Zaphiro, 83; as envoy to England, 104–12, 118–19, 120; and Haile Sellassie's proposed visit to U.S., 113, 114; and Malaku Bayen mission, 117–18, 120, 121, 122, 123; and Ethiopian World Federation, 136
Schieffelin, William J., 71
Schomburg, Arthur, 83
Schuyler, George, 65
Schweinfurth, Georg, 1
Scott, Cyril O., 134
Scottsboro case, 133
Seligman, C. G., 1, 154
Sellassie, Ato Belanghetta Herouy Wolde, 4, 5
Sellassie, Herouy Wolde, 10
Shackleford, Mrs. G. S. Wynter, 35
Shapiro, Lewis L., 67
Shashimana, 152
Shaw, John H.: and fund raising, 70, 73–75, 76, 105, 115, 124, 139, 140; and friction with African Americans, 72, 77–84, 106–108; performance of, as consul, 104; and arms negotiations, 107; and Malaku Bayen, 118, 120
Siefert, Charles, 133
Simmons, Charles H., 53
Simon, Lydia, 128
Simpson, Ian H., 145
Sinkas, Ato, 4
Sirovich, William A., 98
Skinner, Robert P., 2
Smith, Archie, 47
Smith, Arthur, 39
Smoot, Mrs. Ferrol B., 136–37
Social class, 32
Socialist party, 61
Société Nationale d'Ethiopie, 40

Solanke, Lapido, 64
Southard, Addison E.: and United States–Ethiopian relations, 3; and racial discrimination, 4, 10, 29–30; and African-American emigration, 7–9, 14–16, 17; and western education of Ethiopians, 29–30; and Young Ethiopian Movement, 30–33
Spain, 60–62, 158
Star Order of Ethiopia, 7
State Department: and African-American recruits, 9, 143; and racial discrimination, 10, 154; and African-American emigration, 15–16, 18; and enlistment for Italo-Ethiopian War, 42–45, 53; and Malaku Bayen, 46, 129; and loans to Ethiopia, 63, 143; and fund raising, 70–71, 74, 114–15, 124; and visas, 72, 111–13, 114; and Lij Tasfaye Zaphiro, 81; and American League for Italy, 95–96; and H. Murray Jacoby, 99–101; and Phillip Savory mission, 105; and Ethiopian visit to U.S., 109; and Haile Sellassie's proposed visit to U.S., 110–11, 112, 117; and Ethiopian relations, 142; and airplanes, 145; and friction between Great Britain and Ethiopia, 149. *See also* United States
Steen, William M.: and Ethiopian Research Council, 23, 24, 25, 28, 40; publications of, 26; and fund raising, 65, 73, 80, 82, 116–18, 120, 125–26; and Arnold Donawa, 72; and Lij Tasfaye Zaphiro, 84; and Phillip Savory mission, 104–105, 109, 119; and Malaku Bayen, 105, 108, 122, 123; and

John H. Shaw, 107–108; and Haile Sellassie's proposed visit to U.S., 112, 114; and Harry Broome and Pearle Broome, 128; in Ethiopia, 144–45; and Ethiopian relations, 151; and pro-Ethiopian effort, 156
Stevens, Hope, 133, 136
Street speakers, 47–49
Sudan Interior Mission, 70
Sunday Times (London), 36
Suvich, Mr., 101
Sylvain, Benito, 2, 5

Taezoz, Lorenzo, 75
Talbot, David, 144–46, 150–52
Tecle-Hawariate, 64, 65, 154
Tedrous, Lia Workina, 6–7
Tela, Spanish Honduras, 134
Terrell, Mary E., 139
Thomas, Albertha, 151
Thomas, Joseph, 14
Thomas, Matilda, 14
Thomas, Reggie, 48
Thomas, Robert, 47
Thornhill, James, 48
Tibbs, Thurlow Evans, 144, 146, 151
Totten, Ashley L., 133
Tracy, T. H., 47–48
Travelers Aid, 18
Trinidad, 37
Trinidad Citizens Committee, 37
Tsahai, Princess, 138
Tsana, Lake, 6, 13, 27, 74

UAPAD, 118, 122, 126–27
UMA, 51–54
UNIA. *See* Universal Negro Improvement Association (UNIA)
Union Messenger, 134
Unione Italiana d'America, 96

INDEX

United Aid for Ethiopia: and fund raising, 81; and Lij Tasfaye Zaphiro, 82, 126; and Phillip Savory mission, 105, 112, 118; and John H. Shaw, 107; and Malaku Bayen mission, 122, 125
United Aid for People of African Descent (UAPAD), 118, 122, 126–27
United Italian Association, 96
United Presbyterian Mission, 70
United States: Ethiopian missions to, 3–11, 120–27; Ethiopian relations of, 3, 21–22, 108, 142; and Italo-Ethiopian War, 37; neutrality laws of, 40, 71, 74, 76, 95, 107, 111–12, 158–59; and Spain, 61, 62; and fund raising, 109; elections of, 110–12. *See also* Roosevelt, Franklin Delano; State Department
Universal African Union, 137
Universal Ethiopian Students Association, 66
Universal Multitechnic Association (UMA), 51–54
Universal Negro Improvement Association (UNIA): and African-American emigration, 6; and Ethiopia, 12, 27; and street speakers, 48; and fund raising, 63–64; and Ethiopian World Federation, 130, 137, 140

Vann, Robert Lee, 45, 117
Vazquez-Delgado, Obdulio, 144, 145
Verdi, Angelo K., 96
Victory Mutual Life Insurance Company, 105
Vitalien, Joseph, 2

Voice of Ethiopia (VOE), 123, 130–36, 138, 139, 155
Voice of Italy, 93

Walcott, Leonard F., 36–37
Walker, R. R., 42
Walters, Alexander, 2
Walwal incident, 18, 20–22, 27, 46, 99, 126. *See also* Italo-Ethiopian War
Warner, Richard E., 137
Washington *Herald,* 52–53
Washington *Times,* 52, 53
Washington *Tribune,* 47
Watson, James, 140
Watson, Thomas Edward, 144
Watts, Charles, 128
West, Charles I., 13
West, John, 8, 13, 128
West African Pilot, 134
West African Students Union, 64
West Indian Youth Welfare League, 28, 37
West Indies, 15, 22, 35–37, 67
Wheeler, Lloyd G., 144
White Americans, 80, 84, 108, 124, 158. *See also* Caucasians
White (J. G.) Engineering Corporation, 9, 10, 74
Wilkins, Roy, 117
Williams, Henry Sylvester, 19
Williams, Ray, 83
Williams, Vernal, 133, 136, 140
Williamson, Harold H., 50
Willis, N. P., 17
Wilson, Finley, 137, 139, 140
Wolde, Bashawarad Hapte, 8, 33
Wolde, Makonnen Hapte, 33
Woodson, Carter G., 132
Work, Ernest, 26, 31

World War I, 3
World War II, 141
Wright, Richard, 132
Wyatt, Thomas H., 63

Yates, Leonard L., 47, 61
Yergan, Max, 137

YMCA, 63, 136, 137
Young, Reuben S., 8
Young Ethiopian Movement, 28–33

Zaphiro, Lij Tasfaye, 27, 79–84, 126

/963.056H314A>C1/